MAGAZINES, TRAVEL,
AND MIDDLEBROW CULTURE

MAGAZINES, TRAVEL, AND MIDDLEBROW CULTURE

CANADIAN PERIODICALS IN
ENGLISH AND FRENCH, 1925–1960

Faye Hammill and Michelle Smith

LIVERPOOL UNIVERSITY PRESS

First published 2015 by
Liverpool University Press
4 Cambridge Street
Liverpool
L69 7ZU
UK

www.liverpooluniversitypress.co.uk

Copyright © 2015 Faye Hammill and Michelle Smith

The right of Faye Hammill and Michelle Smith to be identified as the authors of this book has been asserted by them in accordance with the Copyright, Design and Patents Act 1988.

All rights reserved. No part of this book may be reproduced, stored in a retrieval system, or transmitted, in any form or by any means, electronic, mechanical, photocopying, recording, or otherwise, without the prior written permission of the publisher.

British Library Cataloguing-in-Publication data
A British Library CIP record is available

ISBN 978-1-78138-140-3

Typeset by Carnegie Book Production, Lancaster
Printed and bound by CPI Group (UK) Ltd, Croydon, CR0 4YY

CONTENTS

	List of Illustrations	vii
	Acknowledgements	ix
	Introduction	1
1	Marketplace	23
2	Pages	65
3	Fashions	109
4	Consumers	146
	Conclusion	180
	Bibliography	185
	Index	205

LIST OF ILLUSTRATIONS

1 Maclean Publishing advert. *Chatelaine* June 1928
2 Packard Cars advert. *Maclean's* 1 Jan. 1930
3 Ford advert. *Chatelaine* Aug. 1930
4 Cover image. *Canadian Home Journal* Aug. 1939
5 Cover image. *La Revue Populaire* Aug. 1939
6 Cover image. *Maclean's* 15 June 1930
7 'Où allons-nous?' article. *La Revue Moderne* Jan. 1932
8 Cover image. *Mayfair* May 1928
9 Cover image. *Mayfair* Aug. 1935
10 Cover image. *Mayfair* Mar. 1947
11 Table of contents. *Maclean's* 15 Jan. 1927
12 Table of contents. *Chatelaine* July 1934
13 Ford advertisement. *Chatelaine* July 1934
14 'Fashions Right for Flight.' *Canadian Home Journal* June 1951
15 Cover image. *Canadian Home Journal* June 1951
16 Cover image. *La Revue Moderne* Aug. 1927
17 Cover image. *La Revue Moderne* Nov. 1927
18 Cover image. *La Revue Moderne* May 1939
19 Cover image. *Chatelaine* Aug. 1929
20 'Shops of Mayfair.' *Mayfair* July 1930
21 'À New-York …' fashion feature. *La Revue Populaire* July 1946
22 'Empress of Britain Fashion Story.' *Canadian Home Journal* May 1956
23 Canadian Pacific *Empress of Britain* advert. *Mayfair* Apr. 1931
24 'The Only Paris.' *Mayfair* May 1927
25 TransCanada Airlines advert. *La Revue Populaire* Sept. 1954

26 Canadian Pacific advert. *Mayfair* Aug. 1929
27 'We Dine and Wine in London.' *Canadian Home Journal* June 1935
28 'Cuisine Française.' *La Revue Populaire* Sept. 1954
29 Canadian Pacific Banff advert. *La Revue Populaire* July 1930

ACKNOWLEDGEMENTS

THIS BOOK emerged from a collaborative research project, and our writing has derived energy and inspiration from all the colleagues who have been involved. *Magazines, Travel, and Middlebrow Culture* was funded from 2011 to 2013 by the Arts and Humanities Research Council, whose support we gratefully acknowledge.

We have many debts to the members of our project advisory board: Ted Bishop, Susan Brown, Peter Hodgins, Dean Irvine, Lise Jaillant, David Kinloch, Valerie Korinek, Eva-Marie Kröller, Victoria Kuttainen, Anouk Lang, Hannah McGregor, Cecilia Morgan, Candida Rifkind, Gillian Roberts, Wendy Roy, Chantal Savoie, Will Straw, and Marie Vautier. They have assisted us with locating material and identifying magazine contributors, with intellectual questions, and with tricky passages in French. The discussions they generated at our 2012 Advanced Research Seminar in Ottawa (splendidly hosted by Peter Hodgins) offered much stimulation to our thinking about Canadian magazines and middlebrow culture. The papers emerging from that seminar, published as volume 48 of the *International Journal of Canadian Studies / Revue internationale des études canadiennes* were invaluable sources of inspiration for our writing. We thank the journal's editor, Claude Couture, for supporting the publication of this special issue.

Anthony Cond at Liverpool University Press has encouraged the publication of this book from the beginning, and we are immensely grateful to him, and to all his colleagues at the Press, for their efficient and enthusiastic work with us. The manuscript reviewers provided us with extremely astute and meticulous suggestions for revision. For carefully commenting on our drafts of chapters and translations, and providing new information, special thanks are due to Rachael Alexander, Nigel Fabb, Sarah Galletly, Carole Gerson, Mark Hussey, Lise Jaillant, Victoria Kuttainen, Anouk Lang, and most particularly Gillian Roberts. Jonathan Percy heroically proofread the entire manuscript.

The book is accompanied by a website, www.middlebrowcanada.org. Research for the website and book have been conducted in tandem, and the visualisations and bibliographical data presented on the site have contributed substantially to the conclusions articulated in the book. We therefore owe many thanks to colleagues at Strathclyde's Enhanced Web Development Service, who built the web resource. In particular: Jim Everett, for many of the initial ideas and for complex development work; Emma Graham, for astute management of this part of our project; Clare Hodgkinson, for patiently fixing all our problems; and especially Cristina Judge, for her imaginative ideas, beautiful designs, and extraordinary level of organisation. Cristina's systematic labelling of our digitised materials and subsequent cataloguing work were crucial to the success of our project, and if we had been left alone with 30,000 unsorted photographs of magazine pages, we would certainly have despaired. We are grateful also to Murielle Jousseau, who translated the site into French and in the process helped us understand subtle semantic differences between our English- and French-language materials.

Our partnership with the Canadian Writing Research Collaboratory (CWRC) at the University of Alberta has afforded essential support. CWRC has not only integrated our digital work into a larger network of projects but also provided an intellectual community. Especial gratitude goes to the project's director, Susan Brown, for practical help and continual encouragement. We have had many useful discussions with the leaders of other projects affiliated with CWRC. Paul Hjartarson and Hannah McGregor of the Editing Modernism in Canada (EMiC) research group at the University of Alberta have been especially generous and wise supporters of our project, providing invaluable ideas and feedback throughout. Exchanges with Karyn Huenemann and Carole Gerson of the Canada's Early Women Writers project, and via them with Peggy Kelly, have been most valuable.

We have presented our work at conferences organised by CWRC, EMiC, the British Association for Canadian Studies, the Modernist Studies Association, the European Society for Periodicals Research, and the University of Newcastle, as well as at the War Studies seminar, University of Strathclyde. We are grateful for the invitations and the excellent feedback provided by audiences.

Primary research for this book was carried out at the Thomas Fisher Rare Books Library, University of Toronto, and at Library and Archives Canada (LAC). Staff at both libraries were immensely helpful; thanks especially to Albert Masters, Graham Bradshaw, and Anne Dondterman at Thomas Fisher, and to Kyle Brownlow, Jean Matthieson, Janet Murray, and David Wax at LAC.

Our colleagues at the University of Strathclyde have been supportive in a whole variety of ways, both administrative and academic, and we are extremely grateful. And most importantly, we both thank our families, and especially Matt

ACKNOWLEDGEMENTS

Smith and Jonathan Percy, for their unfailing interest in, and patience with, this rather all-consuming project.

We are grateful to Mike Macbeth for permission to reproduce the article by her grandmother, Madge Macbeth, and to the Packard Motor Car Company, Canadian Pacific, and AirCanada (formerly TransCanada Airlines) for permission to reproduce the advertisements in our illustration section. For further information on copyright issues relating to this project, see the Copyright and IP notice on our website, www.middlebrowcanada.org.

Some paragraphs in this book are adapted from our chapter 'Mainstream Magazines: Home and Mobility,' forthcoming in the *Oxford Handbook of Canadian Literature*, edited by Cynthia Sugars.

INTRODUCTION

THE 1920s was the decade of flight and speed: it saw the golden age of the ocean liner, the early development of passenger aviation, and the expansion of tourism by rail. It was also the decade in which the word 'middlebrow' came into use, naming the new cultural formations which emerged from the social, material, and intellectual aspirations of the middle classes. And it was the decade when commercial Canadian magazines began to flourish, in the context of a rapid expansion of periodical publishing on both sides of the Atlantic. This book argues that these three developments are connected. We suggest that magazines, by circulating fantasies of travel, were instrumental in forging a link between geographical mobility and upward mobility. They constructed travel as an opportunity to acquire knowledge and prestige as well as to experience pleasure and luxury. And in their repeating patterns and seasonal cycles, the periodicals themselves replicate the experience of travel: the familiar movements and set itineraries, as well as the new discoveries and visual pleasures. As the high society Toronto magazine *Mayfair* put it in 1928:

> Life these days is a sort of merry-go-round! One little sniff of winter, and Canadians of the hothouse variety park their furs in cold storage and silently steal away to bask under southern suns. Meantime, the Dominion, the Switzerland of America, draws devotees of winter sports from all parts. Thus do we swing back and forth—south for the winter—back to Canada to say *au revoir* to the departing snows—then off again on the wing; abroad this time for the season in London or to rove the continent. ('Globe-Trotting Canadians')

The frothy *Mayfair* had been established only the year before, yet its owner, Maclean Publishing, was already on the point of announcing another new magazine. *Chatelaine*, launched in May 1928, took a more serious tone, committing itself to national advancement and to serving the needs of Canadian women. The new titles joined four other mainstream Canadian magazines,

Maclean's, *La Revue Moderne*, the *Canadian Home Journal*, and *La Revue Populaire*, which had started publishing in the first two decades of the century and were beginning to transform themselves and expand their circulation.

These six magazines were the most widely read in Canada in an era when print was the dominant form of mass media. Their rise kept pace with the growing urban, professional class, who sought out such periodicals for advice, information, and entertainment. They maintained their leading positions well into the 1950s, and three have survived into the present. Yet they are hardly ever discussed, and their histories are almost unknown. These magazines are important because they illuminate the relationships amongst nationalism, consumerism, and print culture, three defining features of the last century. The ways in which they addressed their intended audience tell us about an emerging demographic that still defines the norm in Canada: white, middle-class, and aspirational. Their contents tell us about gender divisions that continue to determine contemporary social structures, and their advertisements tell us about the development of consumerism and its role in modern print culture. The fiction and poetry they circulated tell us about shared ideals and value systems, while the disappearance of many of their authors from literary history hints at cultural hierarchies that came into play as the magazines went into decline. In their pages, images of travel and cosmopolitanism are continually set against ideals of nation and domesticity. By focusing on the dynamic between home and mobility in mainstream magazines, this book considers how they engaged with foreign cultures in both responsive and resistant ways.

Print culture and periodical studies in Canada

In their introduction to *Transatlantic Print Culture, 1880–1940: Emerging Media, Emerging Modernisms* (2008), editors Ann Ardis and Patrick Collier point out the inevitable gaps in their collection of essays. Although this is a particularly ambitious book, ranging widely over British and American culture, nineteenth- and twentieth-century periodicals, mainstream and niche titles, newspapers and magazines, it is of course unable to present a comprehensive account. It contains nothing on Ireland, Wales, or Scotland, all of which, Ardis and Collier note, 'saw movements for national self-definition carried out through print culture in the period, to say nothing of Canada, which remains surprisingly invisible in discussions of print culture in English' (8–9). Indeed, most academic studies with a transnational scope still tend to 'say nothing of Canada.' However, several major projects focused specifically on Canadian print culture have been launched in recent years. The monumental 'History of the Book in Canada / Histoire du livre et de l'imprimé au Canada' project, directed by Patricia Fleming, was completed in 2007. Its three published volumes each contain chapters on the serial press. An ongoing collaborative project, 'La Vie littéraire au Québec,' led by Maurice Lemire, is publishing a multi-volume history of literature and literary culture in Quebec. It, too, offers an overview of serial publications.[1] Our research builds on this foundational work in order to produce an in-depth study of a specific genre of periodical. We take up Ardis and Collier's call for a more expansive notion of transatlantic print culture by reinscribing Canada's most important modern magazines into the history of periodical publishing in North America. Our book seeks to explain how the mainstream magazine functioned as a cultural and commercial force in twentieth-century Canada, and to provide a model for such investigations in other cultural contexts.

This study is sorely needed, since the mainstream magazine has so far received even less critical analysis than other genres of Canadian periodical. The little magazine in Canada has begun to attract serious attention, and there have also been articles and dissertations on pulps, newspapers, leftist journals, and feminist periodicals.[2] But the archive of mainstream magazines has, in general, been explored only by researchers aiming to locate contributions by major literary authors. This bibliographical work is most important, since *Chatelaine*, the *Canadian Home Journal*, and *Maclean's* published many of the writers who now make up the canon of early and mid-century literature, such as Mazo de la Roche, Dorothy Livesay, Raymond Knister, L. M. Montgomery, Laura Goodman Salverson, Gabrielle Roy, Robert Stead, W. O. Mitchell, Martha Ostenso, Charles G. D. Roberts, and Nellie McClung.[3] Yet what is needed, in addition, is scholarship on the magazines themselves, in the context of periodical studies. In their influential article 'The Rise of Periodical Studies,' Sean Latham and Robert Scholes point to the dangers of seeing magazines

---

[1] For the volumes in the 'History of the Book in Canada' and *Vie Littéraire au Québec* series we have used, see Gerson and Michon; Lamonde, Fleming, and Black; Saint-Jacques and Robert.

[2] On little magazines, see Irvine, *Editing*. On newspapers, see Distad; Dornan; Gallichan; Sotiron; Steward. On pulps, gossip magazines, and tabloid weeklies, see Houston; Michelle Smith, 'From "The Offal"' and 'Guns, Lies'; Strange and Loo; Straw. On left-wing journals, see Rifkind, *Comrades*. On feminist magazines, see Jordan.

[3] We mention only these three titles since the fiction in *La Revue Moderne* and *La Revue Populaire* was mostly reprint material by authors from France (though much of the journalistic content was by French-Canadian authors). *Mayfair* did not publish fiction.

'merely as containers of discrete bits of information rather than autonomous objects of study' (517–18). Following the guiding principles they set out, this book concentrates on interrelationships between form and content in the chosen magazines. We are committed to a reading practice which treats the magazine as a distinct genre, and also as a material object. We take direction, too, from Jeremy Aynsley and Kate Forde's notion of the magazine as a 'designed object' produced through a collaborative process involving 'a division of labour between editors, advertisers, journalists, illustrators, typographers, designers, art directors and, in more recent years, stylists' (2). Reading the magazine as a multi-authored, multi-genre collage foregrounds the ways in which different types of material (visual and textual, commercial and editorial) compete for readers' attention and work together to generate meaning.

The six magazines we have chosen to focus on are sufficiently similar to be discussed as a group or genre, yet each one developed its own distinctive identity. Their audiences overlapped, but were not identical, since they variously addressed English- and French-speaking Canadians, female, male, and family audiences, and class fractions ranging from upper class to lower middle class. Both the general interest *Maclean's* (launched as a monthly in 1911 before becoming a fortnightly and then a weekly news magazine in the 1960s), and the women's magazine *Chatelaine* (established 1928) are still thriving under these titles; the lifetime of the others corresponds roughly to the decades covered by our study. *La Revue Populaire*, a Quebec family magazine, appeared from 1907 to 1963, and the Toronto society and fashion periodical *Mayfair* from 1927 to 1958. The *Canadian Home Journal*, established in 1910, was absorbed by its rival *Chatelaine* in 1958, while *La Revue Moderne*, launched in 1919 as an intellectual magazine but soon moving towards a more popular format, merged in 1960 with the new French-language *Châtelaine*, which is still published today.

The differences between the magazines in French and in English should not be underestimated, since of course they emerged from different sociocultural contexts. Yet the many preoccupations which were shared across English – and French-speaking Canada in the twentieth century were also shared across their periodicals, and we were very much surprised to find that no comparisons have been attempted by previous critics.[4] We have devoted somewhat less space to Francophone than to Anglophone material because there were only two large mainstream magazines in French during the period we are focusing on, and because they did not cover travel quite so extensively as some of the English-language titles did. Yet our research has always been conceived in

---

[4] Except for Kröller, in her essay on coverage of Expo 67 in *Chatelaine* and *Châtelaine* ('Terre').

terms of cross-cultural reading. We have found it highly productive to bring the two sets of magazines into the same framework of analysis, exploring their joint engagement with, for instance, middle-class aspiration, modern consumerism, and American cultural imperialism, whilst acknowledging their different orientations towards questions of nationalism and cultural belonging. The term 'French-Canadian' is generally used in this study in preference to 'Québécois' because it fits better with the way in which Francophone identities in Canada were understood during the period we focus on. As Erin Hurley explains:

> Before approximately 1960, francophone residents of Quebec identified as French Canadian / *canadien-français*, as did their counterparts in other Canadian provinces (e.g., franco-ontariens and franco-manitobains). The appellation indicates a shared language among French speakers across the country and even throughout the continent stemming from the period of French colonial expansion in North America. [...] As Canadian francophones became more invested in political self-determination, the continental vision of *l'Amérique française* gave way to a national, territorial vision [... because] the French-Canadian identity would be politically viable only as Québécois. (33–34)

Certainly, since around 80% of French-speaking Canadians lived in Quebec during the mid-twentieth century (Richard Jones), it makes sense to understand *La Revue Moderne* and *La Revue Populaire* and their audiences as centred on the province of Quebec. But though the magazines were published in Montreal, they addressed readers living across the country, as well as expatriates accessing the magazine from abroad.[5] The Acadian cultures of the Maritimes and Louisiana were often mentioned. Articles and illustrations reference communities, geographical features, tourist sites, and events located in all of Canada's provinces.

The present volume emerged from a larger project, 'Magazines, Travel and Middlebrow Culture in Canada, 1925–1960,' on which a number of scholars have collaborated.[6] When the project was begun, none of the six magazines was available in digital form, and there were no existing catalogues, excepting

---

[5] See the examples given in the section introducing *La Revue Moderne* in Chapter One.
[6] See the project website at www.middlebrowcanada.org, which includes a bibliography, sample digitised material, a timeline and timemap, pages on magazine authors, and other material.

a printed index to *Maclean's* covering the years from 1914 to 1937 (Mitchell). Now, the complete run of *La Revue Moderne* is accessible online via the Bibliothèque et archives nationales du Québec. It is not surprising that this is the first of the six magazines to have been digitised, since it was—especially in its earlier phases—the least commercial among them, and the most literary, and it was also the most purposeful in its articulation of a political and ideological agenda. Yet, though *La Revue Moderne* is quite often referred to in discussions of literary culture in Quebec, hardly any extended discussions of it have been published. In its later incarnation, as the French-language *Châtelaine* (1960–), it has attracted more attention. Indeed, nearly all the in-depth studies of Canadian mainstream magazines which have appeared to date focus on *Chatelaine* and *Châtelaine* in the second half of the twentieth century.[7] By contrast, we have chosen to explore the period from the 1920s through to the 1950s, when the mainstream magazine marketplace was at its most diverse and vibrant, and to end our study at the point when the six magazines were consolidated into three, all owned by the same company. What is certain is that, taken collectively and over their entire runs, these magazines represent a largely untapped resource, offering extensive possibilities for new research from the perspectives of disciplines including literary criticism, book history, Canadian studies, social and cultural history, consumer culture studies, and fashion and material culture studies. Since our primary expertise is in literature and Canadian studies, our analysis is framed mainly in those intellectual contexts. Yet in drawing, where appropriate, on approaches derived from other disciplines, we aim to suggest ways in which these magazines could be used as source material for research projects in a range of areas. While we have read through a very large amount of magazine content, we could discuss only a tiny fraction of that content in

---

[7] See Des Rivières; Korinek, 'It's a tough time' and *Roughing It*; Kröller, 'Terre'; Mathieu; Mendes. The survey chapter on 'Women's Magazines' in the *History of the Book in Canada* focuses on *Chatelaine* and *Châtelaine*, saying little about *La Revue Populaire* and dismissing the *Canadian Home Journal* (Des Rivières, Gerson, and Saint-Jacques). The other publications devoted to our six chosen magazines are: two articles on *La Revue Moderne* (Pleau; Ricard), one on *Maclean's* in the 1990s (Hutchinson), an MA thesis on *Mayfair* (Potvin), a book chapter on French-Canadian magazines in relation to American and French models (Saint-Jacques and Des Rivières), one article on race in *Canadian Home Journal* adverts in the 1910s (Kinahan), and Michelle Smith's article on the *Journal* and *Chatelaine* ('Fiction'). The special issue we have co-edited on 'Mobility, print culture and the middlebrow' includes a piece on *La Revue Populaire* (Savoie, 'Femmes'). The only existing general survey of Canadian magazines, though most useful, dates back to 1988 (see Sutherland), though Vipond's *The Mass Media in Canada* also includes some discussion of magazines.

detail. This book, then, should be considered as an opening statement rather than a comprehensive or final account.

Middlebrow culture

The title of this book points to its three primary contexts: current research on magazines, on travel, and on middlebrow culture. Among these, it is 'middlebrow' which requires the most extensive introductory discussion, because our theoretical framework derives from current thinking on this topic. We offer here an in-depth account of the contested term 'middlebrow,' outlining its specific resonances in a Canadian context and exploring its relation to periodical culture. Our research begins in 1925, the year the word 'middlebrow' first appeared prominently in print.[8] Each of the terms 'highbrow,' 'middlebrow,' and 'lowbrow' is, as David Carter explains, 'an artefact of a specific historical period and a product of cultural transformation. The terms in opposition emerged to name what was new about divisions in the field of culture in the 1920s and to stake out territory in an early form of culture war' ('Mystery' 176). All three were generally terms of abuse, but 'middlebrow' was always the most contentious. Its use by early twentieth-century intellectuals such as Virginia Woolf and Q. D. Leavis had a clear edge of contempt,[9] and at the centre of what were often called the 'brow wars' were fears that ordinary, unsophisticated people were bidding in some illegitimate way for cultural goods which were 'beyond' them. Pierre Bourdieu, whose sociological work has proved valuable to nearly all theorists of the middlebrow, is nevertheless just as dismissive as earlier commentators: he judges that 'middle-brow art is characterized by tried and proven techniques and an oscillation between plagiarism and parody most often linked with either indifference or conservatism' (*Field* 128). It is hardly surprising, then, that the word 'middlebrow' continues to provoke controversy and embarrassment among scholars (see Grover). Yet recent reassessments of the middlebrow cultures of the earlier and middle twentieth century are increasingly affirmative, emphasising the democratising aspects of the project of bringing high culture

---

[8] In 1925, in *Punch* ('Charivaria'). The OED now identifies one earlier usage, in the Irish *Freeman's Journal* in 1924.
[9] See Leavis; Woolf, 'Middlebrow.' Woolf's account, though, does succeed in troubling the assumption that popular culture was working class, while intellectual culture belonged to the upper classes. As Cuddy-Keane notes in her valuable account of the brow wars, while Woolf was not 'totally free of the entrenched constructions [...] she was able to envision possibilities for moving beyond them in a way that most others involved in the cultural debates could not' (18).

to large audiences and the potential of the non-experimental, realist fiction of the period in negotiating new class and gender identities.[10]

Some critics use the term 'middlebrow' to describe books or artworks which are conventional rather than experimental in form, and accessible rather than challenging to audiences, yet which are not formulaic or sensational. This model assumes that 'middlebrow-ness' is an aesthetic property of a text or a work of art. Its advantage is that it encourages attention to a set of cultural products which were widely known in their own era, but have since been erased from literary and cultural history because they do not fit dominant critical paradigms and cannot be understood as belonging to either high or mass culture. As Carter remarks: 'The heroic modern, the postmodern, and the popular have been researched into centre field, but not the mundane, respectable middlebrow' ('Mystery' 173). In response to this problem, a number of recovery projects have been undertaken. In a British context, the reissue series published by Virago Press and Persephone Books, together with critical monographs such as Nicola Humble's *The Feminine Middlebrow Novel, 1920s to 1950s* (2001) and Erica Brown's *Comedy and the Feminine Middlebrow Novel* (2013), have generated renewed interest in such writers as Elizabeth Taylor, Dorothy Whipple, Monica Dickens, and E. F. Benson.

From the point of view of academic study, the difficulty with this approach is that the set of works which are categorised as middlebrow varies over time. The same novel or piece of music can at first be claimed as a contribution to high culture, but later be seen as an artefact of the middlebrow or popular, and this process can also happen in reverse. To use Canadian examples: Mazo de Roche's *Jalna* (1927) was initially received as a serious, groundbreaking literary novel, but was later recategorised as popular and conservative. Conversely, Martha Ostenso's *Wild Geese* (1925) was written for submission to a competition and became a bestseller and a successful film; decades later, it achieved recognition as a founding example of prairie realism.[11] Elizabeth Smart's *By Grand Central Station I Sat Down and Wept* (1945) underwent a more complex trajectory, beginning in a small edition with Editions Poetry before appearing as a mass-market paperback, presumably on the basis of its sensational quality and erotic power, and was finally canonised as a late modernist classic. In *Literary Celebrity in Canada*, Lorraine York, discussing authors including de la Roche and Ostenso, as well as contemporary stars such as Margaret Atwood and

---

[10] See for instance Blair; Botshon and Goldsmith; Harker; Hammill, *Women*; Hilliard. For a full annotated bibliography of critical work on the middlebrow, see http://www.middlebrow-network.com/.

[11] For discussion see Hammill, 'Sensations'; Panofsky; York 58–75.

INTRODUCTION

Michael Ondaatje, comments that they have all 'agonized over losing cultural capital in the process of supporting themselves as writers.' She adds:

> The term 'middlebrow' comes closest to capturing this refusal of the ends of the cultural production spectrum, and yet this study suggests to me that what is happening is a constant, nervous juggling of the two forms of capital rather than the formation of a stable in-between category of literary value. (176)

While York expresses 'trepidation' (22) about the term 'middlebrow,' we would argue that it is particularly appropriate here. The dynamic model of interaction between different forms of cultural capital, described so well by York, is exactly what produces the anxieties and aspirations of the middlebrow.[12]

Ten years after the publication of her influential book on the feminine middlebrow novel, Nicola Humble wrote an article reflecting on her earlier project of recovery, and offering a fresh perspective on the topic. She argues that the uncertainty over which novels 'count' as middlebrow leads to:

> the trap that yawningly awaits critics seeking to understand the phenomenon of the middlebrow: we will make sense of it not by replicating the elaborate processes of ruling in and out which the guardians of the highbrow pursued so obsessively, but in understanding that those *acts* of inclusion and exclusion were absolutely the point. ('Sitting' 43)

When the process of ruling in and out is applied to periodicals rather than novels, the results can be even more problematic. This is partly because of the diversity of content which might appear in a single magazine, and partly because of the way a magazine's character tends to alter over time, whether in response to external factors or as a result of staff changes. In 2006, a proposal from the Modernist Journals Project (MJP) at Brown University to categorise the titles listed in its online Periodical Directory as 'highbrow,' 'upper middlebrow,' 'lower middlebrow,' or 'lowbrow' provoked a heated debate on the Modernist Studies Association email discussion list.[13] The 'value-laden' nature of these labels was a

---

[12] On middlebrow in relation to Canadian literary celebrity, see also the chapter on L. M. Montgomery in Hammill, *Women, Celebrity*.

[13] The discussion extended from December 2006 to January 2007. It can be viewed by MSA members on the list archive at http://chaos.press.jhu.edu/pipermail/msa-members/2007-January/thread.html by following the thread 'Another question.'

cause for concern: they seemed to invoke an elitist worldview, and whilst 'brow' levels do not correspond directly to social classes, these terms inevitably sound classist. The categories eventually adopted by the MJP were 'little,' 'mixed,' and 'popular,' as well as 'bibelot,' for very small magazines, and 'intermediate,' for generalist titles established before the modernist era but still publishing during that time.[14] Their invented category, 'mixed,' points to the fundamental problem with producing a typology of periodicals. The appeal of most magazines is based on the varied selection of content they offer, and this means that they can literally transmit 'mixed messages,' in ideological terms as well as in terms of cultural level. Additionally, editors, contributors, and advertisers often worked across different types of title. In his discussion of North American magazines of the modernist era, Andrew Thacker notes that they 'might be sorted into many different categories (pulps, slicks, highbrow, quality, avant-garde, little, mass, radical, bibelot, middlebrow, etc.) and, following Bourdieu's model of the cultural field, we might construct a *periodical field* upon which they are placed in different locations.' Yet, he goes on, such an exercise would 'ultimately raise more questions than it answers' (19), because 'the dominant feature of the periodical field of American magazines in 1920 is that of a "cross-fertilization," shown in the multiple networks of connection between and across supposedly distinct categories of publication' (20). Evidently, then, magazines cannot be categorised into a stable hierarchy of low, middle, and highbrow titles.

What we find much more useful is to consider the middlebrow as a mode of circulation, reception, and consumption of cultural products, and also as a space where high and popular culture meet, and where art encounters consumerism. The magazines explored in this book provide just such a space: they publish, sell, or comment on products from opera to romance fiction, haute couture originals to department store bargains. Richard Ohmann explains that the readers of early mass-market magazines 'wanted in their homes and in their conversational repertory the cultural capital that would signify and project their class standing' (244). He adds: 'That the venue of mass culture stood in a vexed relationship to such a project of cultural distinction barely received notice' (245). Our own argument is that this relationship actually generates

---

[14] However, the MJP Periodical Directory does use the word 'middlebrow' in its descriptive notes on some of the magazines, designating five of the British titles—*Belgravia*, *Chambers*, *Good Words*, *Pearson's* and *The Idler*—in this way. This label seems to relate primarily to the type of fiction printed in these periodicals. Interestingly, they are all placed in different categories in the MJP's taxonomy: *The Idler* is classed as 'little,' *Pearson's* as 'mixed,' *Good Words* as 'popular,' and the other two as 'intermediate' (*Modernist Journals Project*).

middlebrow culture. The magazines frame and present the artefacts they contain in such a way as to construct their readers as intelligent interpreters and consumers of modern culture, and simultaneously to provide them with a covert education in these practices. As John Guillory writes: 'Middlebrow culture is the ambivalent mediation of high culture within the field of the mass cultural' (87). Ambivalence is crucial to this definition. The magazines often reported on high culture in its various forms, yet they exhibit a resistance to its perceived difficulty. The fiction and artwork which they actually published (rather than just talking about) was nearly always conventional and accessible; often, it was formulaic and sentimental. So there is a gap between the materials which the magazines offered for the reader's entertainment, and the type of art and literature they thought readers ought to know about and be able to discuss.

This gap should be understood in terms of the firmly middlebrow purpose which these Canadian periodicals have always articulated in their editorials and promotional materials: that is, to combine pleasure with self-improvement. One indicative example comes from the September 1934 issue of *Chatelaine*, in which Byrne Hope Sanders's editorial focuses on 'The right use of leisure,' a phrase which, she says, 'is fast becoming one of the keynotes of the period.' She explains it in terms of finding: 'Time enough to carry forward the new realization of friendliness with children, that most mothers receive as a heritage of an intelligently spent vacation. Time enough to make new friends; to read new books; to experiment with new household ideas; to discuss and work for community problems.' These subjects, of course, were all covered in *Chatelaine*. At *Maclean's*, Blair Fraser, a staff writer and later editor of the magazine, explicitly invoked the dynamic between pleasure and learning in his report to the Royal Commission on Broadcasting in 1956: 'We think of a *Maclean's* reader as a serious person in a relaxed mood, and much of what we offer is intended only for his entertainment and not for his improvement. However, we have serious purposes. We want to report Canada and the world through the eyes of Canadians' ('Joint Submission' 16). *La Revue Moderne*'s editors tended to focus more narrowly on their purpose of improving the minds and taste of the readership. A 1931 editorial commented:

> Il existe chez nous des périodiques plus volumineux, faisant la part plus large à la science et aux lettres, à l'économie politique et aux questions sociales. Mais ces périodiques s'adressent à des petites groupes; ils n'atteignent pas la masse des lecteurs qui, elle aussi, cherche à s'instruire, dont il faut former le goût, à qui il faut donner le culte des choses de l'esprit. ('*Revue Moderne* a douze ans')

This passage makes explicit a process which, at some level, was at work throughout all the magazines. The editors laboured continually to achieve distinctiveness within the periodical marketplace, but also to align their publications with recognisable sets of values which would appeal to readers. Each of the six titles was distinctive in the way it located itself in relation to cultural hierarchies, and each of them shifted position over the course of its existence. They sought, in various ways, to avoid contamination from the lowbrow end of the market, and to appropriate elements of high culture whilst remaining wary of the 'highbrow.'

Self-improvement is the central ideal of middlebrow culture. We understand the mainstream magazines we are studying as part of the middlebrow project because they are aspirational, addressing an upwardly mobile readership. This is achieved partly through advertising of luxury products, partly through editorial material such as travel features and society reports, and partly through commentary on high cultural forms. The various magazines prioritised different elements of this mix—for instance, the greatest coverage of expensive shops and elite society events was found in *Mayfair*, while the most detailed reporting on travel and foreign affairs was provided by *Maclean's*. The Francophone magazines were the most open to intellectual culture and modern art,[15] whereas the form of high culture which held the greatest appeal for the Anglophone women's magazines was haute couture. The term 'middlebrow' in our book title, then, does not categorise the magazines within a supposed hierarchy of periodicals; rather, it indicates the aspirational culture with which they engaged.[16] We invoke this term because it brings with it precisely the cultural baggage which interests us. Part of our intellectual project is to interrogate 'brow' categories, and to understand the magazines' self-reflexivity about them.

The existing body of research on the middlebrow tends to centre on the early and mid-twentieth-century period, when the term was most influential and most hotly contested. Almost all this research is restricted to British and American contexts, though three recent collections—Brown and Grover's

---

[15] See Saint-Jacques and Robert 60–61 on the magazines' attention to modern art in the late 1920s. This was maintained in later decades: to cite two among many examples, *La Revue Populaire* ran a piece on Virginia Woolf in 1946 ('Virginia') and one by Jean-Paul Sartre in 1947.

[16] These magazines are most often described as mass-market or popular. The label 'middlebrow' is occasionally used—see, for example, Granatstein's *Canadian Encyclopedia* entry on *Maclean's*. There may be a gendered implication here, since *Maclean's* was, at least initially, addressed to a mainly male audience, so might tend to be ranked higher up the scale of cultural value.

Middlebrow Literary Cultures (2012), Macdonald's *The Masculine Middlebrow* (2011), and Sullivan and Blanch's 2011 special issue of *Modernist Cultures*—have diversified the field by including essays on middlebrow cultures in Australia, New Zealand, Canada, and France, as well as on contemporary Holocaust representation. 'Middlebrow' is certainly not yet a salient theme in Canadian studies. In French-speaking Canada, Bourdieu's phrase 'la culture moyenne' seems unknown, although the middlebrow ethos of self-improvement is clearly identified in commentary on the French-language magazines included in this project.[17] For example, Jocelyn Mathieu writes in her article on *Châtelaine*: 'L'encouragement incessant à s'instruire et à se cultiver, à se préoccuper de sa santé dans une perspective d'épanouissement personnel et collectif caractérise le discours de plusieurs magazines populaires qui s'adressent plus spécialement aux femmes' (257).

In Anglophone literary and historical studies, a small number of scholars—notably Len Kuffert, Victoria Kuttainen, Heather Murray, Candida Rifkind, Gillian Roberts, and Amy Tector—have explicitly recognised the significance of Canadian middlebrow culture, and the need for analysis of it.[18] Rifkind, in her essay on the poet Edna Jaques, who was commercially successful in Canada between the 1930s and 1950s but was never granted canonical status, argues:

> Jaques's status as outsider to the literary centre of power, then, has as much to do with the large-scale, female, and middle-class consumption and exchange of her poems as it does with her nostalgic idealization of everyday life. Her popularity signified the growing importance of the domestic economy in the marketplace as her readers bought into two traditionally masculine, elitist, and eastern Canadian spheres: property and print. ('Too Close' 109)

Jaques published most of her work in newspapers, but her verse did also appear in magazines; indeed, her poem 'After Summer Holidays' appears on the same page as Byrne Hope Sanders's September 1934 editorial for *Chatelaine*, quoted above. Rifkind's account reveals that for Canadian intellectuals, Jaques

---

[17] On Bourdieu and *art moyen* in French culture, see Pollentier.
[18] Among these, Roberts is the only one to concentrate on contemporary (rather than early twentieth-century) culture. She considers the 'insertions into the middlebrow' (227) of writers such as Yann Martel and Rohinton Mistry, who have achieved wide audiences and extensive media exposure through winning literary prizes. For additional brief references to the middlebrow in relation to the Canadian culture of the later twentieth and twenty-first centuries, see Martin; York 22, 176.

and her enthusiastic readers represented the menace of 'a self-improving and half-educated middle class,' which 'threatened elite culture by poaching some of its elements in efforts at self-improvement and class mobility' (102). Arguably, the mainstream periodicals themselves, as well as the popular authors published in their pages, embodied a similar threat, and this is doubtless one reason why their influence and power have not yet been fully acknowledged by Canadian literary critics or cultural historians.

The term 'middlebrow' usefully connects the mainstream magazines with other cultural products which shared their aim of combining education with entertainment within a Canadian nationalist frame. Literary anthologies, for instance, performed these same functions. Robert Lecker notes that the inclusion of advertising in mid-twentieth-century anthologies of Canadian literature 'altered the status of the book itself, bringing it closer to a magazine format and diluting its authority as a self-contained literary work divorced from consumer culture' (160). In a Canadian context, 'middlebrow' takes on particular resonance through its entanglement with cultural nationalism, and with the debates over modernism and cosmopolitanism in the middle decades of the twentieth century. Canadian middlebrow culture is also distinctive in other ways, since Canada is often constructed in terms of middleness. It is inevitably seen an intermediate space between the imperial powers of the UK and the US, but with the advantage of being able to combine and adapt American and European styles and traditions. In addition, there is a clear emphasis in Canadian literary and public discourse on mediation, moderation, and the avoidance of excess and extremes. All these dimensions of middlebrow culture are evident in the content of our six chosen magazines, and will be foregrounded in the chapters which follow.

Travel and mobility

Travel, in the earlier twentieth century, was a symbol of achievement, cultural literacy, *savoir faire*, and personal means, as its extensive promotion and discussion in mainstream and 'smart' magazines demonstrates. Yet among all the recent studies of middlebrow culture and middle-class taste—which between them cover fashion, food, gardens, and interior decor, as well as literary taste and cultural consumption—there is not one which addresses the close connections between travel and the aspirational culture of the middlebrow. The theme of travel or—more broadly—of mobility provides a focus for our readings in the vast archive of 35 years' worth of Canadian magazines. We are especially interested in Canadians as potential or actual transatlantic tourists, though domestic holidaymaking was also important for the mainstream magazines and their audiences.

While numerous historians and literary critics have discussed the experiences and writings of visitors to Canada, surprisingly little research has been done on Canadians themselves as travellers. There are two books, however, which we have found especially helpful. In her foundational study *Canadians in Europe 1851–1900* (1987), Eva-Marie Kröller provides a valuable prehistory for our own research, as well as a model for transcultural comparison. She explores imaginaries of transatlantic travel in the writing of both French- and English-speaking Canadians, drawing extensively on unpublished sources as well as on travel books and journalism, and emphasising the extent of public interest in European cultures:

> Europe inspired *both* French and English-Canadians. Essays on British, French, Italian, and German art, architecture, city-design, and topical political and social events filled the periodical press. [...] Authors used European settings as backdrops for historical and suspense novels and for fictionalized travelogues, not only because these settings offered escapist entertainment, but also because they had a direct or indirect bearing on Canada's own growing culture. (2)

Historian Cecilia Morgan's *'A Happy Holiday': English Canadians and Transatlantic Tourism, 1870–1930* (2008) is more directly pertinent to our work, since its narrative extends into the early twentieth century and concentrates, as we do, on the aspirations of upwardly mobile Canadians. For source material, Morgan uses archived and published diaries written by Anglophone Canadian tourists, together with some accounts by travellers who went overseas for professional reasons. She frames her study in a way which resonates with the themes of our book:

> for middle- and upper-middle-class English Canadians, transatlantic tourism was desirable for its own sake, as well as offering multiple opportunities for reflection on, and perhaps for testing and questioning, social and cultural sensibilities. This is not to argue that a trip overseas became de rigueur for all those who thought of themselves, and were seen by others, as middle class. [...] However, the press and periodical literature, texts that helped constitute the public spheres of the nineteenth-century middle classes, constantly and consistently invited those who might never venture further than Truro, Hamilton, Selkirk, or Victoria to imagine themselves as doing so, to acquire and share in

> the social and cultural tastes, knowledge, and customs of like-minded men and women. (5)

While Morgan centres her attention on autobiographical texts which recorded journeys actually taken, we prioritise the periodical texts which engendered the desire to travel. Like Morgan, we focus on leisure travel rather than the enforced displacements of the war years, but unlike her, we include sources in French as well as English.

Dean Irvine's study of women and Canadian little magazines, one of the few previous monographs to be devoted to a specific genre of Canadian periodical, provides another model for our research. It is also relevant to the theme of mobility, since one chapter contains a detailed account of Flora Macdonald Denison's *Sunset of Bon Echo* (1916–20), a feminist literary magazine which, curiously, was published out of an Ontario summer resort. As Irvine notes, the magazine was 'in effect, a literary travel brochure' (189) which promoted the Bon Echo Inn, owned by Denison. Other critical material on Canadians and travel takes the form of focused studies of individual writers or destinations. These include Karen Dubinsky's *The Second Greatest Disappointment: Honeymooning and Tourism at Niagara Falls* (1999) and Wendy Roy's *Maps of Difference: Canada, Women, and Travel* (2005). Both books range over a period extending from the nineteenth century through to the late twentieth, and both foreground questions of gender. Dubinsky explores the sexualisation of place through tourism, while Roy's detailed analysis of three authors (Anna Jameson, Mina Hubbard, and Margaret Laurence) concentrates on 'one of the fundamental problems of women's travel writing: conflictual representations of gender and imperialism' (9). Julia Harrison's *Being a Tourist: Finding Meaning in Pleasure Travel* is an anthropological study based on interviews with 33 Canadian travel enthusiasts. Harrison categorises them as 'the new middle class,' a group who 'take pride in the degree of antimaterialism generally reflected in their mode of travel' (10). Nicole Neatby's extended article on the social history of tourism in Quebec covers the same period as we have chosen for our book, and compares the perspectives of visitors with the images of the province offered in government tourist publicity. There are also, of course, numerous published discussions of Canadian travel writing in both English and French, and a still larger body of material in the general field of travel and tourism studies. While *Magazines, Travel and Middlebrow Culture* is not a study of travel writing as a literary genre, nor of tourism as a sociological phenomenon, we do, naturally, draw on these wider academic contexts during the course of our analysis of periodical texts.[19]

Almost all the secondary sources and literary anthologies on Canadians and travel focus primarily on the exploration and settlement eras (pre-twentieth century) or on the post-1960 period. This book concentrates on the decades in between, which tend to be left out. As Victoria Kuttainen notes: 'Remarkably, the record of interwar travel is almost absent in the history of Canadian literature' (149). This is indeed curious, since the period from the 1920s to the 1950s saw not only a vast expansion in tourism across the Atlantic world and beyond, but also rapid technological advances which increased the speed, comfort, safety, and affordability of travel in all modes. As a result, the meanings attached to mobility gradually altered over this period. During the First World War, technologies of transport by air, sea, and land advanced rapidly, with far-reaching effects on international and domestic travel in the period following the conflict (Pearce). The holiday industry expanded during the 1920s, and transatlantic and Pacific leisure travel, which had of course been suspended during the conflict, was resumed with vigour.

In terms of Canadians in particular, Cecilia Morgan reflects that, while 'it might be logical to think that Canadians' travel across the Atlantic underwent a fundamental shift in quantity and quality after the first World War,' there is in fact no solid evidence as to whether the 'numbers of tourists who visited Britain and Europe in the 1920s or 1930s decreased, increased, or remained the same' in comparison to the pre-war years (317). She argues, though, that 'men and women from across English-speaking Canada still saw going abroad as a significant aspect of being both a "Canadian" and, equally importantly, an educated member of the middle class' (317). In addition, 'Europe still held much of the same cultural and social fascination it had before the war, although other ways of seeing the Continent and other considerations also came into play. Transatlantic tourism in the 1920s was marked by both change *and* continuity' (318). Among the changes was the rise of 'battlefield tourism' (see Lloyd), and

---

[19] For surveys of Canadian travel writing, see Kröller, 'Exploration and Travel' and 'Travellers and Travel-Writing.' There are anthologies of travel writing by visitors to Canada (see Gatenby; Carol Martin) and of travel writing by Canadians (Dobbs; Mulhallen; Rooke). Among the most relevant sources on the cultural history and sociology of travel are MacCannell; Rojek and Urry; Urry. Urry's theorisation of the 'tourist gaze,' the process by which tourist experiences are constructed and organised, is especially helpful. On travel and the construction of Canadian authorship, see Kuttainen. Other references are given in the following chapters.

the influence of memories of wartime mobilisation on the present perceptions of visitors to Europe.

The 1920s also witnessed a substantial growth in tourism into, and within, Canada itself, which was by then accessible by car to American visitors. Americans particularly favoured Quebec, and the number of tourists coming from the US increased rapidly during the decade (Dubinsky, 'Everybody' 13; Neatby 466–67). Holidays were increasingly promoted to, and affordable for, the middle classes, and the existing accommodation choices—luxurious hotels in lake, mountain, and urban resorts—began to be supplemented by cheaper options such as boarding houses. Although plane travel was promoted in Canadian magazines from the mid-1930s, vacations during this era were generally taken by car, train, or steamship.[20] Indeed, the interwar period was the heyday of the luxury transatlantic steamship, and at this time, Canadian Pacific changed focus from emigration to tourism.

Magazines increasingly presented tourism—and especially foreign travel—as a status symbol, and also offered a covert training for would-be travellers. *Mayfair*, for instance, regularly featured photographs of wealthy Canadians boarding cruise liners, often using them to illustrate features on shipboard fashions and etiquette. The most favoured European destinations were the same ones which, as Kröller demonstrates, had been popular with Canadians throughout the nineteenth century: Paris, London, and Rome (*Canadians in Europe* 25). Morgan points out that Scotland and Ireland were also important, because so many white Canadians could trace their ancestry to those countries (59–77; 124–60). France, Britain, and Ireland seemed—for the descendants of immigrants from those countries—to combine a sophistication unavailable in Canada with a degree of cultural familiarity and shared historical experience. The magazines offered a complex representation of major European cities as centres of nostalgia and origin, on one hand, and sites of modern urbanity and glamour, on the other. In this way, they contributed to the construction of a racially and linguistically exclusive version of Canadian identity, reinforcing the notion of the two 'founding nations,' and erasing the experience of First Nations people and of ethnic minority immigrants from Asia, eastern Europe, and other regions.

During the 1940s, leisure travel stood in stark contrast to military mobilisation. Vacations within Canada were heavily promoted, not only as a means for Canadians to discover more about their own country, but also in terms of a necessary rest from taxing war work. During this period, Quebec

---

[20] On the history of Canadian Pacific (CP) and Canadian National railways, see Tom Murray. On the history of CP's shipping, see Pigott; Stevenson.

INTRODUCTION

City became a substitute for Paris, and the BC mountains for the Scottish highlands, and coverage of these destinations in the magazines relates in intriguing ways to mythologies of nation, region, and wilderness. New York was also a favoured destination at this time. Like London, its desirability—at least for white Anglophone Canadians—was enhanced by its combination of the exotic and the familiar. Following the war, leisure travel became accessible to an increasingly wide group of consumers who began to be subdivided into different markets according to tastes and means. Dubinsky comments on 'the good life of plenty and optimism attained by a surprisingly large number of white North Americans after World War II' (*Second* 2). Indeed, the middle class was rapidly expanding during this era, and incorporating recent immigrants and others who, in earlier decades, would have been excluded from privileged practices such as leisure travel. During the 1950s, outdoor activities were strongly emphasised in magazine features. Summer camps, lakeside cottages, hiking or canoeing tours, wilderness travel, camping, and youth hostelling all received coverage, in *Maclean's* especially, but also in the family-oriented titles.

Our research has traced the expanding range of the destinations which were regularly promoted to Canadians in the pages of magazines.[21] In 1927, for example, Paris, Rome, Pisa, Naples, Florence, and New York were the subjects of travel features in *Mayfair*. By 1935, Bermuda, London, Gleneagles, Edinburgh, Lisbon, Palermo, Algiers, Dubrovnik, and Naples were among the international destinations covered, while an increasing number of articles on domestic travel showcased resorts including Lake Muskoka and Beaumaris in Ontario, Murray Bay (now La Malbaie) in Quebec, Lake Windermere in BC, and St Andrews-by-the-Sea in New Brunswick. In the 1940s, most travel pieces focused on Canadian tourist regions and cities, or occasionally on Mexico. By the 1950s, quite a wide range of places in North and South America, the Caribbean, and western Europe were being featured, although the emphasis was on 'safer' destinations such as those with a British colonial heritage—British Guiana, Jamaica, Barbados—and those in the supposedly more sanitary parts of Europe like Austria, Scandinavia or, as the title of one article had it, 'Clean, orderly Switzerland.'

In examining this history of travel through the lens of periodical texts, we uncover its intersections with, and responses to, shifts in Canadian class structures and unfolding debates about taste. We also point to the ways in which it illuminates Canada's relationship with the wider world. Canadian

---

[21] For a visualisation of this data, see the timemap on the 'Magazines, Travel and Middlebrow Culture in Canada' website (http://www.middlebrowcanada.org/timemap.aspx).

culture is generally overshadowed by US culture, because of America's much greater power to export its identity beyond its own borders—through global brands, Hollywood film, and so on. Yet the magazines considered in this study demonstrate the influence of Canadians abroad—the internationally famous authors whose careers were launched in *Chatelaine* and the *Canadian Home Journal*, for instance, or the cosmopolitan, worldly figures represented in *Mayfair*'s 'Globe-Trotting Canadians' feature. Our theme of mobility locates Canadian magazines in the context of an increasingly global modern culture, and our study is therefore relevant to other 'overshadowed' cultures, including those of many Commonwealth countries.

Structure of the book

The first two chapters concentrate on the magazine as a material object in a marketplace, while the third and fourth chapters explore some of the themes which dominated the magazines' content. The subject of travel therefore becomes increasingly prominent as the chapters succeed one another, while the notion of middlebrow culture frames the discussion throughout. The amount of attention given to each magazine, and to each period of its history, varies in proportion to the extent of its coverage of travel and related topics. (For instance, *Mayfair* focused on leisure travel throughout its run, so is important to all our chapters, while the family-oriented and Francophone magazines increased their attention to holidays and tourism in the 1950s, and therefore become more central in our accounts of post-Second World War developments. To give another example: the women's magazines often approached the theme of mobility via fashion features, so these titles are prominent in Chapter Three, while *Maclean's*, which never covered fashion, is omitted from this chapter.)

'Chapter One: Marketplace' delineates the mainstream magazine marketplace in Canada over the period from the 1920s until the 1950s. It explores pricing, circulation, and the important role of advertising, which increasingly financed the magazines as well as enabling them to shape and address their target audiences. The chapter also examines the nationalist orientation of the magazines, and the ways in which they differentiated themselves from one another and from their foreign competitors. It concludes with a concise history of each of the magazines, with detail on their changing formats, their most influential editors and contributors, and the type of travel material they included. Given the dearth of information on these six titles, this chapter on its own represents a substantial addition to North American periodical history. 'Chapter Two: Pages' examines the relationship between the physical characteristics of the magazines and the type of material they published. Ardis and Collier call for 'new theoretical

INTRODUCTION

models and methodologies' to make sense of the 'radically transforming print ecology' of the late Victorian and modern eras (2). In response, the method of analysis used in our 'Pages' chapter is proposed as a contribution to print culture studies. Moving from detailed dissection of individual pages and single issues up towards broader surveys of an annual volume and of a full run, we demonstrate the different types of insight which each level of analysis makes possible. The sequential use of these four methods also shows up the elisions and absences which are inevitable in each type of reading. A close reading of a page or issue tells us important things about the interaction of adjacent items, but nothing about the way that periodicals situate themselves in time—by, for instance, pointing towards past or future issues (Parkinson). A more 'distant' method, surveying a year or several decades' worth of issues, reveals larger patterns but blurs the detail and relies on generalisations which can never take full account of all the data.

'Chapter Three: Fashions' considers not only the magazines' association of fashionable clothes with mobility and the exotic, but also their presentation of travel itself as a fashionable practice. The chapter offers close readings of different types of fashion report, ranging from the 'Paris Letters' of the 1920s to the staged photo shoots, taken on location, which featured in the 1950s. We argue that it is in their fashion writing, with its conceptual vocabulary of newness, authenticity, originality, difficulty, and eccentricity, that the magazines engaged most closely with discourses of modernism. The fashion journalism in the magazines was framed by advertising for clothing and beauty products, and our discussion of the relationship between these editorial and commercial materials prepares the way for 'Chapter Four: Consumers.' This chapter focuses on the magazines' construction of travel as an opportunity for consumption, a chance to experience luxury as well as to accumulate social and cultural capital. The aspirational figure of the traveller-consumer was constructed through a collaboration between fiction authors, travel writers, advertisers, and editors. Fantasies of mobility, we argue, were used to sell not only trips and holidays, but also consumer products and, indeed, copies of the magazines themselves. For readers who could not afford a trip across the Atlantic or across Canada, these glossy, illustrated periodicals offered proxy access to the glamour and prestige of travel.

Chapter One

MARKETPLACE

> *Ceux qui n'aspirent à rien, sont des ratés. Il faut toujours vouloir aller plus haut, et plus haut encore. Et pour gravir jusqu'au sommet, sachons se tenir par la main et monter ensemble, étroitement unis les uns aux autres, afin d'éviter les obstacles, de trouver la pente moins rude, le sentier plus sûr, de côtoyer, sans danger les précipices et d'arriver jusque là-haut, en pleine lumière, à toucher les étoiles sans jamais songer à les éteindre, mais à leur éclat somptueux, nous allumerons nos rêves qui sont tout d'amour pour la patrie, tout de tendresse pour la famille, tout d'espoir pour la race!*
> —Madeleine, editorial for *La Revue Moderne*, January 1926

In the first decades of the twentieth century, middle-class, consumer-oriented magazines were typically seen as a middle ground between the pulps and the avant-garde magazines of the period. The first pulp magazine, *Argosy*, was created by Frank Munsey in 1896. It was 7 x 10 inches in size and printed on inexpensive pulp paper. The magazine was a huge commercial success in the US and beyond, and was followed by a large body of similar periodicals. They were usually monthlies, and while they had garish covers, their internal pages consisted of densely packed type with few illustrations. The success of the pulps was entwined with the development of several popular genres, most notably hard-boiled detective fiction. But they were dismissed as 'lowbrow' publications that proved, in the rather snobbish words of H. L. Mencken, cultural critic and one-time owner of the pulp *Black Mask*, that 'nobody ever went broke underestimating the taste of the American people' (Douglas 90).[1] By contrast, mainstream magazines, which emerged in the US in the

---

[1] *Black Mask* was the birthplace of the hard-boiled detective genre, publishing Dashiell Hammett and Raymond Chandler. Its co-owners, Mencken and George Jean Nathan, sold the magazine after eight issues, using the profits to subsidise their elite

1880s and in Canada in the first decades of the twentieth century, targeted a wide middle-class audience with increasing amounts of disposable income.[2] This was the audience advertisers most wished to reach, and mainstream magazines proved an effective medium for promoting consumer goods and services, partly because their glossy paper stock was ideal for printing colour images and partly because they addressed a national audience. Usually 11 x 14 inches in size, these monthly or twice-monthly titles contained not only advertisements, but also lavish illustrations and, later, full-colour photo spreads. Their contents typically consisted of several discrete departments, including fiction, features, correspondence, travel, home décor, and—depending on the type of magazine—business and foreign affairs, or society reports and fashion, or cookery and child-rearing. These diverse contents cohered around the magazines' encouragement of readers' upwardly mobile instincts, particularly when it came to discriminating and sometimes luxurious consumption. The third group of periodicals, avant-garde or little magazines, have their origins in the 1890s, and were a part of what Kirsten MacLeod calls a 'revolution in print.' She argues: 'While the little magazines clearly styled themselves in opposition to these mass-market publications on one level, at another, they were implicated in the broader transformations to the field of magazine production' (8). These periodicals adopted diverse print formats, and published literature that was often experimental and, at times, controversial. They sought out intellectually elite audiences, and literary critics have located them at the top of the cultural hierarchy; certain publications have received sustained scholarly attention.[3]

The division of periodical publishing into pulp, mainstream, and little magazines is largely derived from American print history. Yet the general principles are useful to the Canadian context, in which pulps (both American imports and Canadian publications) circulated alongside mainstream titles and a host of home-grown little magazines that proved central to the formation of a specifically Canadian branch of modernist culture. The tripartite model offers a starting point for understanding the complexities of both authorly and readerly

---

magazine, *The Smart Set* (see Sharon Hamilton). On the history of pulps, see Erin Smith.

[2] 'Slicks,' 'glossies,' and 'smart' or 'quality' magazines are alternative labels for what we are calling 'mainstream' magazines (see Douglas; Hammill and Leick; Michael Murphy), though these terms are somewhat more appropriate to an American context, as they apply best to magazines such as *Vanity Fair* or *Esquire*.

[3] Among the many projects and discussions focusing on little magazines, see especially Edward L. Bishop; Irvine, *Editing*; Modernist Magazines Project; Modernist Journals Project; Morrisson.

communities as they took shape in conjunction with broader commercial and cultural forces. The boundaries between the three categories of periodical are, however, rather porous, and it is perhaps more useful to think in terms of a continuum rather than a fixed hierarchy. To use Andrew Thacker's words, the 'interplay between high and low circulations, between mass and minority publications, or between "pulp" and "slick" or "quality" magazines' (12) has been crucial to shaping scholarly work on periodicals.

Mainstream English-language magazines in Canada were markedly influenced by their American precursors, particularly *Munsey's Magazine* (1889–1929) and the *Ladies' Home Journal* (1893–). Richard Ohmann notes that the producers of these titles were the first to achieve a genuine mass circulation, by means of identifying a large aspirational audience, appealing to its desires, keeping the price to readers low, and selling advertising space to accrue profits.[4] He argues that this approach was the result of cleverly fusing together different periodical formats as the new mass-market monthlies:

> took from the weeklies the idea of a lively pictorial appearance, from these and a few of the monthlies a willingness to hustle ads and let them be splashy, from the women's magazines and the mail order journals the idea of a very low price that would attract a large audience of people with only a little extra money to spend. Some publishers of magazines from each of these genres had already discovered that such an audience could be delivered to advertisers at prices that would pay a major share of costs. And from the literary monthlies, the entrepreneurs of 1893 took the idea of offering this audience participation in mainstream culture, though they rechanneled that stream in such a way that it no longer implied life membership in an elite club; it was no longer rooted in family, old money, the past. (29)

Other magazines to adopt the same strategy included *Cosmopolitan* (1886–), *Good Housekeeping* (1885–), *Harper's Bazaar* (1867–), *McCall's Magazine* (1897–2001), and *The Saturday Evening Post* (1897–). The first four of these periodicals primarily targeted women, while *The Saturday Evening Post*, which appeared twice a month, initially targeted men.[5] When this proved unprofitable,

---

[4] *Munsey's* had a circulation of 40,000 in 1893. In October of that year, Munsey reduced the cover price from 25 to 10 cents, and by the following February, circulation had climbed to 200,000, rising to 500,000 by April. In 1898, Munsey claimed the magazine had the largest circulation in the world (Ohmann 25).

[5] *McClure's* (1893–1929), a literary and political magazine, was somewhat similar,

it reoriented itself as a family magazine—a pattern also seen in the history of *Maclean's*.[6] Indeed, *Maclean's* is markedly similar to *The Saturday Evening Post*, while *Chatelaine* and the *Canadian Home Journal* bear a striking resemblance to the *Ladies' Home Journal*. As the American periodicals expanded into foreign markets, they were increasingly identified as competitors for the Canadian titles they had so clearly influenced.

Magazines and the language divide

During the period covered by this study, the key Anglophone monthly and twice-monthly magazines published in Canada consisted of *Canadian Magazine* (1895–1939); *Canadian Home Journal* (1905–58); *Maclean's* (1911–), published as *The Busy Man's Magazine*, 1896–1911; *Everywoman's World* (1913–23); *Canadian Homes and Gardens* (1924–60); *Mayfair* (1927–59); *Chatelaine* (1928–); and *National Home Monthly* (1932–51), published as *Western Home Monthly*, 1899–1932. The major Francophone monthlies were *La Revue Populaire* (1907–63) and *La Revue Moderne* (1919–60).[7] In the later decades of their runs, these two titles were, likewise, strongly influenced by the high-quality American women's magazines. Initially, however, they were modelled on rather different types of publication. Denis Saint-Jacques and Lucie Robert note two precursors for *La Revue Moderne*: *L'Action française* (1917–28), which aimed to generate 'un sentiment d'appartenance nationale' (208), and *Le Terroir* (1918–40), which was originally published by La Société des arts, sciences et lettres de Québec, but had, by 1924, adopted a more mainstream format (209). *La Revue Populaire*, by contrast, was primarily a fiction magazine, and therefore must have taken its inspiration from the pulps.

The six periodicals chosen for discussion in this book intersected in format

---

though best remembered for its muck raking. Initially targeting a mixed audience, it later tried, unsuccessfully, to reinvent itself as a women's magazine, and was eventually merged with *The Smart Set*.

[6] Damon-Moore says of the *Post*: 'the commercial milieu of the late nineteenth century—informed as it was by an emphasis on the female consumer—demanded a broadening of the newer magazine to target women as well' (2). By 1910, it had a circulation of 1 million. It is worth noting that Thomas B. Costain, editor of *Maclean's* during the First World War, became a successful talent scout for *The Saturday Evening Post* during the 1920s.

[7] The Canadian weeklies, notably *Le Samedi* (1888–1963) and *Saturday Night* (1887–2005), fell between magazines and newspapers in terms of format and mix of content.

and type of content, and though the slant of editorials and articles varied, the topics discussed often coincided. A single company, Maclean Publishing (which, in 1945, became Maclean-Hunter) owned *Maclean's*, *Chatelaine*, *Mayfair*, and *Canadian Homes and Gardens*. The Francophone and Anglophone magazines were similar in many aspects of their content, ethos, and design, yet there seems to have been very little interaction between the two groups of publications until 1960, when *La Revue Moderne* was turned into a sister publication for *Chatelaine*, named *Châtelaine*. Geographically, the English-language magazines were usually published in Toronto, and the French-language ones in Montreal,[8] discouraging day-to-day exchange amongst editors, managers, and production staff. Magazines in the two languages assumed that they were speaking to distinct audiences, to the extent that editors and writers often discussed the culture of the people on the other side of the perceived divide, or pondered questions of unity and difference.

Many authors and journalists wrote for more than one Anglophone title, or for both the Francophone magazines, but we have found only two who contributed to magazines in both languages. Monique Bosco (1927–2007) was of Austrian origin and a native speaker of German, but following her emigration to Canada in 1948, she developed a career as a journalist and researcher, primarily working through the medium of French but sometimes writing in English (Toussaint). She also published poetry and novels in French. Between 1952 and 1955, Bosco contributed six articles on literature and the performing arts to *La Revue Moderne*,[9] and between 1963 and 1969 she worked as a columnist for *Maclean's*. A better-known author with an important presence in both the Anglophone and Francophone magazines was Gabrielle Roy (1909–83). In 1939, she began contributing to *La Revue Moderne* as a freelance writer, and wrote numerous pieces during the war years. Her story 'Sécurité' appeared in *La Revue Moderne* in March 1948, but it had been previously published in an English translation in *Maclean's* on 15 September 1947. Three months earlier, *Maclean's* had published Roy's story 'Dead Leaves,' this time in the original French but with an English version on the facing pages. Roy's international fame granted her the glamour and prestige that Maclean-Hunter wished to associate with their leading magazine: an editorial paragraph placed alongside the story identified her as a 'young Quebec writer whose novel "The Tin Flute" has skyrocketed her to literary fame' (21). The use of the English title

---

[8] There are some exceptions: *Western Home Monthly* was published in Winnipeg, and *Mayfair*, while initially published in Toronto, relocated to Montreal in December 1936.

[9] For a list, see the catalogue search facility on our website, www.middlebrowcanada.org.

for *Bonheur d'occasion* (1945) hinted at the adoption of her work by Anglophone audiences. As Marie Vautier notes, literary historians identify Roy as 'a representative of an evolving French Canada, and, later, Québec. Roy, however, was strongly committed to the bilingual readership that her work fed' (196). Rosemary Chapman, outlining the importance of Roy's work (in translation) to the English-Canadian canon, locates her 'somewhere *between* English and French Canada' (153).

The publication of the original text of Roy's short story in *Maclean's* is a rare instance of an item in French appearing in one of the Anglophone magazines. English texts hardly ever appeared in the Francophone titles either, although there are a few isolated examples in *La Revue Moderne*. For instance, the 15 December 1919 issue featured an article by Montreal author John Boyd, 'The Secret of National Unity.' In his article on the political orientation of *La Revue Moderne* in its early years, Jean-Christian Pleau, after pointing out that Boyd's piece was presented without translation or explanation, comments:

> Ce fait n'est pas unique dans l'histoire de la revue, mais demeure néanmoins singulier. On peut y voir d'abord le reflet d'une réalité sociale, à savoir que la bourgeoisie mondaine qui formait le lectorat de la revue pouvait fort vraisemblablement lire sans trop de difficultés un texte en anglais. Mais dans le cas de l'article de Boyd, l'utilisation de la langue anglaise n'était pas non plus dépourvue d'implications symboliques, dans la mesure où il s'agissait d'en appeler à l'unité nationale. (218)

In the early years of its existence, *La Revue Moderne* vigorously advocated Canadian national unity, and launched several attacks on the French-Canadian nationalism which had gained strength during and after the First World War. The magazine's political positioning easily explains Madeleine's choice to print the essay by Boyd, who was President of the Canadian National League and author of a biography of George-Étienne Cartier, one of the 'Fathers of Confederation.'

Three decades later, and in the aftermath of another world war, *Chatelaine* published an article, 'We're closer than we think,' by French-Canadian novelist and journalist Roger Lemelin (1919–92). It appeared in the July 1951 issue and reflected on the apparent divide—and underlying bond—between French and English Canada. Lemelin explains how he went on his first trip to Paris in 1949, initially feeling 'happy to visit the land of my forefathers, and what seemed to me to be my true *patrie*' (33). Yet, within a few days, he was longing for the Canadian landscape: 'my Laurentian mountains, my immense Canadian sky' (33). He meets an equally homesick Anglophone in a bar, and the two men excitedly introduce themselves as simply 'Canadian' to one another. They agree that they have much in common: an admiration of French-Canadian hockey player Maurice Richard, a respect for both Wolfe and Montcalm as 'two courageous warriors,' and an appreciation of fishing, skating, and 'those Quebec girls—they certainly outclass all the *Parisiennes*' (33). The foreign setting of Paris, then, puts pressure on the identities of Canadians abroad, and pushes them to recognise that their nostalgia for a supposed homeland is hollow, whereas their connection to Canada's past and present is a source of meaning and unity. Lemelin bolsters this argument by reflecting on the new threat posed by nuclear arms, insisting that this will force Canada to take a united stance in world politics and so define what 'Canadian' will come to mean for future generations of both language groups.

While moments of direct cross-cultural exchange, such as the publication of Lemelin's article in an Anglophone periodical, are rare, we have nevertheless found that certain key characteristics of mainstream Canadian magazines work across the language divide. At the commercial level, companies ranging from Canadian Pacific to Magic Baking Powder used identical advertisements in the different magazines, generating a common consumer ethos that ignored linguistic, religious, and cultural differences. Many of the advertisements were placed by US companies, and the influence of American popular culture was evident across all six of the Canadian magazines. Yet resistance to Americanisation was equally evident, and all the magazines appealed to patriotic feelings about Canada as a whole, even though the particular forms of nationalist discourse they espoused varied between titles and over time. Whilst the Francophone titles looked to France, and the Anglophone ones to Britain, for cultural resources and a sense of heritage, all six titles nevertheless used Paris as their primary reference point for high culture, fashion, and sophistication. The magazines 'weave shared emotional repertoires' (Hurley 6) through affective appeals to their readers' presumed attachment to France, Britain, and Europe more generally. These gestures work to privilege Canada's white population, circulating a vision of national belonging which excludes Native and ethnic minority citizens.

There is an important convergence, then, in that magazines in both languages traded in nostalgia for the old world while marketing a modern lifestyle to a readership it addressed as middle class. In part, this lifestyle and class identity was defined visually: fashion illustration, for instance, presented very similar images of women to English- and French-Canadian readers. It is important to remember that both Francophone titles marketed themselves primarily as family magazines up until the 1940s, and it was not until after the war that they began to target women specifically (see Des Rivières, Gerson, and Saint-Jacques 249).[10] Nevertheless, within the family magazine format, content aimed at women resonated with similar content in *Chatelaine* and the *Journal*. At the level of print production and layout, *La Revue Moderne* and *La Revue Populaire* both came to look more like the Anglophone and American women's magazines over time. For most of the 1930s, for example, *La Revue Moderne* had a simple monochrome cover with a small inset photograph, and the contents consisted primarily of text, with relatively little advertising. By the 1950s, covers typically featured a photograph of a female model in fashionable attire, and on the inside pages, the proportion of space devoted to illustration and to advertising had markedly increased.

Constructing an audience: circulation and advertising

Throughout the 1930s, the nationally oriented magazines—*Maclean's*, *Chatelaine*, and the *Canadian Home Journal*—each proclaimed, on their front covers, a net paid circulation (subscriptions and newsstand sales) of about 130,000. This rose to approximately 250,000 per title in the 1940s, and again to just under half a million in the 1950s. *Mayfair* had a more restricted, but decidedly affluent, audience centred on Toronto and Ottawa; its circulation did not rise above 20,000 (Sutherland 248). *La Revue Populaire*'s circulation increased from 5,000 to 125,000 over the period of its existence (Sarfati and Martin), while *La Revue Moderne*'s stood at 23,000 in the early 1920s, and had grown to over 100,000 by 1960.[11] As early as 1930, *La Revue Moderne* claimed to have 100,000 readers (as opposed to purchasers); this is perhaps plausible, since copies of magazines were shared within and between families, so that the number of readers greatly exceeded the net paid circulation. Towards the end of the 1950s, however, mainstream magazines went into a steep decline: both the *Journal* and *La Revue Moderne* were sold to Maclean-Hunter Publishing and merged with *Chatelaine*, which, from 1960, appeared in both English and French. Meanwhile, *Mayfair*, *Canadian Homes and Gardens*, and *La*

---

[10] This shift was less to do with social change in French-speaking Canada, which didn't gather force until the 1960s, and more to do with the demands of the periodical marketplace. Before the war, the English-speaking population of Canada was just about large enough to support a magazine aimed primarily at men (*Maclean's*) alongside the women's titles, whereas the smaller French-speaking population could only sustain generalist titles which appealed to everyone. As advertising revenue became increasingly necessary to the funding of all mainstream magazines, however, the focus turned more and more towards women, as the primary consumers.

[11] Beaulieu and Hamelin vol. 5: 294–95; Ricard.

Revue Populaire went out of print. There are several possible explanations for this, notably the availability of other forms of mass culture such as television and cheap paperbacks, the fragmentation of periodical publishing into niche markets, and the migration of advertising to other venues, such as television and newspaper colour supplements.

During the early twentieth century, advertising became the primary source of funding for mainstream magazines.[12] In *Selling Themselves: The Emergence of Canadian Advertising* (2001), Russell Johnston notes: 'Raymond Williams has dubbed advertising "the magic system," a term that invokes both sides of advertising's social role. Advertising is "magic" in so far as it endows material objects with identifications and associations that they otherwise would not have.' At the same time: 'Advertising is also a system, in that it provides financial support to cultural publishing, broadcasting, and now new media. Hence, advertising's role in society is both cultural and structural' (9). In North America, the establishment of the Audit Bureau of Circulations in 1915 indicated the growing influence of advertising over periodical culture. A cross-border organisation based in Chicago, the Bureau's purpose was to ensure the accuracy of the circulation figures that magazines provided to advertisers (Johnston 130–32). In the early 1920s, the newly founded Magazine Publishers' Association of Canada (MPAC) began a campaign to persuade advertisers that Canadian magazines had large audiences which were interested in their products and capable of purchasing them.[13] A full-page advertisement in the 15 September 1932 *Maclean's* explained that:

> with a net paid circulation totalling more than 780,000 copies each issue, the five magazines listed on this page now provide a coverage of better than every second urban home from coast to coast. Their circulation is more than two and one-half times what it was ten years ago.

---

[12] In the US, the shift from subscriptions to advertising as the main source of income for periodicals began in the 1890s (see Damon-Moore; Garvey; Ohmann; Scanlon). The orientation towards consumerism came later to Canada, with print culture historians highlighting a decisive shift in the 1920s (see Johnston; Sutherland; Vipond, *Mass*).

[13] *Mayfair* did not participate in this campaign, suggesting that its goal was to seek out a more refined and restricted audience. It may also have wished to eschew the crass process of selling itself to advertisers, despite its heavy concentration of commercial content. Alternatively, since its circulation was relatively low, it may simply not have been strategic for the Maclean Company to include this magazine in its claims to large readerships.

Their prestige and influence has been enhanced accordingly. (Magazine Publishers)

The magazines in question were *Canadian Home Journal*, *Western Home Monthly*, *Maclean's*, *The Canadian Magazine*, and *Chatelaine*. Collectively, they promised to reach a nationwide audience, and the reference to their prestige and influence implies that their respective (and, to some extent, overlapping) audiences likewise possessed these qualities. Advertisers were more interested in urban householders, as they would be more likely than rural dwellers to have access to shops and less likely to rely on home production to supply the needs of their families. In their effort to promote themselves as advertising venues, the magazines constructed their audience as modern, mobile, and at least moderately affluent. An advertisement in *Chatelaine* from June 1928 entitled 'Straight to the Heart of Canada's Buying Power' (see Figure 1) proclaimed that the magazine's readers consisted of 'the leadership families of the Dominion from coast to coast' (Maclean Publishing). The idea of a 'leadership family' was highly suggestive, encompassing everything from being well educated and possessing political or commercial influence to having an awareness of consumer trends and a willingness to invest in products as a means of social display.

Advertisements were often identical across the different Canadian magazines, consolidating their shared aspirational quality. Advertising constituted roughly one-third of the content of each magazine in the 1930s, and this percentage increased steadily over the decades; by the mid-1950s, roughly half of the content was commercial material. There was some variation across titles. The percentage of advertising in *Mayfair*, for example, typically worked out to 30% in the late 1920s and early 1930s, and this figure rose to roughly 45% by the 1950s. *Maclean*'s, by comparison, consisted of about 40% advertising content in the early 1930s, and maintained this level fairly consistently in later decades. The overlaps and divergences in commercial content between the titles are telling. As we discuss in Chapter Three, while five of the magazines reported extensively on fashion, these columns were accompanied by very different types of advertisement. The women's and family titles ran ads for patterns, fabrics, and sewing machines, whereas *Mayfair* sold advertising space to department stores such as Holt Renfrew's and Eaton's, and to exclusive boutiques. Apart from *Mayfair*, all of the magazines contained many advertisements for foodstuffs (Ritz crackers, Campbell's soups, Heinz baby foods), household cleansers (Chipso, Listerine, Old Dutch cleanser), and beauty products (Cutex nail varnish, Woodbury soap, Ipana toothpaste). *Mayfair* did not run advertisements for these kinds of product at all; rather, its advertising sections contributed to the construction of its audience as leisured, monied people who did not have to do their own housework, sewing, or cooking.

For readers of the more domestically oriented magazines, advertisers promised to make life simpler by providing effective household products and appliances, and to assist in improving health and appearance. Such advertising incites, and trades on, fears that one might fail as a housewife and mother, or that one might fall out of fashion (either in dress or home décor) in ways that reflected social or material shortcomings.[14] The desire for advancement meant that, in Russell Johnston's words, 'advertising played upon the anxieties of readers by suggesting that specific products would help them to achieve the status or acceptance they desired. It worked its magic to articulate and reinforce the relationships between lifestyle, status, and material possessions' (17).[15] This 'magic' cut across language boundaries, as identical advertisements with translated copy appeared in the Francophone and Anglophone magazines. This also holds true for wartime government adverts which, by playing on patriotic feelings, marked an assumption that readers shared a common Canadian identity.

The most telling advertisements of all—the ones that dominated the magazines and most clearly portrayed consumers as concerned with upward mobility—were for cars and leisure travel. Of the total advertising content, a remarkable 40% is for cars and car-related products, consistently, across decades and across all six titles. Advertising for leisure travel (cruises, hotels, rail journeys, and, in the 1950s, air travel) took up another 10%, making the theme of geographic mobility central to half of the consumer advertising in the magazines. Moreover, the boundary between the upper-crust *Mayfair* reader and readers of other magazines collapsed when it came to the aspiration to achieve greater mobility, whether it was in the form of a rail ticket or a Studebaker. An advertisement for Packard Cars in the 1 January 1930 issue of *Maclean's* focused on luxury and status. It combined an exotic scene depicting 'the splendour and luxury of Cleopatra's barge' with a description of Packard owners as patrons, rather than consumers, 'who know and appreciate fine things' (see Figure 2). A Packard, then, indicated social prestige by drawing from a notion of the

---

[14] On advertising in women's magazines, see Korinek, *Roughing* 139–41, 158–60; McCracken.

[15] We are concerned to distinguish between Canadian and American contexts, yet on this topic, there are many similarities. Indeed, Johnston argues that Canadian adworkers looked 'south for inspiration and confirmation of their abilities,' adding: 'The Canadians did not view this as a process of acculturation. They were not adopting American business practices. They were adopting modern business practices' (60).

ancient past to endow the car with a mythical royal status. While advertisements in the women's magazines tended to place greater emphasis on the reliability of the cars, they often depicted them against a backdrop of dramatic scenery, suggesting—especially to Ontario-based readers—that the cars might take them on an ambitious journey across Canada (see Figure 3).

Tapping into the twin themes of travel and upward mobility, products as different as Jergens hand lotion, Westclox clocks, and Canada Dry ginger ale were promoted using the imagery of travel. An advertisement for Canada Dry that appeared in the June 1934 issues of several of the magazines ties together home and mobility with class and consumer desire. Beneath an image of a family dining out, the copy reads:

> there scarcely is a place you'll go where you won't find Canada Dry waiting to cheer and refresh you. It's an honored guest at all the better hotels, clubs, and restaurants. On dining cars. On ocean liners. And you can enjoy it in virtually every port and city of the world. […] And for the home, buy The Champagne of Ginger Ales by the case.

The ad copy suggests continuity between the private home and the glamorous environments of modern travel. Ginger ale was far more affordable than an ocean cruise or a trip to a hotel, yet it seems to bring the inaccessible prestige of luxury travel into the ordinary household. The visual image of the Canadian leadership family is cheerfully aspirational—comfortable with their everyday lives, they are nonetheless both outward- and upward-looking.

Where consumer goods relied on linkages between mobility and luxury to make a product appealing, travel advertisements explicitly encouraged readers to purchase the experience of luxury itself, an experience which was portrayed in lavish illustrations and narrated through ebullient ad copy. A Depression-era advertisement for the Jasper Park Lodge declared that guests would enjoy 'trail riding, motor trips to scenic wonderspots, tennis, swims in a warm outdoor pool, and the restful formal luxury' of the hotel, along with 'evenings of bridge, music, dancing, and social contacts with friendly folk from all over the world.' The realities of Depression-era poverty are absent, with a fantasy of leisured sociality offered in their place. Advertisements like this resonate strongly with Roland Marchand's argument, in *Advertising the American Dream*, that:

> the 'society' of the wealthy […] was an organized society. As revealed in advertisements, it had distinct boundaries and standards of admission. People who were 'in society' could be confidently labelled as such; others could be described as seeking to 'break in.' For their own tactical

purposes, advertisers simultaneously stressed both the clarity of such boundaries and the ease of crossing them—the first to enhance the exclusiveness and desirability of the life of the rich, and the second to suggest how easily the advertised product would eliminate barriers to upward mobility. (194–95)

In this light, travel advertising became a particularly compelling means of conceptualising one's position in the social world, for it reinforced social divisions by things like first-, second-, and third-class tickets, while simultaneously suggesting that people from all different backgrounds could be brought together in front of the Mona Lisa and share in the same experience. It was as if crossing a geographical border were a magical means of crossing a socio-economic border, and the traveller could subsequently bring home a degree of cultural capital that might translate into social and economic capital.

Advertisers, trust, and the ideal reader

In order for these notions of advancement and improvement to take hold, advertisers first needed to gain the trust of periodical readers, and editors participated in this process by mentioning specific products in their columns or reminding readers to read the advertisements as closely as they presumably read the fiction, features, and other materials. The placement of advertisements was also very important. For example, *Chatelaine*, the *Journal*, *La Revue Populaire*, and *La Revue Moderne* all had cookery sections that were framed by advertisements for baking supplies, sauces and soups, and kitchen appliances, while the travel sections of *Maclean's* and *Mayfair* abounded with advertisements for luggage, cruises, hotels, and travel clothing. More overtly, issues of *Chatelaine* in the thirties and forties included a page called 'This Month With Our Advertisers,' which bore a striking visual resemblance to the editorial and table of contents page. An index listing all the advertised products, with page numbers, appeared alongside a column in which Sanders enthused about various products. In the December 1931 issue, Sanders presents an image of the *Chatelaine* reader as a woman attuned to advertising, an understanding of which is deemed essential to a modern outlook:

> When advertisements are planned for *The Chatelaine*, the writers have a definite picture of the audience they are addressing—the modern chatelaine, 'mistress of a little castle.' She is young, alert, eager for the best, trained in values, and conscious of her great profession as a modern wife and mother.

Sanders goes on to draw attention to certain advertisements, analysing the relationship between text and image, and concluding that, like editorial content, advertising 'can only drop ideas, like pebbles in the water. [...] I can only suggest ways for you to consider the advertisements: you must do the exploring yourself.'[16] In April 1941, the *Canadian Home Journal* launched a similar column, 'Advertising Newscast,' placing it in the centre of the back page, in between the table of contents and the index to advertisers. The first instalment suggested that: 'Some of the best news, the smartest ideas, the most helpful instructions, are in today's advertising columns. In this new JOURNAL department, we shall have a chance to discuss a few items each month' (News Scout).[17]

Editors thus intervened in a way that both extended the construction of readers as consumers and helped advertisers appear trustworthy. Indeed, a series of advertisements in the *Canadian Home Journal* entitled 'Why You Should Buy Advertised Products' highlights the role of editors in vetting advertising content for the benefit of readers, on the one hand, and encouraging readers to engage with advertisements for the benefit of businesses, on the other. A note at the end of the first piece, in October 1930, informed readers that the *Journal* had:

> for over a quarter of a century, been doing business with manufacturers of advertised commodities. It has always maintained a strict censorship over its advertising pages. Like other reputable magazines we must be satisfied that an article has merit before we permit it to be presented to our readers. In exercising this careful vigilance we are protecting your interests, just as you can safeguard them yourself by purchasing only those articles that are nationally advertised and of established quality. ('Why You')

Subsequent pieces in the series, published over the period from 1930 to 1932, cited a variety of specific benefits to be derived from paying close attention to advertisements, such as the assurance of value for money and the protection of one's health. Advertisers aimed to convince readers that they had their best interests at heart, and editorial staff were complicit in this aim. Moreover, magazines tied together the work of shopping, which involved self-education in

---

[16] Garvey argues that magazines participated in training readers to interpret advertisements and 'to appreciate and respond to the kinds of narratives that advertising came to use' (15).

[17] See Scholes and Latham (especially 521) on the use of advertisers' indexes and accompanying text in magazines such as *Scribner's*.

an ever-changing marketplace, with the competition for money and status that underpinned middle-class aspiration.

In the French-language periodicals, there was a relative editorial silence regarding advertising. There are no promotions of the 'Straight to the Heart' variety, and no recommendations that readers look closely at advertisements. This absence suggests two possibilities: on the one hand, the magazines may have been averse to becoming vehicles for advertising; on the other, their lower circulation figures, combined with a perception that their readers were on average less affluent than English-Canadians, and more likely to live in rural areas, may have made it difficult for these magazines to attract advertising. As Denis Saint-Jacques observes in his essay on popular magazines in Quebec around the turn of the century:

> the American formula for success, that of the magazine as a vehicle for advertising, gradually became dominant. This was not yet obvious, however, in *La revue populaire*, which sold for $1 [annually] in 1909 and claimed 'to rival any other American magazine of the same price.' It was a monthly and then a fairly thick semi-monthly (96 to 148 pages), providing the usual columns, a long serial novel, illustrations, and wide-ranging information presented in an accessible form; the model was that of the mass-circulation magazine, but the proportion of advertising was small. (320)

In fact, it would not be until the 1950s that advertising would comprise a high proportion of the contents of *La Revue Moderne* and *La Revue Populaire*. During the interwar period, the small number of adverts that did appear were not visually striking: they were typically printed in black and white, and relegated to small spaces at the sides of the pages. The advertisements in the January 1932 *La Revue Moderne*, for instance, were for an eclectic assortment of things: travel to Bermuda, Quebec newspapers and magazines, strawberry ice cream, the Hotel Strand in Atlantic City, Bluenose Skis, a biography of Wilfrid Laurier, cotton fabric, Desjardins furriers, and Vicks VapoRub. While some products spoke to a desire to escape (to the Caribbean, America, or the ski slopes), others were attuned to domestic demands (food, fashions, medicine) and still others had more to do with French-Canadian culture (periodicals, the biography of Laurier). On the inside front cover, a Chevrolet advertisement linked magazine reading to conspicuous consumption and being in-the-know: 'Aux lecteurs de *La Revue Moderne* qui veulent savoir ce qu'il y a de plus nouveau en automobile.' The other two cover adverts in this issue point to the fact that *La Revue Moderne* was the most literary and intellectual of the six magazines. The inside back cover promoted the 'Journaux, Revues, Livres, Catalogues' printed by La Compagnie d'Imprimerie des Marchands, publisher of *La Revue Moderne*. The advertisement on the back cover was for the new *Petite Revue*, and proclaimed that '10,000 personnes ont acheté le premier numéro.' It promised prospective readers 'une magnifique publication de format commode contenant 112 pages de matière à lire. Ses romans moraux, ses articles intéressants, avec ses illustrations de bon goût, comprenant photos d'artistes de cinéma, vous feront agréablement passer votre moments de loisirs.' Good taste, an awareness of contemporary culture, and the pleasurable use of leisure time were brought together in the construction of the magazine's appeal. Taken together, the advertising items in this 1932 issue appeal to the same needs, aspirations, and patriotic sentiments evoked in the more lavish commercial material in the Anglophone magazines.

Pages devoted to letters from readers give further insight into the editorial construction of an intended audience, as well as the reception of a magazine. As Barbara Green points out, 'letters columns hold great significance for scholars of modern print culture: they reveal the traces of readers' interactions with a paper and highlight the ways in which feminist periodicals addressed their readers, invited them to try on new identities, and engaged them in the debates of the public sphere' (462).[18] *Chatelaine*, for instance, ran a letters page, 'The Last Word: Our Readers Have It,' during 1934. At later points the magazine had an intermittent 'Backchat' column, and in the early 1950s, a regular letters page was established, variously entitled 'Reader Takes Over,' 'You Were Asking *Chatelaine*,' and 'The Last Word is Yours.' These pages offered a space for feedback on the magazine's contents, and correspondents generally give their names and towns of residence, providing a useful snapshot of the geographical spread and gender balance of the readership. *Maclean's* published responses to its content in a semi-regular column entitled 'Brickbats and Bouquets' (1930–33), while enquiries from correspondents appeared in its 'Financial Queries' column. This is of particular interest for the insight it offers into the

---

[18] Green also acknowledges that 'correspondence columns certainly count as some of the more ephemeral aspects of weekly papers—their authors largely unknown, their reference points sometimes too distant to resonate today. And they are among the least likely materials to circulate in any manner after the periodical ceases publication: letters are unlikely to find their way into an anthology' (462). On the importance of correspondence columns for scholars of print culture, see also Shevelow, especially 37–38; Korinek, *Roughing* 79–87. For a discussion of reader letters as historical sources (focused on *Western Home Monthly* and the *Family Herald*) see Azoulay, especially 9–12.

socioeconomic status of regular readers, and even if some of the letters were perhaps redacted or faked, they are still revealing in terms of the way *Maclean's* positioned itself in the periodical marketplace. The magazine addresses an ideal reader who is prosperous yet thrifty, and letters from such readers are prioritised in the 'Financial Queries' column. This example is from 1927:

> *I am a constant reader of your magazine, and take this opportunity of seeking your advice regarding investment of my small savings. I am a civil servant, age 32; wife and four children; salary, $3,000 per year. Five per cent. of salary is deducted towards superannuation. I have $10,000 civil service insurance, costing $265.56 per year; $4,000 15–20 pay life insurance; $1,000 endowment costing $163.50 per year. All this insurance will be paid up between 40–45 years of age. Would you advise more insurance, or what would you suggest as an investment for my savings amounting to $700–$800 per year.—R. G. N. British Columbia.* ('Financial' 61)

This correspondent, like many of those who requested money advice from *Maclean's*, offers very detailed personal information. In comparison, those writing in to the women's advice columns tend to give away very little about themselves. The letters from Eleanor Dare's correspondents on the *Canadian Home Journal*'s problem page during the 1950s, for example, were signed with names such as 'Troubled,' 'Uncertain,' or even 'Good-looking' (Dare, 'I'd like'), and few of them revealed more than their age and gender.[19]

La Revue Moderne devoted much space to responses to readers' personal enquiries, but these columns can be hard to interpret, since the letters received from readers were not usually printed. The founding editor 'Madeleine' (Anne-Marie Huguenin) launched a letters page, 'Le Courrier de Madeleine,' with the first issue of the magazine. She promised: 'nos fidèles trouveront ici, avec l'expression de notre sollicitude affectueuse, le mot de conseil, de réconfort, de joie ou de tristesse.' When Madeleine temporarily left the magazine in 1928, the department continued on under the title 'Le Courrier du Mois' until 1938.[20] The page was prepared at first by 'Rosemonde' and then, from 1929 onwards, by 'Marjolaine' (Justa Leclerc). The column maintained its direct address to individual readers, but without reproducing or quoting from their

---

[19] The *Journal* started a letters page in December 1955; it had also established a 'Reader Advisory Board' in 1937.

[20] During 1941 and 1942, *La Revue Moderne* ran a readers' letters column, 'L'Opinion du lecteur,' alongside the editorial. This was similar to the correspondence columns in the Anglophone magazines, but it did not become a permanent feature.

letters. Thus, the editors exercised control over how readers and their concerns were represented, embedding them in their own rhetoric about the process and vision of the editorial department. In the January 1932 issue, Marjolaine comments that the magazine does its best to respond to all the diverse queries it receives, though this entails prioritising information with a general appeal: 'Nous ne pouvons limiter nos articles à quelques questions particulières—les quotidiens ont leur courrier à cet effet—nous devons rester dans la note générale en cherchant autant que possible à intéresser toutes celles qui lisent nos pages.' Yet, while catering to a broad audience, the correspondence columnists also treated each individual reader as someone important who should have a say in the development of the magazine. Marjolaine writes to her correspondent 'Lili': 'Nous avons beaucoup apprécié l'intérêt que vous témoignez à notre revue et nous prenons note de vos remarques.' On the same page, she replies to a reader signing herself 'Brune Maman': 'vos bons mots sont autant d'encouragements qui nous sont précieux.' 'Le Courrier du Mois,' then, continually praised readers, and expressed pleasure in meeting their needs as well as hopes about the role that *La Revue Moderne* played in their intellectual lives. The attitude resonates with *Chatelaine*'s, especially during the tenure of editor Byrne Hope Sanders. The solicitous attitude demonstrated by Marjolaine and Sanders, combined with their edifying comments on the work of editing a magazine, offers one way of understanding the middlebrow reading public as it was constructed through periodicals: readers were given a flattering feeling of control over the contents of these mass-produced objects. Such positioning elevated the reader above the status of mere consumer, but avoided granting her elite status. Rather, the sense of belonging to a large audience offered pleasure and security by situating the reader as a part of a community made visible through periodical culture.

Pricing, politics, and nationalism

Deducing the meaning of magazine pricing is complex: there is no direct correlation between price and production quality, format, cultural value, or audience appeal. In the late 1920s, for example, *Mayfair*, *Maclean's*, and *La Revue Moderne* all commanded an annual subscription fee of $3, but this price was attached to three very different magazines. *Mayfair* was the glossiest among them, its 100-page issues filled with advertisements, illustrations, and photographs. It was unabashedly upward looking, frequently profiling diplomats, industry leaders, and socialites, and offering coverage of topics (sports, travel, shopping, society gossip) thought to reflect the interests of this group. *La Revue Moderne*, at only 50 pages per issue, was not glossy at all, had an intellectual slant, and gave less space to advertising. *Maclean's* came in between in terms of production quality, and its scope was general interest, with an abundance of advertisements. A typical issue was 70 pages long, but it was published semi-monthly, so that an annual subscription included 24 issues. At this period, *Chatelaine* and the *Journal* each asked for $1 per year, whilst *La Revue Populaire*, which was essentially a pulp magazine in the 1920s, surprises with its relatively high annual subscription price of $1.50. *La Revue Populaire* maintained this price for the rest of its print run, even though it changed its format in 1932 to resemble the other magazines discussed here. Subscription fees dropped for *Mayfair*, *Maclean's*, and *La Revue Moderne* in the 1930s and '40s, but remained the same for the lower-priced monthlies. This was presumably because the more expensively produced titles were increasingly able to finance their production via advertising and wished to maintain subscriber numbers through the period of depression, in order to continue to attract advertising. Prices begin to climb in the 1950s ($2.50 for *Mayfair*, $2 for *Maclean's*, $1.50 for all the others), a decade in which advertising and reader attention was increasingly diverted into other media, forcing magazines into collapse or redesign.

American competition led, at times, to political intervention aimed at protecting the Anglophone Canadian magazine marketplace. In 1926, MPAC agitated for federal tariffs on imported American magazines, arguing that a healthy magazine industry was necessary to national self-definition and progress. In 1928, the Advisory Board on Tariffs and Taxation conceded an 80% reduction on duty paid on some paper stock and printing materials. The change contributed to the increases in circulation that mainstream magazines were quick to promote to advertisers in the 1930s. Magazines were further aided in 1931, when the federal government imposed a tax on magazines with more than 20% advertising content, thus targeting American titles such as *Ladies' Home Journal*, *Saturday Evening Post*, and *Colliers*. The tax was abolished in 1935, when the Liberals replaced the Conservatives, prompting MPAC to ask, in one aggressive 1936 advertisement, 'Should Canadian Publishers Move to Buffalo, Detroit, or Minneapolis?' The copy declared:

> Canadian periodicals have made a great contribution to the welfare of the people of Canada. They plan to make further advances in the production of a periodical literature that stamps Canada as a nation outstanding in cultural, governmental, and industrial achievements. Standing between Canadians and the full development of a Canadian periodical literature, adequate to Canada's growth and needs, is the legislative handicap of added costs of raw materials and equipment, as compared with similar costs in foreign countries. (Magazine Publishers)

MPAC argued that it was the patriotic duty of Canadians to support the publishing industry of their own nation in order to preserve a cultural body that was fundamental to national progress. Similar concerns were prevalent in the French-language periodical market. As Mary Vipond notes: 'laments about newspapers have arisen from intellectual and cultural nationalist sources, with an emphasis on the need for a diversity of voices on the Canadian scene. The title of a Quebec report on press concentration expressed the key idea: "De la précarité de la presse ou le citoyen menace"' ('Major Trends' 247). Language difference did not necessarily protect Francophone periodicals from the influx of American cultural products. Rather, the Montreal magazines faced a parallel problem of reaching out to an audience that was surrounded by English-language periodicals and under constant threat of having its own culture and language eroded. It was an issue they addressed in their own pages. For example, in an open letter published in *La Revue Moderne*, Maurice Quedrue explores the tension between Anglophone and Francophone speech and printing in Quebec. The piece notes that young Québécois, in particular, seem to think that English is more stylish than French: they throw English phrases into party conversations, and use it in everyday situations. Quedrue worried that: 'ils sont en train de délayer leur nationalité, ils ne sont ni français ni anglais, ce sont des hybrides, c'est-à-dire des êtres qui ne créeront rien, ils sont vides.' He added: 'N'oublions pas que la langue est l'expression extérieure de la mentalité et qu'un esprit français qui ne parle qu'anglais est un esprit "prisonnier"' (20). Quedrue argued that families and educators must work together to maintain the French language and uphold its importance to the development of Canada.

The Second World War brought both challenges and opportunities to Canada's magazine industry. Subscription revenue was restricted when, in 1942, a Wartime Prices and Trade Board measure ordered that magazines could not raise prices higher than they had been between the dates 15 September and 11 October 1941. Yet, magazine circulation in North America increased markedly during the war years (see Peterson 54–59). Paper rationing reduced all of the Canadian magazines in length: *Mayfair* slimmed down from 144 pages in 1930 to 68 by 1945. But this would not necessarily have reduced advertising revenue: John Bush Jones, in his study of advertising in American magazines during the war, cites complaints from magazines that paper shortages were forcing them to turn down ads, but notes that 1944 and 1945 saw 'tremendous gains' in advertising revenue, due to the prevalence of war-related ads (21). In Canada, government presence within magazines was inescapable, as advertisements for the Canadian Women's Army Corps, Victory Bonds, and War Savings Certificates, as well as advisory notices on everything from inflation to the prevention of venereal disease, became staples of advertising content (see

Keshen 33). These advertisements, of course, drew on the patriotic sensibilities the magazines were already employing to market themselves.

Whether it took the form of presenting Canadian authors, exploring Canadian politics, or surveying Canadian regional distinctions, the discourse of national identity was always prominent in these periodicals. They were thus uniquely positioned to cater to Canada's emerging middle class, and they contributed significantly to the construction of that class's identity—one that was predicated on upward mobility. In the early to mid-twentieth century, the conflation of national identity with aspiration and self-improvement can be seen at work across all six titles included in our study. The connections between mainstream magazine content and Canadian patriotism are, indeed, baldly laid out in the March 1929 issue of *Chatelaine*, in which an advertisement for *MacLean's* (as the magazine was then titled) claimed that 'Canadian Daily Newspapers Voice Public Sentiment.' The promotional text quoted a selection of newspapers from across Canada. An extract from the *Fort William Times-Journal* ran:

> Col. Maclean had an ideal and an ambition. He intended to become the publisher of a Canadian magazine which should measure up, not only in its style and matter, but also in its circulation in Canada, with anything that the United States could send in. Moreover, the Colonel is an intensely patriotic Canadian, and was determined that, so far as it was in his power, MacLean's Magazine should be essentially Canadian in its entire make-up and outlook. (MacLean's)

The advertisement linked the success of the magazine to the intelligence and taste of Canadian readers, including another extract, this time from *The Edmonton Journal*, to consolidate the point:

> The figures indicate that Canadians are reading their own magazines in ever increasing numbers; that where they do read American products, they prefer those of the highest quality and these [sic] with a universal appeal; and that 'trash' gets scant attention from the general public. In the growing Canadian-mindedness of the people of the dominion, combined with the steady improvement in the quality of our own publications, lies the explanation of the change of conditions as compared with five or ten years ago.

Discernment and good taste are, then, identified as defining features of 'Canadian-mindedness,' since it is the ability of Canadians to choose high-quality publications that underpins a successful magazine industry.

Moreover, magazines presented themselves as investors in Canada's broader economic, social, and cultural development: they supported Canadian authors and journalists, profiled politicians and other public figures, and reported on issues that affected the everyday lives of readers. Each magazine did so in its own unique way, inflected by different aspects of Canada's evolving middlebrow culture. The remaining sections of this chapter offer individual histories of the six magazines, considering aesthetics, editorial slant, and target audience.

Canadian Home Journal (1905–58)

The *Canadian Home Journal* was the first of the six magazines to be founded, and offers fascinating insights into how mainstream periodicals addressed female readers, promoted Canadian authors, and engaged with consumerism. Almost all previous discussions of Canadian women's magazines have focused on *Chatelaine* while ignoring the *Journal*, so it is worth outlining their similarities and differences here. Whilst the layout, selection of contents, and advertising material in the two magazines were nearly identical, the *Journal*'s demographic was apparently slightly older than that of *Chatelaine*, which, from the start, adopted a youthful, chatty, sisterly tone. The *Journal*, by contrast, evinced an attitude of authority over its readers, particularly in regard to relationships, politics, cultural tastes, and home management. In short, *Chatelaine* presented itself as a magazine in dialogue with its readers, whilst the *Journal* aimed for one-way communication. Also, the *Journal* was more overtly religious than *Chatelaine*. Christian beliefs certainly ran throughout *Chatelaine*, which assumed that its readers regularly attended church and subscribed to mainstream Christian views, but the *Journal* was much more likely to publish articles written by ministers, and to refer to religious authorities, or directly to the Bible, when it came to questions of child-rearing, marriage, and community.

The *Canadian Home Journal* is the only one of the four Anglophone titles we discuss that was not owned by Maclean Publishing. It was originally published as *The Home Journal* by The Home Publishing Company, which was formed in Toronto in 1905. At this point, it appealed primarily to residents of central and eastern Canada, since the *Western Home Monthly* was already serving the western and prairie provinces. From the 1930s onwards, both periodicals aimed at national coverage. James Acton bought the magazine in 1906, but the *Journal* would change hands again 1907, when its advertising manager, Bill Rooke, bought it. Rooke owned the magazine for five years, changing the title to *Canadian Home Journal* in 1910, and selling it to Harold Gagnier in 1912. His company, H. Gagnier Ltd., was already the publisher of *Saturday Night*, together with a variety of trade journals, including *Women's*

Wear, Canadian Baker and Confectioner, and *Dominion Dental Journal.* Gagnier retained ownership until his death in 1922, when Miller McKnight took over the company. He oversaw H. Gagnier Ltd.'s transition to Consolidated Press Ltd., which was a publicly traded company, making it the first Canadian magazine publisher whose shares were listed on the stock market (Barbour 94). The *Journal* was published by Consolidated Press for the rest of its print run, although the Press itself was purchased, by Jack Kent Cooke in 1952. Cooke was a self-made millionaire who had started out operating radio stations and newspapers in Canada. He eventually sold the holdings of Consolidated Press to the Maclean Publishing Company in 1958. Over the period of its publication, the *Journal* consistently increased its readership. In 1925, it had 68,000 net paid subscriptions. By 1930, this number had nearly doubled, rising to 132,000 and thus staying ahead of its new competitor, *Chatelaine*, which had a subscription base of 122,000. By 1940, monthly circulation was listed as 260,000, and during the 1950s, the *Journal* boasted subscription figures between 400,000 and 500,000 households throughout the 1950s (Sutherland 156, 160, 249).

The *Journal*'s first long-term editor was Jean Graham, who remained in the post until 1930. She encouraged many Canadian authors (see McClung 370), and after the end of her tenure, the *Journal remained* strongly committed to promoting Canadian writing. Its importance to literary history has, however, been rather underestimated. It published many authors who were popular novelists in their own time, such as Louis Arthur Cunningham and Leslie Gordon Barnard, as well as several who have since become part of the Canadian canon (Mazo de la Roche, Nellie McClung, L. M. Montgomery, Laura Goodman Salverson, and Martha Ostenso). The *Journal* had ties to the Women's Canadian Club of Toronto, notably in relation to the Club's annual short story competition—the prize-winning story and two runners-up were published in the magazine. The magazine also ran features on contemporary social issues, and offered suggestions for recipes and home decoration.

Improvement, whether of oneself, one's home, or society, was a theme that ran through the *Journal*'s content. As Marjory Lang notes in *Women Who Made the News: Female Journalists in Canada, 1880–1945*, Jean Graham gave an address to the alumnae of McMaster University in which she argued that 'given the influence of the press, it was a great advantage to "philanthropic work and public morals in general to have women in newspaperwork"' (78).[21] The feeling Graham expresses here correlates with the prevailing attitude

---

[21] Lang notes that the quotation is from a 'scrapbook (presented by Pat Groves 1928), undated clipping, 67,' which is part of the National Archive Media Club of Canada collection.

evinced by the *Journal* towards women and their work, whether in the home, for charity or the church, or in paid labour. This attitude remained consistent throughout Graham's editorship and those of her successors, Catherine Wilma Tait, Mary-Etta Macpherson, and Rosemary Boxer. Indeed, when Tait took over from Graham in 1930, there was little fanfare, and judging from the content and layout, the new editor's work was defined largely by a desire for continuity. Tait would remain relatively silent throughout her editorship. Where *Chatelaine*'s editors—Byrne Hope Sanders, Mary-Etta Macpherson, Doris Anderson—maintained lively editorials that sought out readers' opinions, the *Journal*'s editorials were less frequent, and were typically unsigned, suggesting that they were presented as the view of the magazine, based on consent, rather than offering the quirky perspective of an individual.

The *Journal* often included generalised images of female mobility (see Figure 4) but since its focus was primarily domestic, it presented the experience of travel as an exceptional and yet meaningful event, rather than as a part of ordinary life. In some cases, travel took on a relatively extreme quality. For instance, Allen Roy Evans's postwar pieces, which had striking titles such as 'She Collects Mountains' (July 1948) and 'She Hunts Big Cats' (May 1949), were profiles of women who had unusual occupations, such as mountaineering or gamekeeping. In concluding his essay on the hunter Joan Yates, he sardonically asks, 'is there a woman who has wished for a holiday that is "different," or who has at times longed to "get away from it all?" A few days with the lions on Vancouver Island may be the answer. But it's no dainty, pink-tea affair' ('She Hunts'). His final remark implicitly evokes advertisements for the Empress Hotel, famous for its English-style afternoon tea, and located within the picturesque urban landscape of Victoria—the kind of landscape in which magazine writers and advertisers persistently asked women to picture themselves during this period. Another typical representation of the foreign, in the pages of the *Journal*, consisted of features on the royal family. These combined domestic interest with the rather exotic allure of the English nobility. For example, Mollie McGee's 1949 piece 'They're a Happy Family' showcased the royal family at home in Buckingham Palace, whilst Grace Garner's 1947 article 'Princess Elizabeth Comes of Age as a Fashion Personality' discussed the princess' wardrobe for a trip to South Africa. In both instances, visiting a faraway place, whether England or South Africa, was portrayed as out of reach for ordinary Canadians. By contrast, a point of connection between royalty and ordinary Canadian readers could be found in the *Journal*'s representation of the Windsor family's everyday affairs.

During the Second World War, the *Journal* fell in line with other Anglophone magazines, advocating national patriotism and individual courage:

MARKETPLACE

You can keep your self-respect (and nothing in the world will ever mean as much to you as that) if you rise above the strain and make yourself a tower of strength to your husband and family. There's heroism in that which equals the courage of the soldier on the battlefield. (Dare, 'Smiling')

In May 1948, Mary-Etta Macpherson took over as the magazine's editor. Macpherson had written for *Mayfair*, and had also served as co-editor (with Sanders) of *Chatelaine* during the war. Like Tait, Macpherson seems to have been expected to maintain the status quo. The *Journal*'s tone and content remained consistent with previous issues. It regained some of the gloss it had lost due to wartime constraints, and expanded from a wartime average length of 48 pages up to 92; this increased in the 1950s, though remaining shy of the pre-war length of 120 pages per issue. The baby boom was reflected in a proliferation of features on birth, infant care, and child development. Rosemary Boxer replaced Macpherson in April 1956, and from this point, the *Journal*'s layout took on a more spacious quality and employed more modern-looking typefaces and photographs. The articles also had titles that made them appear in tune with changing times, though the underlying attitudes remained more conservative than those of *Chatelaine* or *Maclean's*. It is tempting to attribute the demise of the *Journal* in May 1958 to its conservatism, yet we know that it had a loyal readership, suggesting that the values it represented continued to resonate with many Canadians. It is more probable that the sale of the magazine to Maclean-Hunter happened because the owner, Jack Kent Cooke, was finding that magazine publishing was less profitable than he had expected.

La Revue Populaire (1907–63)

La Revue Populaire was launched by Poirier, Bessette, publishers of the successful illustrated weekly *Le Samedi*. It was owned by the same company during the whole of its run, but its appearance and mix of content changed considerably over time. During the 1920s, *La Revue Populaire* was in effect a pulp magazine, printed in a 7 x 10 inch format, with a large proportion of its pages devoted to fiction; cover lines described it as a 'Magazine Littéraire Mensuel Illustré.' In September 1930, the magazine changed to an 8.5 x 10.5 size; it was the only one of the six magazines to use this format, which is similar to that of most twenty-first-century magazines but smaller than its mainstream contemporaries. In the 1930s, the cover proclaimed *La Revue Populaire* to be 'La plus grande revue canadienne,' and listed 'arts, lettres, sciences, histoire' as the topics covered. The magazine maintained its traditionalist outlook, but there was increasing coverage of Canadian topics during this period, as opposed to the stories of adventure and exotic 'fait divers' which had been staples of the magazine in its earliest years. New features, such as a children's page, horoscopes, and columns on cinema, cookery, and Canadian art, were gradually introduced. For most of its lifetime, *La Revue Populaire* printed a complete romantic novel or novella in each issue, as well as serial fiction. The vast majority of the fiction was by popular French romance writers such as Max du Veuzit, Claude Jaunière, or Magali (the pseudonym of Jeanne Philbert), who was one of the most frequently published novelists in *La Revue Populaire* across its whole run. Occasionally, translations of English or American stories appeared.

La Revue Populaire positioned itself as a family magazine; advertisements often suggested that a gift subscription was appropriate for one's parents and friends alike. The appeal to both men and women was evident in the presentation of different materials along stereotypically gendered lines: a page in the January 1932 issue, for instance, was divided in two, with the top section advising on home manicures and the bottom section offering items of news relating to cars and driving. The fact that women were being instructed to manicure their own nails hinted at the less-than-luxurious lives of readers—a magazine such as *Mayfair*, in contrast, ran adverts for beauty salons. That said, *La Revue Populaire* did pay increasing attention to fashionability, describing itself as 'la revue à la mode!' in its 1932 subscription advertisements (Revue Populaire). Distinguishing itself from the more intensive, politically driven atmosphere of *La Revue Moderne*, *La Revue Populaire* focused on enjoyable and novel aspects of contemporary life, bringing together pictorial features on locations both abroad and within Canada, romance and adventure fiction, and a miscellany of one-page articles on fashion, food and wine, books, films, celebrities and artists, and sports.

The January 1932 issue, for instance, included photographic features on Quebec City after a heavy snowfall and on the ruins of Egypt, Greece, and Rome. The images of ruins were provided by Canadian Pacific as a form of subtle advertising; the fine print beneath explained that 'ruines que verront les touristes qui feront la croisière de la Méditerranée, à bord de la *L'Empress of Australia*. Départ de New-York, le trois février' ('Plus Belles'). The issue's articles covered seal-hunting in Newfoundland, the decline of the bison in Alberta, the work done by 'le refuge Meurling,' a homeless shelter that served some of the most impoverished residents of Montreal, and a travel piece on the churches of Mexico City. The reader was thus taken on a journey around the Americas, but not simply in order to admire picturesque scenes—indeed, a majority of the articles encouraged engagement with social and environmental issues. In the same issue, celebrity culture mingled with 'serious' culture, with a page devoted to Hollywood stars Norma Shearer, Buster Keaton, and Marion Davies appearing after a review of a new book by political economist Edouard Montpetit. Much of *La Revue Populaire*'s advertising was based on domestic concerns, with soap, cigars, beer, cough and cold remedies, soup, toothpaste, and baking ingredients figuring prominently, although full-page car ads and CP or Canadian National Railway promotions brought out the magazine's emphasis on worldliness and mobility. This was reinforced by the travel-themed covers which were increasingly used from the late 1930s onwards (see Figure 5).

Poirier, Bessette's other magazines *Le Samedi* and *Le Film* were also routinely advertised in *La Revue Populaire*. One advertisement promised 'chaque mois, un ROMAN-FEUILLETON sensationnel choisi pour plaire à tous ses lecteurs and lectrices' (Le Film). This dedication to the new popular culture of cinema may have located *Le Film* in the realm of mass rather than middlebrow culture, the advertisement of *Le Film* in *La Revue Populaire* helping us to understand the periodical as a site in which the popular and contemporary conversed with the educative and traditional. That is, articles designed to inform readers about current issues (such as urban poverty and declining bison populations) and things of lasting value (such as the architecture of Mexican churches) mingled with sentimental fiction and photographs of film stars. All this content related back to an overarching desire to be conversant with contemporary culture, but the idea of culture was a multi-faceted one that constructed readers as pleasurably engaged in the essential process of remaining in-the-know.

Circulation for *La Revue Populaire* stood at 4,672 in 1910, and at just over 6,000 in 1916, but had grown to 25,000 by the mid-1920s. By 1941, a circulation of 40,532 had been reached, and this figure doubled over the next 15 years. In 1963, the circulation was 127,363 (Beaulieu and Hamelin vol. 5: 266; Saint-Jacques 320). The annual subscription price of $1.50 was maintained across the magazine's run; this was possible because *La Revue Populaire* was increasingly financed by advertising. Roughly 30% of the magazine's content consisted of adverts in the 1930s. This percentage increased steadily over the decades, with commercial material comprising 37% of the content of a typical issue in the 1940s, and climbing to 43% by the mid-1950s. In effect, magazines such as *La Revue Populaire* moved away from selling themselves, as attractive printed products, to their readers, and towards selling their readerships, as a market, to advertisers.

The magazine was never shaped by the individual vision of an editor-in-chief to the extent that other Canadian periodicals sometimes were, but there was one particularly influential editorial director, Jean Chauvin, who held the position from 1929 until 1956. Another key member of staff was Thérèse Surveyer, widow of the celebrated journalist Jules Fournier, who signed herself 'Francine' (see Dumont and Toupin 112). From the 1920s until the 1940s, she contributed the enduring 'Chronique féminine' column, and when the magazine expanded this into a whole section, 'Pages féminines,' its editor was listed as 'Madame Jules Fournier.' In the more competitive, and more fragmented, periodical marketplace of the later 1940s and 1950s, *La Revue Populaire* attempted to convert itself into a women's magazine, with greatly increased coverage of fashion and the domestic realm. But *La Revue Moderne*, soon to become *Châtelaine*, was already occupying that segment of the magazine marketplace in Quebec. Though it abandoned its conservative ideology and embraced more modern concerns, *La Revue Populaire* nevertheless found it impossible to survive in the cultural climate of the Quiet Revolution (Beaulieu and Hamelin vol. 5: 269), and folded in 1963.

Maclean's (1911–)

Maclean's was publisher John Bayne Maclean's first foray into producing a commercial magazine. He had established himself as a trade journal publisher, but *Maclean's* would prove to be not only the first of four successful consumer-oriented titles (*Mayfair*, *Chatelaine*, and *Canadian Homes and Gardens* were the others), but also his flagship periodical: it was the one that attracted serious literary authors (Martha Ostenso, Morley Callaghan, Stephen Leacock, Thomas Raddall), important artists (A. J. Casson, Arthur Lismer, and J .E .H. MacDonald), and high-profile editors (Scott Young, Blair Fraser, Pierre Berton, W. O. Mitchell). According to Korinek, 'within the Maclean Hunter Consumer Magazines Division, *Maclean's* and *Chatelaine* were regarded as sibling publications. Yet all the glamour, prestige, expensive talent, parental encouragement, and pride went to *Maclean's*' (*Roughing* 49). *Maclean's* was addressed to a mixed audience of men and women, and aimed to provide in-depth analysis of current affairs and issues of importance to Canadians. It presented itself as more serious than the company's other title. Its nationalism was generally geared towards constructing and consolidating an Anglophone identity, although as we have noted above, there were occasional moments of cultural exchange with Francophone Canada.

Originally a monthly, titled *The Business Magazine*, and published by an advertising agency, the periodical was bought by Lieutenant-Colonel Maclean in 1905. He retained the title for two issues, published in October and November, before changing it to *The Busy Man's Magazine* (Aston and Ferguson). Previously, the focus had been on reprints of articles from other business journals, but by 1910 Maclean had begun to include original, commissioned features. In 1911, he renamed the magazine *MacLean's* and turned it into a general interest title, adding new departments designed to appeal to female readers. This appeal was crucial. There was increasing pressure within the mainstream magazine industry to attract finance from advertising, and advertisers wished to address female readers since their research indicated that most shopping was done by women. At the same time, *Maclean's* paid much attention to questions of Canadian identity, singling out this theme as the one that distinguished the magazine from its American competitors and could therefore aid in building up a strong subscription list in Canada (see Johnston 242–48).

Johnston suggests that between 1913 and 1917, Maclean apparently 'elected to run *MacLean's* on a deficit in order to build its profile' (245). This soon led to an era of prosperity for the magazine. From February 1920, *MacLean's* was published twice a month. It boasted 70,000 subscribers (Sutherland 143) at the time, and by the early 1930s, was proclaiming a net paid circulation of 130,000 on its covers. In 1934, the figure had reached 200,000, greater than the Canadian circulation of any of its US competitors (Karr 203). The circulation of *Maclean's* (the upper-case L had been dropped in 1931) continued to increase steadily over the next decade, and was boosted above the quarter-million mark in 1945, when the magazine ran the celebrated journalist and politician Beverley Baxter's diary of a 5,000-mile cross-Canada trip. An advertisement for the magazine that appeared in the 1 January 1948 issue claimed that it: '1. Is independent in politics. 2. Puts editorial service first. 3. Insists upon efficient circulation methods. 4. Sells advertising space on merit and proven readership' (Maclean-Hunter). The advert concluded that adhering to these four principles made the periodical 'a leader in its field,' echoing the emphasis on leadership that defines MPAC's 1930s campaigns to attract both readers and advertisers. At the end of the year, the regular column 'In the Editor's Confidence' drew attention to the cover itself as an important indicator of the identity of the magazine. All 24 of the 1948 covers were reproduced on a single page, and an inset paragraph invited comment:

> We ask you to tear out this page, mark a figure one over the cover you liked best, a 2 on your second choice, a 3 on your third and so on up to 5. If you'd like to enclose a letter about our covers in general or any cover or covers in particular we offer you a fighting chance to get your postage back. We'll pay $25 for the best letter—pro, con, or neutral—and $10 each for the three next best. (4)

As an informal marketing ploy, the invitation served several functions: it engaged readers with the production of the magazine, thus promoting a spirit of ownership and the feeling that readers influenced its look and contents; it created an opportunity to gather opinions from readers which could inform the magazine's design; and it could, potentially, elicit demographic details on the gender and location of regular readers. In this sense, *Maclean's* took pains to reflect reader tastes, although the magazine was equally engaged in constructing those tastes, too.

Gertrude Pringle's 1926 profile of interior decorator Minerva Elliot, 'Making a Business of Good Taste,' brought together domesticity with travel in a discussion of style that was predicated on the life story of a self-made woman. According to this account, Elliot's fascination with décor began when she was a teenager, and prompted her to enrol in a two-year course taught in Montreal by 'a Great English authority' on 'Foreign Architecture' (71). Elliot is quoted as saying that she

> read everything I could lay my hand on about the subject, too, so that when I made a trip abroad I 'did' the British and South Kensington Museums, the Louvre and the Cluny in Paris, and the Pitti and Uffizi in Italy with a very fair knowledge of the treasures they contained. (71)

She thus combines formal instruction with autodidactic study that culminates in travel. Elliot went on to work in a Toronto department store, a job that entailed 'many trips to New York buying lovely and costly things wherewith to furnish many Toronto homes' (71). Drawing attention to this cross-border commerce, the article implies that high style depends on cosmopolitanism. Next, Elliot left to work in Philadelphia, and then took a trip through England, France, and Italy during which she 'established valuable contacts with a number of exclusive dealers' (72), enabling her to set up a business in Canada. The piece concludes with the sober reminder that her success 'had been brought about by the grinding slavery of incessant work which alone makes for mastery in the technique of any art.' But this is supplemented by Pringle's inspirational final comment: 'Her influence in the community is a valuable one; from her hundreds of Canadians are learning that the business of living is immeasurably brightened and enriched by surroundings of true beauty' (72). Elliot's is a story of aspiration achieved, though the heady fantasy of travel and autonomy is balanced by an emphasis on effort which is characteristic of a middlebrow ethos. Ultimately, Elliot places her international, artistic flair in the service of Canadians, whose tastes she hopes to elevate.

Maclean's frequently promoted such edifying and pleasurable aspects of travel abroad, yet, equally often, it urged readers to tour their own country. In the spring of 1930, readers were encouraged to share their holiday photographs,

MARKETPLACE

and *Maclean's* had received over 6,000 by the time the 15 June 1930 issue appeared. Those selected for the 'Summer Snapshot Album' took readers on a coast-to-coast tour of the Dominion (see Figure 6). The feature wove together images of Canada into a visual narrative that offered readers a sense of community and shared landscape, as well as ownership in what was ostensibly 'their' magazine. Two decades later, a piece by Grattan Gray titled 'Banff: A Paradise for Sultans and Stenos' celebrated Canada as a destination that was worthy of visits not only by Canadians, but also by foreign tourists. In his words, 'as anyone capable of reading a travel folder knows, the town of Banff, Alta., and its environs are one of North America's great tourist paradises. Close to half a million visitors from all over the world descend on Banff each year—and leave behind untold thousands of dollars' (17). The accompanying photographs (provided, unsurprisingly, by Canadian Pacific) showed views of the Rocky Mountains, a stereotypical image of Stony Indians in ceremonial dress, and the outdoor hot springs of Banff Springs Hotel. This combination of unspoilt natural beauty, voyeuristic exoticism, and luxury was discussed as something unique to Canada that ought to be a source of pride (and profit) to Canadians.

Like many mainstream magazines, *Maclean's* struggled in the 1950s, as advertisers and readers turned increasingly to television, but the adoption of a news magazine format in the 1960s revitalised the periodical. It had changed to fortnightly (rather than twice-monthly) publication in March 1955, but had to revert to monthly publication during the period from 1967 to 1975, due to financial pressures and competition from Canadian editions of American weeklies such as *Time* and *Newsweek*. *Maclean's* reinvented itself as a weekly news magazine in 1978.

La Revue Moderne (1919–60)

We analyse *La Revue Moderne*'s 41-year print run in detail in Chapter Two, examining editorial strategy, design, contents, and positioning within the marketplace. The history provided here is therefore more succinct than those for the five other magazines. *La Revue Moderne* was founded by Anne-Marie Gleason, later Huguenin, who wrote under the pseudonym 'Madeleine.' She served as editor for the magazine's first decade, and was a pioneer of women's journalism in an era in which women were only just beginning to become visible in public arenas in Quebec (see Baillargeon 11). Yet, in the context of the conservative social and political climate of the province, where women were not accorded provincial voting rights until 1940, *La Revue Moderne* could only achieve wide support if it maintained a moderate position. As Jean-Christian

Pleau observes, 'la position de Madeleine sur des enjeux tels que le droit de vote des femmes était souvent d'un conservatisme prudent' (209).

The content of Madeleine's magazine was varied, including literary, political, arts, and general interest material, as well as a 'Fémina' department that featured advice columns, dress patterns, and articles on home management and beauty. In this respect, the periodical resembles two of its Paris-based precursors, *Femina* (launched in 1901) and *La Vie Heureuse* (launched in 1902).[22] In *Having It All in the Belle Epoque: How French Women's Magazines Invented the Modern Woman*, Rachel Mesch explains that these two magazines 'celebrated achieving women in dazzling feature stories sandwiched between elaborate fashion plates and advertisements for beauty creams, corsets, and high-end furniture. Regardless of the nature of their achievements—not just as writers, but as lawyers, doctors, actresses, explorers or athletes—their femininity remained fully intact' (3). Moreover, their circulations encompassed both Paris and the provinces, both upper-crust and aspirational readers. As a result, they produced:

> a fusion of the exclusiveness of the salon with the openness of the department store, displaying for an aspiring public the amenities of the upper classes. The luxuries associated with this milieu, however, were not limited to high-end goods. Quite remarkably, *Femina* and *La Vie Heureuse* made available and desirable for a broad female readership the creative, intellectual endeavours of the *monde littéraire*; they encouraged readers not only to dress and shop like the social elite, but to be reflective and literary themselves. (5)

This balance of commerce and culture is instructive in understanding the role of the mainstream magazine. *La Revue Moderne* likewise juxtaposed creative and intellectual work with fantasies prompted by holiday features and fashion pages.

In her January 1926 editorial, Madeleine clearly expressed her attitude towards her readers: 'En effet, le lecteur est l'ami, l'ami sûr et absolu, sur lequel, nous devons compter, et sans lequel notre action resterait stérile. Et ce lecteur, nous voulons le remercier et nous assurer de la constance de sa sympathique attention' ('Plus haut'). The magazine's success, she says, is attained 'en nous tenant en communication constante avec lui, en questionnant ses goûts, en nous inspirant de ses suggestions, comme de ses conseils, en nous mettant

---

[22] *Femina* is spelled without an accent. On this magazine, see also Rogers 19; Stewart 37.

enfin à la disposition complète de tous ceux qui aiment la Revue Moderne.' Her description of the magazine reveals her aspiration, not only to mediate French-Canadian culture for a local audience, but also to showcase that culture for the benefit of the rest of Canada and the rest of the world:

> la Revue Moderne avec son souci de dignité, l'élégance de son allure, la discrétion de ses propos, la solidité de ses articles, la Revue Moderne qui porte un peu partout à travers le monde, la pensée canadienne-française, et qui est accueillie comme la représentante d'une race éclairée, fait un peu partie de la fierté nationale.

The magazine emphasised that Francophone culture extended into every province of Canada, and it addressed readers living in all areas of the country, as well as expatriates, especially those in the US and France. Just to cite a couple of indicative examples: in 1925, Madeleine contributed a long article, 'Chez les Canadiens de France,' recounting her visit to Paris and her encounters with some of the six to seven hundred Canadians (mostly French-speaking) who lived there. During the economic crises of the early 1930s, *La Revue Moderne* frequently commented on the problems of the prairie provinces. In the March 1932 issue, for instance, the columnist exhorted readers 'de ne pas oublier les Canadiens français de Saskatchewan' and noted the generous donations which readers had recently sent to Edmonton in response to an appeal for 'la défense de l'école française de cette province de l'Ouest où les nôtres, missionaires et colons, ont été des pionniers'. He thanked 'tous ceux qui ont répondu, même du lointain Colorado' (Jean-Baptiste). In its early years, then, the magazine was at once preoccupied with the distinctive qualities of French-Canadian culture and also strongly committed to Canadian national unity (see Pleau 206–07).

Nevertheless, American influences on the magazine were discernible even during Madeleine's era. For instance, a regular column that ran throughout the 1920s and early 1930s, 'Eve au miroir' by Celia Caroline Cole, was a translation of a feature from the American fashion magazine *The Delineator* (1873–1937), published by the Butterick company. In the January 1932 issue of *La Revue Moderne*, Cole's piece, headed 'Où Allons-Nous?' is illustrated with skiing, boating, and beach scenes (see Figure 7).[23] It begins: 'Nous sommes tous des voyageurs,' and is constructed around notions of progress: 'Veillons-nous à nous habiller d'une manière plus attrayante, avec plus de *chic*, plus de goût? Notre figure, est-elle plus agréable à regarder que l'année dernière? Et notre

---

[23] The illustrations were unsigned, but bear a striking resemblance to drawings from the same period that appeared in *Mayfair* and were signed 'Ricardo.'

vie, cherchons-nous à la vivre avec plus de compréhension, de profondeur et d'efficacité qu'avant?' (20). Expanding outwards from fashion to self-cultivation, Cole emphasises—as she does in all her contributions—the intimate connections between appearance and personality. This reinforces the middlebrow emphasis on self-improvement visible elsewhere in *La Revue Moderne*, and reveals its connection with discourses of travel and (upward) mobility. The magazine did not, however, offer extensive coverage during its first three decades, though it always paid attention to foreign cultures. Holiday features focused principally on Canadian destinations, while articles on other countries tended to be informative rather than promotional. In the 1950s, the space devoted to travel features, tourist advertising, and travel-themed fiction increased dramatically. By this time, *La Revue Moderne* had become increasingly commercial, with a marked growth in advertising and an increasing orientation towards female consumers. This made it attractive to Maclean-Hunter, and the company purchased it and turned into *Châtelaine* (1960–), which initially bore the subtitle 'La Revue Moderne.'

Mayfair (1927–59)

Mayfair was launched in May 1927, with the declaration that:

> those of us whose problem was the selection of a name for another MacLean publication were confronted with unguessed considerations. First of all there were our own publishing traditions. As a publishing house with an established reputation over a period of years this was a matter of deep concern. Then we had the traditions of Canadian life in its most gracious aspects, with which to reckon.
> So we chose Mayfair—Mayfair with its long line of culture, fashion, and social distinctions. Actually the name of a fashionable neighbourhood in the West End of London, England, adjoining the equally fashionable Belgravia, east of Hyde Park, Mayfair has, however, taken, on a broader—but invariably exclusive—interpretation. (Hodgins, Editorial)

In this inaugural editorial, J. Herbert Hodgins, who would serve as *Mayfair*'s editor until September 1945, set out the ways in which the magazine intended to distinguish itself from other mainstream periodicals, including those already published by the Maclean Publishing Company. (Hodgins himself had previously written for *Maclean's*.) He explained that *Mayfair* would 'interpret the life of Canadians in their most gracious moods,' but made it clear that 'Canadian' meant upper-crust, white, and Anglophone. There was a focus on

MARKETPLACE

debutantes and diplomats, society weddings and sporting events, and in general, on the activities of Canada's elite. For this reason, the magazine was hailed by reviewers across Canada as a periodical whose 'appearance and contents are the fruits of enterprise and good taste,' and as 'a final contradiction to the frequent claim that Canada is not mature enough, not cosmopolitan enough to inspire a publication of this sophisticated type.'[24] *Mayfair* signalled a coming of age in Canadian magazine publishing, and is affiliated with the middlebrow through its intensely aspirational character, and its balancing of sophistication and fashionableness with conservative values.

Hodgins remained at *Mayfair* for 18 years, with Bertram M. Tate taking over in September 1945. The editorial changeover received no fanfare, and long-time contributors and advertisers continued to appear in the magazine. The same holds true for later editorial changes, with Tate being replaced by Herbert C. Manning in September 1951, and Manning by Eric Hutton in January 1954. While a change in editorship sometimes signals a decisive shift in a magazine's outlook, *Mayfair*'s editors seemed cast in the role of maintaining what Hodgins had established. Even when *Mayfair* was sold to the Crombie Publishing Company in December 1955, and David B. Crombie took over as both publisher and editor, the magazine continued to deal primarily with elegant fashions, society weddings, and taste (sometimes literally, as discussions of tea, breakfast customs, and gourmet dishes appeared throughout *Mayfair*'s print run). Indeed, the leading article in Crombie's first issue resonated with Hodgins's first editorial three decades earlier:

> Mayfair and its famous thoroughfare Bond Street, possessing a pervading air of exclusiveness, sophistication, and fashion, are to London what Fifth Avenue is to New York. The names bear a peculiarly indefinable ring of quality, quality that has matured for centuries to earn universal acknowledgement. (Clark 23)

The piece featured black-and-white photos of the shopping arcades, gardens, and clubs to be found in the district, and was one of four articles in this issue to focus on England. It is difficult to read Clark's piece, along with others in the issue, without sensing that *Mayfair*, like the neighbourhood from which

---

[24] These are extracts from other periodicals which Hodgins quotes in his June 1927 editorial. The first was from *Scribe*, a publication of the T. Eaton Company; the second from Toronto's *Mail and Empire*. Other passages expressing similar sentiments were taken from seven more regional papers.

it took its title, saw itself as having matured over the years in a manner that consolidated its initial claims to exclusivity.

Visually, *Mayfair* was distinguished from the rest of the magazines considered here by its heavy paper stock and its abundance of sumptuous illustrations and advertisements. Where the others all had a slightly utilitarian feel resulting from compressed text printed on cheap paper and, indeed, had utilitarian features on topics such as cookery and finance, *Mayfair* distanced itself from the demands of everyday life. Instead, it offered a fantasy of an elite lifestyle that was grounded in representations of individuals who were fortunate enough to belong, in reality, to an elite class. It thus generated an ethos of aspiration, underwritten by a blithe assurance that the attainment of material wealth and social status was fulfilling and therefore a worthwhile pursuit. If you did not belong to Canada's elite, you were tempted to imagine yourself as part of it, with all of its privileges sketched out for you by the magazine's contents. Chief among these privileges was geographic mobility. Of the six magazines, *Mayfair* was the one most focused on travel. The preoccupation took many forms: European travel memoirs; photo features such as the long-running column 'Globe-Trotting Canadians,' which reported on the overseas journeys of Canadian politicians and industry leaders; fashion reporting, particularly from Paris; special issues dedicated to representing London and Paris; and much travel-themed advertising. This included direct advertising for cruises, flights, and hotels, and also adverts that used travel imagery to promote consumer goods. Travel, then, was intimately linked to the upward mobility and *savoir faire* that *Mayfair* made its purview.

In style terms, *Mayfair* did undergo certain shifts, moving away from its initial art deco style to a clean, concise look during the Second World War and on to a whimsical series of cover typefaces and illustrations that contrasted with a blocky internal layout in the 1950s. But during its whole run, *Mayfair*'s covers evoked fashionability, mobility, and cosmopolitanism, visualising the 'gracious moods' that Hodgins named as central to the magazine (see Figures 8, 9, and 10). Photographic images became more prevalent on other magazine covers during the postwar era, yet *Mayfair* continued to use illustrated covers, a choice that set it apart. *Mayfair*'s look and contents bear a striking resemblance to Britain's *The Tatler* (1901–), which is still in print, and continues to report on elite lifestyles. During the early and mid-twentieth century, both periodicals featured frivolous cover illustrations, pages devoted to society gossip and fashion, and black-and-white photographs of aristocrats on holiday in exclusive locations like Cannes and Monte Carlo. For all of *Mayfair*'s attention to aesthetics, there is no question that the printed quality of the magazine gradually declined. By the 1950s, its glossy pages had given way to low-grade paper, and its length—

typically 144 pages in the 1930s, and 92 in the 1940s—had dropped to a scant 44 pages by the last issue, in December 1959. *Mayfair*'s collapse may owe something to its determined consistency of tone and content. Its ideas on social hierarchy and good breeding, and its implicit exclusions (along racial, ethnic, and class lines) may no longer have seemed suitable, or even tasteful as the 1960s began, and *Mayfair*'s reign as Canada's society magazine drew to a close.

Chatelaine (1928–)

Chatelaine, the third and last mainstream title launched by the Maclean Publishing Company in the 1920s, arrived in March 1928, four years after *Canadian Homes and Gardens* had been established, and just ten months after *Mayfair*'s appearance. *Chatelaine*'s declared purpose was to serve the needs of the Canadian woman. Editorials discussed this figure in what appeared to be broadly inclusive terms, citing a desire to reach readers from coast to coast, whether living in remote farms or urban centres. Yet silently present was the notion that the Canadian woman was white, middle class, and heterosexual, and that her chief preoccupations were marriage, child-rearing, health and beauty, and home management. These were the magazine's overarching concerns, although *Chatelaine* also constructed its readers as women who wished to keep up with current events and engage with Canada's arts and letters.

The new magazine was titled *The Chatelaine* until March 1932, when the definite article was dropped. The way in which the name was selected marked the newest periodical as populist rather than—as in *Mayfair*'s case—elitist. Potential readers were asked to submit suggestions, and there was a $1,000 prize for the winning title. This generated a feeling that the magazine would belong to Canadian women, its contents determined by the expressed interests of its readers. At the same time, the publicity surrounding the competition—which attracted 75,000 entries—was already creating an audience. In its first issue, the magazine published a piece by the winner, Mrs Hilda Pain, reflecting on how the name 'The Chatelaine' came to her. She wanted, she says, to express 'the noble dignity of maternity, the presiding genius of the home—for these are the aspirations of every woman.' Then inspiration came:

> I pictured, in my mind's eye, the cover of the new women's magazine decorated with the gracious figure of a chatelaine, standing at the head of the flight of steps, inviting with outstretched hands the women of Canada to enter and enjoy the restful charm of her home. The Chatelaine seemed exactly to fill the need. It covers those attributes a woman naturally desires to possess. And another thing, while the name has

long been incorporated into the international vocabulary, it still holds that touch of native chivalry dear to the hearts of our fellow Canadians of the French tongue.

Pain's vision outlines the narrow limits imposed upon women, yet her choice of title was celebrated as universally appealing, not least because aspiration was its essence. The figure of the chatelaine, characterised by charm, noble dignity, and even genius, was one to emulate.

Chatelaine appealed to the women of Canada's expanding middle class—and to those who aspired to belong to it. Readers were constructed as participants in their country's transition from a predominantly rural, agrarian culture towards an urban, consumer-based economy. This positioned them as part of Canada's first 'professional managerial class,' to use Richard Ohmann's phrase (118). *Chatelaine*'s first editor was Anne Elizabeth Wilson. Previously, she had contributed to nearly every issue of *Maclean's* in the late 1920s, and worked as an associate editor at *Mayfair*. She stayed with *Chatelaine* for eighteen months, but it was her successor, Byrne Hope Sanders, editor for the next 23 years, who would define and consolidate the magazine's ethos. In her first editorial, in September 1929, Sanders wrote that 'from the first issue of *Chatelaine*, I have studied and watched this magazine, not only with the reader's point of view, but with an editorial slant.' Moreover, she had 'spent several evenings minutely checking the answers to the questionnaire sent out to many of our readers, to discover just what you liked best in the magazine.' The answers, she comments, 'were astonishing, in that they showed a wide unanimity of opinion in likes and dislikes.' Sanders thus constructed her audience as a cohesive community of women with shared values, interests, and desires.

The typical contents of an issue of *Chatelaine* from the late 1920s through to the late 1950s consisted of four works of fiction, articles on topical events, and departments on home management, beauty culture, and fashions. *Chatelaine* positioned itself as a champion of Canadian literature, publishing big names such as L. M. Montgomery and Martha Ostenso, but also taking risks on new authors, and even printing short stories submitted by readers. For example, Eva L. Bruce's first short story, 'Pyjamas,' appeared in June 1932, accompanied by Sanders's declaration that Bruce was 'a brand new writer who is, I believe, in the jargon of the printing world, "a comer"' (2). Some of the new writers who appeared in *Chatelaine*, such as Dorothy Livesay and Alice Munro, went on to become major figures. The literary material included poetry, though poems tended to be integrated into the magazine wherever space allowed, and were not consistently included in the table of contents. The stories chosen for *Chatelaine* tended to be set in Canada and plots were often driven by a conflict that reflected a contemporary problem, whether it was labour strikes or the Second World War. Yet the magazine's selection of fiction was decidedly constrained. It was chosen, under Sanders's leadership, to uplift the reader, and romance was the key genre. The assumptions about what women preferred to read dovetailed nicely with the articles and columns on marriage and the home. Advertisements for foodstuffs, cleaning products, and beauty preparations appeared in every issue. During the War, advertisements for Victory Bonds and the Canadian Women's Army Corps were prevalent; indeed, Sanders was seconded to the Wartime Prices and Trade Board on the assumption that she had the ear of Canadian women and could persuade them to comply with rationing.

Despite the emphasis on domesticity, many articles and advertisements in *Chatelaine* looked outward, discussing journeys to Europe, as well as travel within Canada. The articles can be divided into two groups: memoirs by Canadian authors and journalists who had visited Europe, and practical pieces offering advice on arranging trips. *Chatelaine*'s coverage of travel emphasised family holidays, and rarely presented travel as a fantasy in the way that *Mayfair* pieces did. Rather, the articles dealt with the work involved for a wife and mother in managing a holiday, and offered guidance on everything from immunising children to planning meals and packing clothes. The June 1941 *Chatelaine*, for instance, was subtitled 'Your Canadian Holiday Number,' and included short pieces on each of Canada's provinces as well as a fashion column which explained how to 'shuffle three simple ensembles into a whole handful of different get-ups' ('Travel Light'), a cookery article entitled 'Menus for a Three-Day Motor Tour,' a piece on 'How to Pack,' and a feature about running a bed and breakfast establishment during the summer. The emphasis in these pieces was on economy rather than extravagance, effort rather than leisure, and planning rather than spontaneity.

When Sanders retired in January 1952, she was replaced by Lotta Dempsey, who had been a freelance writer for both *Chatelaine* and *Mayfair* since 1935. She held the post for only seven months, after which John Clare, the only man ever to edit *Chatelaine*, took over. During his tenure, which lasted until August 1957, he tended to maintain the status quo. However, Valerie Korinek critiques his editorial contributions as 'self-centred, patronizing, and sexist, although not atypical of the era,' and notes the particularly critical tone of readers' letters during this era (*Roughing* 268). Clare's replacement, Doris Anderson, would reverse this attitude in her lengthy tenure, from 1957 until 1977. She is famous for reinventing *Chatelaine* as a venue for second-wave feminism, and ensuring that the magazine engaged in depth with Canada's changing gender economy and political climate. During the late 1950s—the part of her editorship which comes within the purview of our study—she commissioned articles on topics relating to health, equality, sexuality, and social issues affecting women. They included: 'What's New in Natural Childbirth?' (January 1958), 'Are We Winning the War Against Cancer in Women?' (October 1958), 'The Invisible Barrier Between Canadian Men and Women' (June 1958), 'Do Women Like Other Women?' (August 1958), 'Why Aren't There More Canadian Women in Science?' (November 1959), and 'The Scandal of Women's Prisons' (November 1958). Korinek observes that Anderson, in her editorials, often 'criticized women for being complacent' (*Roughing* 269), and the pieces she selected for publication were certainly edgier than those *Chatelaine* had featured in earlier decades. They challenged the status quo and pushed women to take on an increasingly active (or, indeed, activist) role in determining both their own fates and the direction of the nation. In the midst of these concerns, travel articles continued to feature prominently. Pieces on European tours, train travel, and camping holidays offered advice and anecdotes that reveal changes in economic conditions and point to the shifts in aspiration that attended them. The emphasis, in these pieces, was on relaxation, fun, and private family time, rather than on networking, prestige, or self-education. The design of *Chatelaine* also altered during this period. Korinek notes: 'During the Sanders and Dempsey years, cover art design appeared stuck in an earlier era, with illustrations of dewy-eyed ingenues in their new Easter bonnets.' It was not until the 1950s, she adds, that *Chatelaine* upgraded its paper stock and began to run covers which were 'more confidant, more colourful, with more upscale images' (108).

Chatelaine is still in print, but in the 1980s it moved away from its feminist self-definition, re-imagining itself around the idea of the 'superwoman' (a woman with both family and career). Its longevity has led it to be identified as 'Canada's most prominent women's periodical—and perhaps all-time magazine success story' (Des Rivières, Gerson, and Saint-Jacques 249). This success results in part from the talents of its editors, and also from its ability to adapt to marketplace pressures by increasing advertising revenue and also by acquiring its competitors and their subscription lists. Its eightieth anniversary issue, in May 2008, included a special feature, 'The Way We Were,' put together by Katie Dupuis and presenting the magazine's own version of its history. Since it was sponsored by Kraft Canada, it is difficult not to read the nostalgic renderings of cookery pages from the past, situated as they are opposite pages advertising cream cheese and cookies, in a rather cynical light. Yet, the feature's many sections—'How *Chatelaine* got its name,' 'Notable *Chatelaine* editors,' 'Writers and Reflections' (highlighting Morley Callaghan, L. M. Montgomery, June Callwood, Germaine Greer, Margaret Atwood, Nellie McClung, Barbara Frum, and Margaret Mead), 'Fashions,' 'Beauty,' 'Décor,' 'Famous Faces,' 'Health,' 'Family and Relationships,' 'Politics,' 'Society,' and 'Careers'—remind us not only of how many concerns were taken up and explored in mainstream magazines, but also of the complexity of their readers' lives. Indeed, *Chatelaine* has long been adept at presenting itself as a 'beam of light [that] has never dimmed on the path it marked' (Dupuis 321), illuminating the changing societal, professional, and domestic pressures faced by readers seeking to situate themselves within the culture of modernity.

Conclusion

In 1951, the report of the Massey Commission (officially, the Royal Commission on National Development in the Arts, Letters and Sciences) noted the challenges faced by the magazine industry: Canadian magazines had collectively achieved a circulation of 42 million, but US titles had a combined circulation in Canada of 86 million.[25] The Massey Report commended the Canadian industry for its resilience in the face of competition, but the 1950s would turn out to be a time of flux that resulted in the closure of *Mayfair*, the *Canadian Home Journal*, *La Revue Moderne*, *La Revue Populaire*, and also *Canadian Homes and Gardens* between 1958 and 1963. The failure of so many mainstream magazines was one reason behind the establishment, in 1960, of a Royal Commission on Publications, also known as the O'Leary Commission after its chairman, Grattan O'Leary. Its task was to examine the problems that Canadian magazines faced with regard to foreign competition. In 1961, the Committee tabled its report, which included recommendations that would make it more costly for American publishers to export their magazines to Canada, thus rendering some economic protection for Canadian periodicals. One of the commission's chief recommendations was that expenditures made for advertisements in imported publications aimed at the Canadian market be disallowed as income tax deductions. The recommendation, though accepted in principle by the Conservative Party, would not be implemented for another 16 years, as it was shelved by the Liberals when they came into office in 1963.

Nevertheless, of the six magazines profiled here, three have evolved and are still in print: *Maclean's*, *Chatelaine*, and *Châtelaine*. They are all owned by the Rogers Media conglomerate. *Chatelaine* has become a much more frothy production, heavily focused on cooking, health, and beauty, and its French-language sister *Châtelaine*, while offering a comparable mix of content, also includes coverage of cultural events and international topics. Both titles run a book club. *Maclean's* maintains a strong nationalist agenda and an emphasis on in-depth investigative reporting. It is complemented by *L'actualité*, a Quebec

---

[25] For discussion see Doig 26–28.

current affairs magazine likewise owned by Rogers. In 1976, *L'actualité* absorbed the French-language edition of *Maclean's* which had started in 1961 under the title *Le Magazine Maclean*. All of the surviving titles have a strong online presence. They no longer publish fiction or poetry, and they devote an even higher proportion of space to advertising than they did in earlier decades. Yet there are notable continuities between the current and earlier incarnations of these magazines. As Imre Szeman notes in his article on Canadian magazines and globalisation at the start of the twenty-first century: 'Form and content overlap in the audience's cultural aspirations, which are addressed by advertising as much as by the articles in the magazine' (222). This comment would have applied, equally, in the decades covered by our study. The magazines published by Rogers Media still address a class with disposable income and a desire for consumer goods, tasteful entertainment, and types of knowledge that will advance their economic and social standing. The histories of the magazines are central to understanding this aspirant middle class as it came to stand in as a normative Canadian identity.

Chapter Two

PAGES

The techniques of discontinuous juxtaposition in landscape poetry and painting were transferred to the popular press and the popular novel.
[…]
The children of technological man respond with untaught delight to the poetry of trains, ships, planes.
                    —Marshall McLuhan, *Counterblast*

THIS chapter concentrates on the magazine as a material object. Its contribution is partly methodological: the multi-levelled analysis practised here might be applied to magazines from other countries and other eras. At the same time, the focus of the chapter is determined by the primary themes of our research, so we consider the material dimensions of our chosen periodicals in relation to middlebrow culture and travel. In general terms, the way that any magazine places itself and its audience in relation to cultural and class hierarchies may be discerned through analysis of its design and layout, internal organisation, pricing, mix of content, and mode of address to readers. More specifically, one aspect of the Canadian magazines' engagement with the middlebrow project is their presentation of travel—whether actual or vicarious—as a pleasurable form of self-improvement. This may be explored in relation to the format of the magazines by examining interactions between text and image, commercial and editorial content. Travel features and travel adverts are often structured by common image sets associated with, for example, sophistication and the exotic, or heritage and nostalgia. The role of the editor can also be imagined in terms of the practice of travel. Richard Ohmann's comment on turn-of-the-century American mass magazines is pertinent here: 'The editor or his implied persona […] was like a tour guide, pointing to this thing as interesting, that as notable, another as worrisome, still another as curious' (230). This is a helpful analogy, not least because it emphasises one of the qualities which the golden-age mass magazines inherited from their nineteenth-century precursors: the miscellany format. These earlier magazines were often made up of collections of largely unrelated facts, illustrations, and anecdotes, many of them offering information about far-off places.[1] In the first decades of the twentieth century, the newly established Canadian magazines (especially *La Revue Populaire* and *Maclean's*) continued to draw on this periodical format. And if, as Ohmann suggests, the editor can to some extent be positioned as a tour guide, then the reader becomes a tourist, collecting impressions. Indeed, across the six magazines examined in this study, the rhetoric of travel is continually intertwined with a middlebrow emphasis on accumulation, whether of knowledge, experience, or material resources.

This accumulated knowledge was organised, to a certain extent, through the structuring and design of the magazines. In the specific context of the periodical, structure can work at different levels, such as column, page, issue, and volume. The reading experience is partly determined by the juxtaposition and ordering of items in a column and on a page, and, at the next level, by the ordering and distribution of items within the issue, and the implicit connections with previous issues which the regular reader will have seen. This repeating structure is indexed, and made visible, in the table of contents. In glossy magazines today, the contents page is often difficult to locate due to the volume of advertising which precedes it and yet which is never listed as part of the official 'contents.' This is a strategy to force readers to view advertisements while searching for the contents page. By contrast, the Canadian magazines of the early to mid-twentieth century were much more visibly structured, and both commercial and editorial materials were presented as a resource for readers. The table of contents was nearly always placed prominently at the very front or back of each issue, and an index of advertisers was often present as well. Since these magazines were generally addressed to a broad audience—for instance, women of several different generations (*Chatelaine*, *La Revue Moderne*) or all the members of the middle-class family (*La Revue Populaire*, *Maclean's*)—these finding aids were all the more important in helping individual readers locate the items of interest to them. Again, Ohmann's account of the equivalent American titles is helpful: 'The magazines included an astonishing potpourri of material, but organised explicitly and tacitly into categories that implied the diversity and individuality of taste among the readership' (224–25). The form of a periodical works to construct and subdivide its implied audience, and to consolidate its own role as a tastemaker.

---

[1] On the nineteenth-century magazine in relation to genre and miscellany, see Liddle (especially chapter 6); Mussell 59, 140. A good example of a British magazine based on the principle of miscellany is *Tit-Bits*, a popular weekly established in 1881.

Continuities between editorial and commercial items in a magazine are often deliberately reinforced through adjacent positioning,[2] yet seemingly accidental juxtapositions, or discontinuities, can also produce fresh meanings. Periodicals scholars have recently taken up the notion of 'emergence' (see for instance Latham). This is a term from systems theory which refers, in N. Katherine Hayles's words, to 'any behavior or property that cannot be found in either a system's individual components or their additive properties, but that arises, often unpredictably, from the *interaction* of a system's components' (198). This serendipitous generation of meaning works, to some extent, against the organising structures which editors and designers seek to impose. Indeed, this should alert us to one way in which Ohmann's metaphor of the editor as tour guide may be slightly misleading: tour groups have set itineraries and proceed all together at the same pace, whereas periodical readers may each take a different route through a magazine. Though, as Latham and Scholes point out in their influential article on periodical studies, 'editors worked carefully to solicit, craft, and organize the material as part of an autonomous print object' (528–29), their ordering of material does not force, or even invite, readers to proceed through from first page to last, as they would with a novel. Readers are more likely to skim through and pause at items of interest, or read only the headings before returning to look at particular pieces in depth; in the process, they may view some advertisements multiple times.

This embodied relationship with the physical copy of the magazine directs attention to its material dimensions and its visual design. In exploring the significance of these, the notion of the 'bibliographic code,' introduced by Jerome McGann (57) and elaborated by other print historians, is essential. George Bornstein, in *Material Modernism: The Politics of the Page* (2001), explains: 'the literary text consists not only of words (its linguistic code) but also of the semantic features of its material instantiations (its bibliographic code). Such bibliographic codes might include cover design, page layout, or spacing,' as well as 'the other contents of the book or periodical in which the work appears' (6). Peter Brooker and Andrew Thacker have suggested that a version of bibliographic codes specifically relating to magazines—'periodical codes' (6)—should be elaborated. This should include aspects such as price, periodicity of publication, placement of advertisements, editorial practices, and

---

[2] In the modern magazine industry, the term 'adjacency' refers to 'the position of an advertisement next to certain editorial material for which publishers can charge higher rates' (McKay 314). There are also, however, adjacency standards which are espoused by editors of, for instance, consumer review magazines; these require that product adverts are not placed next to reviews of those products.

payment rates for contributors. We contribute to that ongoing work, offering case studies as well as exploring the relationships among different magazines. Competition, we would argue, is an important factor in determining periodical codes. Magazines owned or taken over by the same company (such as, for instance, *Maclean's*, *Mayfair*, *Chatelaine* and, later, *Châtelaine*) have especially complex commercial and editorial interrelations, involving both antagonism and mutual support.

This chapter offers a set of four perspectives on our chosen magazines as complex multi-authored texts and as physical objects. The four sections represent different levels of analysis, moving from a focused reading of the elements which make up a single page or issue towards broader generalisations about shifts over time. The first section works with the individual page, comparing examples taken from *Maclean's* in 1927 and *Chatelaine* in 1934. The second section examines one number of the *Canadian Home Journal*, from June 1951. The third surveys a complete volume of *Mayfair*, for 1935, and the fourth considers *La Revue Moderne* across the whole of its run, from 1919 to 1960. The level of detail inevitably decreases with each section, yet each one offers a different type of insight into the way the materiality of the magazines inflects representations of travel. An anatomisation of a double-page spread reveals how discourses of self-improvement were brought into conjunction with discourses of mobility—through, for instance, a car advert placed beside an editorial on the wise use of vacation time. Attention to the arrangement and categorisation of content in a particular issue offers clues about the range of reader groups the magazine envisaged. An account of a whole annual volume allows insight into a magazine's ideological positioning, the diversity (or otherwise) of its contributors, and the degree of consistency of its month-by-month content. Finally, surveying one title over several decades shows up shifts in style, production values, and editorial strategies, as well as in the extent and type of travel coverage. This summary by no means covers all the possibilities which are opened up by these different modes of investigation, nor is there space in this chapter to examine them all. However, by combining close reading, sampling, and broad survey, and by taking account of available information on audiences and their responses, we can offer an overview, and a demonstration, of several possible approaches to the analysis of the magazine as artefact.

Page: *Maclean's* 15 January 1927 and *Chatelaine* July 1934

The middlebrow emphasis on upward mobility and profit is clearly evident in the relationship between editorial and commercial content in all six of the periodicals, and a broadly patriotic outlook inflects this relationship. This may be related to larger tendencies in Canadian culture of the earlier and mid-twentieth century: L. B. Kuffert, in *A Great Duty: Canadian Responses to Modern Life and Mass Culture, 1939–1967* (2003), writes that this period saw an unprecedented 'willingness to link self-improvement with a decorous patriotism and, most important, to do so in magazines, on radio, and on television' (230). Whilst sustained transnational comparison is beyond the scope of this study, we would suggest that the nationalist dimension of middlebrow culture was apparently more salient in Canada and also Australia (see Carter) than it was in the UK or US. Certainly, the precise colouring of Canadian or Quebec nationalist sentiment, and the extent of loyalty to Britain or France, varied among the different magazines, and still more across the period under review. The ideological structures of nationalism and imperialism were not necessarily taken for granted; rather, they were extensively debated in articles and editorials. Nevertheless, the patterns of travel, shopping, and fiction reading which the magazines promoted were persistently related to their audience's presumed patriotism. This discussion of individual pages will begin by examining a double-page spread with advertisements alongside an editorial column, taken from a 1927 number of *Maclean's*. In presenting travel and mobility as forms of investment, these pages elaborate in several ways on the theme of 'getting ahead,' which was becoming central to *Maclean's* self-presentation. The two pages also emphasise the Canadian–British connection which was likewise important to the magazine's identity. We have chosen a double-page spread because the reader of a paper copy of a magazine is always looking at two pages at once, a verso and a recto. As John Dagenais writes: 'In the real world "the page" is almost always accompanied by a failed mirror image of itself, a lost twin. In the codex form book, we are always aware, peripherally, of what is to come and what has come before, of the past and future of reading' (62). Indeed, this is particularly important to remember when studying magazines, because their pages are often designed in pairs, with articles and even images spread across the fold in the centre (the gutter). Even when the items on facing pages appear unrelated, the reader's awareness of the opposite page will shape her or his response to the page s/he is focusing on.

The discussion in this first section will move on to the table of contents in the same issue of *Maclean's*, considered alongside the contents page in the chosen issue of *Chatelaine*, for July 1934. For many years, both magazines placed an editorial column next to the contents list.[3] A comparison between

---

[3] *Maclean's* sometimes shifted these two elements between the first and last pages, but they were kept together until 1939. *Chatelaine*'s table of contents was initially surrounded by adverts; the issue for November 1929 was the first to place the editorial

MAGAZINES, TRAVEL, AND MIDDLEBROW CULTURE

them reveals certain visual and ideological continuities, and also some key contrasts. Since the two titles were owned by the same company, staff often contributed to both. H. Napier Moore, editor of *Maclean's* from April 1926 until October 1945, was simultaneously (from 1928) editorial director of *Chatelaine*. The editor of *Chatelaine* in 1934 was Byrne Hope Sanders; most editorials during this year were signed by her, though there were two by guest writers and one by Moore. The issue with Moore's editorial has been chosen for study here: this facilitates comparison with the selected number of *Maclean's*, since in both, the same person signed the editorial, and therefore, the differences between them must be due primarily to the strategies adopted by the two magazines in order to appeal to different audience groups.[4] (Naturally, the seven-year gap between the two issues would also explain some of the differences, particularly in visual terms.)

In 1927, *Maclean's*, which at that point still spelled its name *MacLean's*, was published on the first and fifteenth of each month, priced at 10 cents a copy or $2 for a year. It was printed in the standard size for mainstream magazines (10 x 14 inches) and had a circulation of approximately 110,000.[5] Issues varied considerably in length during this year, ranging from 60 to 114 pages. Editorial material and smaller advertisements were all in black and white, but covers were printed in four colours, and numerous full-page adverts in one, two, or four colours were interspersed through each issue. On the chosen double-page spread from the mid-January issue, the 'Business and Investments' section takes up the two centre columns on page 60 and the two left-hand columns on page 61, with a single column of advertisements on either side on page 60, and three advertisements of two-column width on page 61. 'Business and Investments' contains one article, 'Revenue from Tourist Traffic Reaches Total of $194,000,000,' and a 'Financial Queries' department, consisting of questions from readers, with names and addresses (all in italic) and unsigned answers (in roman type). Both pages are dense with text, and only one of the adverts makes use of white space to emphasise its message.

---

on the contents page. From 1947, the magazine started to move and separate these items.

[4] Also, George H. Tyndall was business manager of both magazines, providing a certain consistency of approach. However, Moore's leadership may not have been the primary influence on either title: Sanders would have made most of the decisions at *Chatelaine*, while William Arthur Irwin was at least as important as Moore in determining the direction of *Maclean's*. Irwin joined the magazine in 1925 but did not become editor until 1945 (Berton; Djwa 129).

[5] *MacLean's* 15 Feb. 1927: front cover.

'Revenue from Tourist Traffic' is contributed by J. Herbert Hodgins, who would become managing editor of *Mayfair* a few months later. His article focuses on the profit which may be made from American tourists' admiration of Canada: 'At last we are discovering that we are a little *different*! [...] I have increasing reason to believe that most of those who live across the border consider us a people with manners, habits and customs which absolutely identify us as Canadians. In other words, our trade mark' (60). Hodgins's article, surrounded as it is by advertisements for Canadian firms, and placed in a periodical whose cover announced it as 'Canada's National Magazine,' participates in the promotion of Canada as an independent economic actor. Yet this emphasis not only co-existed with, but depended on, a simultaneous reiteration of Canada's cultural identity as British. Hodgins describes conversations with American tourists who enthused about the politeness of Canadians and their courteous treatment of visitors. He quotes from the writings of Elbert Hubbard, Jr: 'I like the Canadians. They are more natural, serious, unsophisticated, still having much of the pioneer spirit. [...] Maybe it's all because [...] they are British and have a king. There is something about having a king at the head of a nation that preserves the national spirit' (60).[6] Indeed, Hodgins's main theme is preservation—he argues that Canadians should resist the incursions of Americanism, even as they welcome American tourists and 'harvest' (61) their dollars. His conclusion is that 'above all we require to maintain those national characteristics which are the spirit of our people and which [...] have a distinct appeal. In other words, politeness pays profits so let us capitalize politeness' (61).[7]

In its title, and in the accompanying table showing annual numbers of American visitors from 1922 to 1926, the article precisely quantifies the financial gains to be made from the intangible 'capital' of Canadian courtesy. The 'Financial Queries' column, which begins just underneath, concentrates on more traditional forms of asset—the first question, for instance, relates to the Prudential Oil and Gas Company of Calgary. But this column, too, has a clear nationalist emphasis: every suggested investment is in a Canadian business or in government or municipal securities, and one of the strongest recommendations is for Canadian National Railway's 5% bonds.[8] The nine

---

[6] On the presentation of Canada as unsophisticated, in Hodgins's article and elsewhere, see Hammill, 'Wilderness/Sophistication.'

[7] As Dubinsky points out, the post-Second World War period saw exactly the same emphasis on the importance of exploiting the famed Canadian courtesy in order to attract more American tourist dollars ('Everybody' 339).

[8] This column also offers insight into the socioeconomic status of *Maclean's* readers;

advertisements alongside these columns were placed by one American company (the Spencerian Pen Company), one Scottish mail order firm (a bootmaker), and seven Canadian businesses (three investment securities firms; the Cooper Institute of Accountancy; Simonds Saws; *The Financial Post* newspaper; and *Maclean's* itself). There is, then, a direct link between the editorial content on these pages and the area of activity of five of the advertisers (finance), while the remaining adverts have clearly been fitted in to fill small spaces. Yet even these work to reinforce Hodgins's emphasis on Canada's Britishness: the ad for Hogg's 'Fife Shoe' foregrounds Canada's Scottish connection, while the *Maclean's* advert, which asserts that any news dealer in Great Britain and Ireland can now procure the magazine, is aimed at Canadians travelling or living in the UK, and reiterates the extent of exchange between the two countries.

Moving to the table of contents in *Maclean's*: in this period, it was placed on the last page (64 in this issue), across the two centre columns, with the editorial column, titled 'In the Editor's Confidence,' running on either side (see Figure 11). The editorial was headed, during the mid-1920s, with a line drawing of two whispering figures, enclosed between a set of bookends and with open volumes beside them. Both are wearing draped garments rather than modern clothes, and the left-hand figure resembles a mischievous Puck, with pointed ears and a topknot. This character implies a certain continuity with the American humour and political magazine *Puck* (1890–1918); both titles reference Puck from *A Midsummer Night's Dream*, who knows what is happening amongst all the other characters because he travels so fast that he can 'put a girdle round about the earth / In forty minutes' (II.i.75–76). The drawing constructs *Maclean's* in terms of wide-ranging interests, up-to-date information, and an ability to combine serious knowledge with the latest news and gossip. Opposite the contents page was a full-page, four-colour advertisement for the 'Copper and Brass Research Association' in Toronto. Its emphasis on investment in property—the headline is 'Whether you're going to build, buy or remodel a home'—speaks to the financial focus of several of the items listed in the table of contents, and reinforces *Maclean's* address to a prosperous, upwardly mobile audience.

The table of contents was, at this period, divided into three sections. The first (untitled) part presented fiction and features, each labelled as 'serial,' 'short story,' or 'article.' All but one were attributed to an author, and illustrators were named for each fiction piece, with the cover artist identified at the top of the list. *Maclean's*, then, placed a comparatively strong emphasis on individual contributors. (During this period, some of the other magazines included a

---

see our discussion of reader letters in Chapter One.

higher proportion of unsigned content and, among them, only *Chatelaine* named its illustrators on the contents page.)⁹ This particular number of *Maclean's* contains four short stories, by William Merriam Rouse, Archie McKishnie, C. F. Lloyd, and Thomas P. Freney, and one fiction serial by Alan Sullivan. Four different illustrators (H. Weston Taylor, A. C. Valentine, E. J. Dinsmore, and Paul Kossoff) provided the pictures. Most of these worked regularly for *Maclean's*, but the magazine used quite a large number of artists—the preceding issue, for instance, credited six illustrators, of whom only one also contributed to the 15 January edition. However, whilst some of the *Maclean's* cover art was quite striking, the story illustrations drew on a fairly consistent and predictable visual repertoire. This first section of the table of contents also lists six feature articles. One is the second in a set of articles by Norman Reilly Raine on 'Government Service—and You'; another is part of a regular series of 'Cabinet Portraits' by H. C. Crowell. The rest are stand-alone pieces: 'Growing Our Own' by Douglas MacKay; 'Making the Tariff Safe for Democracy' by Grattan O'Leary; 'Evolving the Arctic Cow' by Alan Longstaff; and an unsigned piece, 'The Duncan Prescription,' which was about the Royal Commission of Enquiry into the economic situation of the Maritime Provinces. In the context of the 1920s, the political and economic focus of this set of articles, and the exclusion of women authors from the whole front section of the magazine, constructs *Maclean's* primary readership as male. There is a clear continuity here with its former incarnation as *The Busy Man's Magazine*.

So *Maclean's* does not quite fit into the category of 'family magazine' (a label which perfectly suits, for instance, *La Revue Populaire*). Yet *Maclean's* did explicitly address women's interests in its political columns, and printed letters from female correspondents in its query sections. It also included reading matter directed at women—specifically, one assumes, at the wives and daughters of male subscribers. In the 15 January 1927 issue, the second and third sections of the table of contents are titled 'Special Departments' and 'Women and their Work.' Among the Special Departments were two humour columns—'Wit, Wisdom and Whimsicality' and 'Maybe Adam Laughed at These'—as well as the 'Review of Reviews' (a response to notable articles in other periodicals), and two regular columns, Hodgins's 'Business and Investment' and 'The Home Beautiful' by Anne Elizabeth Wilson (who went on to become the first editor of *Chatelaine*). The other female authors in this issue were Pansy Atkins and

---

⁹ During the late 1920s, in *La Revue Populaire*, an average of just two or three contributions per issue were attributed to authors, though almost all items were attributed in *La Revue Moderne*. In *Mayfair*, a little over half of articles were signed; in *Chatelaine* and the *Journal*, a high proportion were signed.

Edwina Seton, who contributed the two items in 'Women and their Work': a feature article on 'Mind Pictures and their Power,' and the 'Maclean's Question Box,' an informational column which in fact responded to male as well as female correspondents. These section divisions, and many of the regular features within them, persisted for many years. Intriguingly, though, on 15 June 1929, the title of 'Women and their Work' changed to 'Women and the Home.' The content did not alter very much, since the department had always focused mainly on domestic topics, yet the new title does indicate a narrowing of the realm of activity which *Maclean's* envisaged for women. 'Women and their Work' sometimes included articles about, or by, professional women. There was, for instance, one by the naturalist, businesswoman, and politician Martha Munger Black in March 1926, and one on Canada's youngest woman judge in May 1929, but that type of material was dropped from 'Women and the Home.' This may have something to do with the appearance of *Chatelaine* in 1928: the new magazine took a fairly broad view of women's lives, and began to run its own features on women working outside the home. It also took on some of the female staff and contributors who had previously written for *Maclean's*. Arguably, this left the 'Woman and the Home' section of *Maclean's* as a refuge for more conservative female readers: indeed, it increasingly appears to represent a male view of what the woman's realm should be.

H. Napier Moore's editorial in the mid-January edition in 1927 was framed as a response to a letter received from a reader, 'R. H. M. of Montreal,' protesting against the requirement of the *Maclean's* short story contest, 'that all stories submitted must be distinctively Canadian.' The letter (whether real or invented) is quoted at some length, extending over almost half a column. It denies the existence of a 'Canadian type' and proposes a continentalist view: 'So far as habits, customs, environment, scenery, politics, business, hopes and fears, and reading matter, are concerned, we people in the upper half of North America are just a conglomeration.' Moore counters this through reference to the different environments and histories of the US and Canada:

> To take only one phase of life—settlement of the country. The United States West was settled by a different breed to that which settled our own West. The very ingredients of the 'melting pot' are different. Take the Scots and the English who first pioneered in Canada. Consider the life they left and the life they adopted. Consider the influence of Canada on stock such as this. Study the [...] achievements wrought under that influence plus their native and inherited influences. The product, whether it be of themselves or of their progeny, cannot be otherwise than something distinctively Canadian. [...] The romance of Canada,

whether it be of the days of Port Royal or of the business conquest of the Saguenay; whether it be of the Royal Canadian Mounted [*sic*] or of the wheat pool; whether it be of old Montreal or of Vancouver Island, belongs to Canada.

The racialist language here ('breed,' 'stock,' 'native'), and the celebration of the romance of Canadian history is similarly present in many of the short stories published in *Maclean's*. The editorial also directly echoes J. Herbert Hodgins's emphasis, in his contribution to the same issue ('Revenue from Tourist Traffic'), on the ethical and monetary value of a distinct Canadian identity.

It is precisely the question of 'value' which H. Napier Moore and his correspondent debate. The disgruntled 'R. H. M.' laments that a Canadian literary text can easily become 'a sort of advertising booklet' for Canada, 'paying so much attention to Canadian environment and setting that the literary value is completely submerged.' It was often for precisely this reason that Canadian fiction, and especially magazine fiction, was disparaged as middlebrow. Indeed, R. H. M.'s complaint anticipates A. J. M. Smith's 'cosmopolitan' position, as formulated just one year later in the influential essay 'Wanted: Canadian Criticism.' Printed in the *Canadian Forum* in April 1928, Smith's piece protests against the increasing alignment of commerce and art, arguing that the ethical imperative to buy Canadian consumer goods is increasingly being extended to cultural goods:

> If you write, apparently, of the far north and the wild west and the picturesque east, seasoning well with allusions to the Canada goose, fir trees, maple leaves, snowshoes, northern lights, etc., the public grasp the fact that you are a Canadian poet, whose works are to be bought from the same patriotic motive that prompts the purchaser of Eddy's matches or a Massey-Harris farm implement, and read along with Ralph Connor and Eaton's catalogue. (32)

This comment is particularly pertinent to the study of mass-market magazines which, in their physical properties and modes of circulation, have a certain affinity to the catalogues produced by retailers such as Eaton's, P. T. Legaré, or Simpson's. The major mail-order services were established between 1884 and 1928, the same period in which the mainstream magazines were emerging. There was some crossover in terms of staff,[10] and both types of publication were produced in the industrial centres of central Canada and distributed, mainly

---

[10] For example, Byrne Hope Sanders wrote for the Eaton's catalogue before joining

by mail (though sometimes through shops), to a dispersed audience across the country. Like the magazines, the catalogues disseminated images of the model Canadian family (see Béland), but both also targeted specific customer groups through separate publications or by dividing a single publication into sections. For instance, Dupuis Frères created a catalogue specifically for Catholic clergy, while Eaton's produced special catalogues for customers in the western provinces and in the Maritimes. Catherine C. Cole, comparing Eaton's Toronto and Winnipeg catalogues, notes that while the Toronto version 'catered to working women in cities as well as to rural women, the Winnipeg catalogue catered more to rural men and their wives. There were far more single men in the West than women'. Therefore, menswear was given greater prominence in the Winnipeg catalogue, and placed nearer to the front.

In many ways, mass magazines in North America quite literally 'catalogued' aspects of modern life, as Ohmann notes:

> Most of the favored genres other than fiction reinforced discontinuity and discreteness. [...] The vicarious tour (a woman climbs the Matterhorn; hunting walrus in the Arctic) put remote places and strenuous activities on view. The survey of new contrivances (warships, automobiles, submarines) simply cataloged. The celebrity article collected memorable facts into an illusion of intimacy with the great man or woman. The 'visit' admitted readers to the home or country retreat of painter, writer, or statesman, and documented what would now be called his 'life style.' The cultural departments were handy annotated catalogs of new plays, new novels, recent paintings, great singers. Pointing, describing, and enumerating were the characteristic gestures of these articles; taken as a whole they enacted a rhetoric of taxonomy and accumulation. (230)

The magazines were structured according to principles of collection and exhibition, not only of goods but also of facts and ideas. Their displaying function points us towards another way in which magazines and catalogues may be usefully compared: in both, advances in marketing techniques and also in printing technologies are visible in the increasing use of illustrations, photography, white space, and typographical variety.[11] A clear shift in this respect can be seen by comparing the 1927 *Maclean's* to *Chatelaine* in 1934.

Maclean Publishing (Sutherland 160). Mary-Etta Macpherson published a biography of the Eaton family in 1963.

[11] See Belisle, particularly 21–48; 132–55. Library and Archives Canada has digitised a selection of catalogues dating from 1887 to 1975 (http://www.collectionscanada.gc.ca/

At that time, *Chatelaine* was priced at 10 cents per monthly copy or $1 a year for residents of Canada, Britain, or British overseas territories. It was published in the standard 10 x 14 inch format, and had a circulation of 180,000.[12] The readership for this, as for the other magazines, would have been considerably larger than the circulation figure, as a result of library subscriptions and copies shared among family members and friends.[13] A readers' letters page in *Chatelaine* for June 1934 includes a contribution from a woman in Ireland who received the magazine from her Montreal cousin, and another from a British Columbia reader, who wrote: 'My copy is read in no less than a dozen different homes' (Mapes). During 1934, issues of *Chatelaine* ranged from 50 to 90 pages in length, with a majority coming in at around 70 pages. Single-colour printing was extensively used for editorial material: either as part of the design of the page itself (in the form of dividing lines or blocks of background colour), or for 'colouring-in' parts of a fashion or fiction illustration. Covers and cover advertisements were printed in four colours, but nearly all the remaining adverts were in black and white. This meant that the use of colour had actually declined in comparison to the 1927 issue of *Maclean's* examined above, and in comparison to earlier volumes of *Chatelaine* itself. Marie-Louise Bowallius in her essay on the American *Woman's Home Companion*, offers an explanation:

> In 1932 the use of colour decreased considerably; only 42 per cent of the full-page ads contained colour in the March issue. Meanwhile, 54 per cent employed black and white photography. To a certain extent this was due to economic factors as photographs were cheaper than drawings or paintings, but explanations can also be found in the development within photography. From the literal, matter-of-fact realism it had developed its own artistic self-consciousness and begun to manipulate the subjects, using extreme camera perspectives, variant focus, light and shadow, and compositional juxtapositions to startle the eye or evoke a mood. Because of this development, photography became more attractive to advertising

---

mailorder/). An online history of Canadian mail order is hosted by the Canadian Museum of History at http://www.historymuseum.ca/cmc/exhibitions/cpm/catalog/cat0000e.shtml.

[12] *Chatelaine* Jan. 1933: front cover.

[13] It is very probable that rural and suburban public libraries subscribed to magazines such as *Chatelaine*, but we did not find actual evidence of this on surviving copies. However, there are stamps indicating that the runs currently stored in places such as Library and Archives Canada and the Bibliothèque et Archives nationale du Québec originate from subscriptions held by those libraries or their precursors.

agencies and increasingly out-rivalled colour and modern art as a means of arresting attention. (31)

The contents and editorial page for the July 1934 *Chatelaine* (on page 2 of the issue) uses single-colour printing, with pink gridlines above and below the editors' names (see Figure 12). In comparison to the *Maclean's* issue, this gives much greater prominence to the editorial team, and perhaps increases the sense of the magazine as the product of a coherent and distinctive editorial vision. The use of pink, of course, genders the magazine's presumed audience. *Chatelaine*'s national identity is emphasised by a vertical row of photographs, rather resembling a filmstrip, and offering a kind of panorama of travel within Canada.

Another important visual shift was the increased use of white space: this contents page is far less cluttered than the 1927 *Maclean's* example. The typefaces are much more modern: title words are in an art deco style, body text in a clear, sans serif typeface, and items in the contents list are printed in bold rather than capitals. The editorial text is presented in an entirely different way, using a large, attention-grabbing heading—'Holiday Dividends'—and comprised of a series of very short paragraphs with blank lines in between. It is far easier to read than the densely-packed, lengthy text of Moore's earlier editorial for *Maclean's*, discussed above, but this was not an effect of modernisation: the editorials in *Maclean's* in 1934 were just as long, and almost as closely printed, as those in 1927. Rather, it is an effect of the gendered construction of the two magazines' audiences: Moore makes his *Chatelaine* editorials more accessible and less formal than his *Maclean's* ones, presumably because he is envisaging his reader, in the conventional terms of the day, as a distracted housewife rather than a serious businessman. The masthead illustrations in the two examples are not dissimilar: the one in *Chatelaine* also includes two hand-drawn figures on opposite sides of the page, but these figures are not talking together because they belong to different worlds: one is in seventeenth-century dress and holds a large key to the castle which stands behind her; the other is a highly modern figure in trousers, heels, fur jacket, beret, and bobbed hair, standing with her hands on her hips in front of a car. *Chatelaine*'s evident ambition to combine modernity with traditional wisdom, and to blend consumer advice with romantic escape, is reinforced by the subheading 'Mistress of her Castle,'[14] and more strongly by the masthead text beneath: 'This magazine is equipped to serve the chatelaines of Canada with authoritative information on housekeeping, child care, beauty

---

[14] 'Mistress of Her Castle' was the subtitle on the combined table of contents, masthead, and editorial page from February 1933 to December 1934.

and fashions, and with entertaining fiction and articles of national interest.' The emphasis on female mobility is communicated without words, in the drawing of the modern woman. It is made explicit, though, in the full-page advertisement for Ford cars on the facing page, which shows an elegant lady in the driving seat, and describes the V-8 model as 'a grand car for a woman to drive' (see Figure 13). The Ford is endorsed by a customer quotation: '"I used to be afraid of traffic", one woman writes, "but now I go everywhere".' The advert draws implicitly on a discourse of upward mobility—the phrase 'go everywhere' hints at access to the best social circles, and the text also suggests that the owner of a new Ford will be able, quite literally, to get ahead—that is, to differentiate herself from her peers: 'Its quick acceleration enables you to get out in front and escape the jam at every traffic light—its instant, eager speed helps you to pass other cars with greater safety.'

H. Napier Moore's 'Holiday Dividends' editorial likewise invites women, specifically mothers, to become more mobile. It begins: 'Money spent in travel is a sound investment,' a line in which these magazines' dominant attitude to tourism seems to crystallise. Elaborating on this, the next sentence functions as a perfect summary of the middlebrow ethos of enjoyable self-improvement: 'Nothing can take from you the returns it guarantees—broadmindedness, pleasant education, relaxation, recreation and lasting memories.' The third sentence, which like the previous two, is emphasised by being given a paragraph to itself, invokes the reader's sense of duty both as a parent and as a citizen: 'You can render no greater service to your children, derive no greater pleasure yourself, than to enlarge knowledge of your own country.' Following this introduction, the bulk of the editorial performs the function identified by Ohmann as 'pointing, describing, and enumerating' (230), as it surveys the attractions of each of Canada's provinces, moving from west ('Have you sailed the inside passage from Vancouver to Skagway?') to east ('have you tasted of the calm and rest and loveliness of Prince Edward Island?'). There is a strong emphasis on modes of transport, and the modern railways and roads of Canada are celebrated quite as much as the beauties of its landscape:

> Have you [...] followed the Trail of '98 from the observation platform of the train that climbs over the White Pass and into the Yukon? Or driven over the spectacular highways of Vancouver Island from Victoria the Beautiful?
>
> Have you basked in the Okanagan; followed in retrospect the gold seekers plodding the Cariboo trail? (You motor over a smooth road now.)

Picking up on the romance of Canadian history evoked in his earlier editorial for *Maclean's*, Moore suggests that the national past is available as an accessible, 'smooth' experience for middle-class families. The magazines included in this study often raise, or imply, questions about whether leisure time and income should be used for relaxation or for personal development. This editorial is typical in its attempt to balance these competing demands and to intertwine them with a strategic construction of the audience as patriots. The piece concludes: 'Do you know your Canada? Travel, and you make your holiday an investment as well as a joy.' The personal address to 'you' is another aspect of the gendering of Moore's prose. Advertisers often hailed readers in this way, but it is not a mode which Moore used in his more formal, carefully argued *Maclean's* editorials.

Beside this editorial is the table of contents, divided into six sections: Fiction, General Articles, Beauty Culture, The Chatelaine Institute (a section on cookery and housekeeping, contributed by the staff of the institute),[15] Chatelaine Patterns, and Children's Feature. All the listed items, apart from the patterns, are attributed to an author. Those contributing stories to this issue were Ann Morse, Louise M. Comstock, Elizabeth Whiting, Margaret E. Barnard, and Nancy Barnes. General articles were by the actress Madeleine Carroll, the freelance journalist Maud Pettit Hill, and *Chatelaine*'s fashion columnist, Kay Murphy, while staff writers Annabelle Lee, Norah Whitton, Anne Thompson, M. Frances Hucks, Helen G. Campbell, and Anne Elizabeth Wilson each wrote one or more of the beauty, children's, and cookery pieces. This stands in marked contrast to the largely male contributor list in *Maclean's*: the only man listed in the *Chatelaine* contents page is H. Napier Moore himself. The issue exhibits a preoccupation with celebrity: Carroll's piece is entitled 'My Hollywood Diary,' while Norah Whitton's contribution to the 'Beauty Culture' section is headed 'Mary Pickford on Charm.' These pieces point beyond Canada to the world of Hollywood fantasy. (It is worth noting that Pickford's Toronto origins are elided in many of the Canadian media features about her, and she is generally presented as a representative of a foreign world of glamour.) Apart from these items, the contents list of this edition is almost entirely domestic (in both senses of the word), and bears no apparent relation to the emphasis on travel and discovery evident in the editorial and the column of small photographs. However, through the fashion illustrations showing women and children in beach, mountain, and cruise settings, and through the

---

[15] The Institute was located in Toronto, and its staff tested recipes, produced menus, budgets, and schedules, liaised with the members of *Chatelaine*'s Consumer Council, and answered reader enquiries (Korinek, *Roughing It* 186). 'The Chatelaine Institute' was first used as a section heading for the magazine's service departments in May 1930.

advertisements for Canadian Pacific Railway, the Canadian National Exhibition, Kodak, and the Provincial Tourist Board of Quebec, the issue as a whole does encourage aspirations to see the country and to go away on holiday.

Issue: *Canadian Home Journal* June 1951

The June 1951 *Canadian Home Journal* retains the emphases on mobility and on seeing Canada which were so evident in the July 1934 number of *Chatelaine*, but it expands outwards by promoting overseas travel and adventurous holidays. The cover features a large photograph of a cheerful infant, labelled 'Intelligence Tests for Babies,' and carries a second cover line: 'Fashions Right for Flight: A West Coast Holiday' (see Figure 15). This combination of items epitomises the way that the magazine, especially during the 1950s, maintained its primary focus on the domestic sphere whilst simultaneously inviting readers to move outside it through recurrent references to travel, holidays, and faraway places. These observations may be generalised to a broader statement. Both of the Anglophone women's magazines remained grounded in the domestic—in the two senses of the individual home and the Canadian nation. Over the course of the decades covered in this study, they each gradually began to include a little more material on travel and to envisage a wider geographical scope for that travel. Conversely, they gradually reduced the extent of their reference to France and Britain as touchstones of taste in the areas of fashion and culture, embracing a notion of Canadian individuality and independence (though retaining an association between Canadian-ness and a white Anglo-Saxon heritage).

In 1951, the *Canadian Home Journal* was edited by Mary-Etta Macpherson, supported by nine sub-editors, departmental directors, and managers. During the 1950s, the magazine's circulation ranged from 400,000 to 500,000 (Sutherland 249), its cover price was 15 cents, and an annual subscription cost $1.50. It was produced, as it had always been, in a 10 x 14 inch format, and the 1951 issues ranged from 60 to 104 pages, the variation determined largely by changing volumes of advertising. The June edition had 96 pages; of these 13 were printed in black and white, 45 contained material printed in one colour, three included two-colour printing, and 35 featured four-colour illustrations. Four-colour printing was used almost exclusively for advertising, but some of the one – and two-colour images and designs were editorial material. Roughly two-thirds of the advertisements were illustrated with drawings, and the remainder with photographs; a few used both. Editorial illustrations were about equally divided between drawings and photographs. In comparison with issues of the *Journal* from earlier decades, this one was far more visually appealing.

Richard Ohmann points to the importance of advertisements as a component of the 'visual display' (224) offered by magazines, and as one of the methods by which readers were positioned in social space. He notes that: 'Ads consistently addressed readers as belonging to one of the two highest social classes, or as aspiring to be like such people' (206), but at the same time, 'it was hard for any but the poor, rural, or illiterate not to be readers of at least some ads, not to take part in this new literacy of goods' (209). Ohmann's reference to 'reading' advertisements gestures towards another aspect of their role: even in the 1950s, magazine advertisements often functioned as providers of information and advice, however biased. Indeed, as we discuss in Chapter One, the presence of an Advertisers' Index in many volumes of *Chatelaine*, the *Journal*, and *La Revue Moderne* emphasises the status of the advertisements as a resource for readers. The editorial texts accompanying these indexes emphasised the magazines' role as gatekeepers or quality controllers, but they focused entirely on household products, confirming that the authority to which the women's magazines laid claim was primarily located in the domestic sphere. Indeed, most of the 107 firms which advertised in this issue of the *Journal* were manufacturers of household products, foods, and cosmetics, though there were also adverts placed by service providers such as financial or insurance firms, railway companies, or tourist boards.

The table of contents, on page 3, was divided into the following sections: 'Fiction' (three items, by Virginia Oakey, Leslie Gordon Barnard, and Vera Henry); 'General Features' (eight items, of which seven are attributed to authors); 'Foods, Cookery and Home Bureau' (four items, written by contributing editors or groups of staff); 'Beauty and Fashions' (seven items, three attributed to magazine staff and the rest anonymous); and four further sections, each containing one item by a named writer: 'Modern Home'; 'Needlecraft'; 'Well-Baby Centre'; 'Poetry.' (The 'Poetry' component, however, hardly deserves to be called a section, as it consists of a single eight-line piece by an author named Gilean Douglas, taking up 5% of one page.) This issue is quite representative, giving a good indication of the balance of content during this era. The literary material reveals a continued preference for Canadian authors, but also suggests that the magazine's earlier commitment to publishing up-and-coming authors had declined by the 1950s. Barnard, for instance, was a safe choice who had been publishing in the *Journal* since as early as 1911 and had contributed stories and serials almost every year since 1925 (Michelle Smith, 'Mainstream' 9), while Henry was primarily an author of confession stories for the 'love pulps.' Several of the 'General Features' were apparently contributed by freelance authors, while most of the domestic items were probably written by magazine staff. Illustrators are not identified in the contents page, though the illustrator's name is given beneath the author's for the short stories and for those of the features accompanied by artwork. The cover photography is credited to a company, 'Camera Clix.' The relatively high level of attribution demonstrates that the *Journal* was strongly emphasising the good quality and individuality of its contributing journalists and artists. This is reinforced in the unsigned editorial (on the page opposite the table of contents), which focuses on the magazine's editors and writers, and is illustrated with photographs of the *Journal*'s art director and fashion editor.

The editorial starts by announcing an award won by the art director, Nancy Caudle. The pleasure taken by her colleagues in Caudle's award is described in terms of 'pure, doting-family pride,' metaphorically bringing the work of a professional woman back into the context of the home, and perhaps extending the notion of 'family' to include the *Journal*'s readers. (Indeed, this anticipates contemporary commercial rhetoric, which refers to companies with the same owner as 'families' with a common 'parent,' and constructs consumers as the 'guests' of retailers.) The second part of the editorial promises: 'A bit of change of air and scenery is on just about everybody's mind, come June, and in the following pages you'll encounter a nice fresh wind blowing from several interesting directions' ('Among Those'). The items trailed are an account by the high-profile writer Judith Robinson of a 14-month tour around Britain and France, and the cover story, 'Fashions Right for Flight.' This visually lavish fashion story is given great prominence, with two consecutive double-page spreads; by contrast, the other three leading stories and features in the issue each run for only a single page before transferring to the back section.

'Fashions Right for Flight' presents a set of captioned photos of a model named Betty, together with a text on travelling to British Columbia by Margaret Thornton, the *Journal*'s fashion editor (see Figure 14). Combined fashion and travel features were an innovation of the 1950s: this one provides as much detail about Vancouver tourist attractions as it does about clothes. The styling of the piece contrasts with that of the other main fashion item in this issue, a conventional spread based on Butterick patterns. Entitled 'Vacation Varieties,' it consists of four captioned black-and-white drawings of women wearing holiday outfits. It is very similar to the fashion pages of earlier decades, except for a tendency towards fewer, larger drawings. In comparison, the 'Fashions Right for Flight' feature has a far more contemporary, innovative appearance. It consists of a series of elegantly posed photographs, with plenty of white space around them. The page design uses one colour, and one of the photographs is in full colour. The colour picture establishes visual continuity with the advertisements: every other full-colour image in the June 1951 *Journal* is an advert. This emphasises the 'advertorial' nature of the fashion feature, which directly promotes a range of products. The text names not only the clothing designers but also the hotel and restaurants visited. It gives details of flights taken, and the Trans-Canada Airlines logo is clearly exhibited in one of the photographs. Reinforcing this commercial orientation, a luggage advertisement in the back pages reproduces one of the pictures from the 'Fashions Right for Flight' feature, showing Betty standing on a runway beside her McBrine suitcases (McBrine). A slightly more subtle link between editorial and advertising content is evident in the placing of a Canadian National rail advert, with a line drawing showing mountains and totem poles, alongside the continuation of the feature in the back pages.

The commitments of the feature extend beyond the strictly commercial, however. In Thornton's text, the nationalist emphasis of many of the *Journal*'s holiday features is strongly evident:

> Suppose it's you—a career girl, a housewife, a student—with a time limit on your holidays; two weeks perhaps, a month if you're lucky. No world gadding for you! You want to see our own beautiful West Coast. Perhaps you have relatives or friends there. You want to spend every precious minute with them, amid the unbelievable loveliness of Pacific Coast scenery, and so you decide to be air-borne. (Thornton 13)

Even in the midst of a highly consumer-oriented piece, which promotes both designer clothing and luxury travel, there is that note of thrift, that middlebrow emphasis on the profitable use of leisure time. This short passage, with its direct, personal address to a specific segment of the magazine-reading public, manages to construct its audience not only as 'career girl,' 'housewife,' or 'student,' but as middle class, family-oriented, hard-working, solvent, patriotic, and appreciative of beauty. The magazines continually imagine their readers in these terms.

The short story which follows this piece, 'Successor to Laura' by Leslie Gordon Barnard, begins:

> More even than the salty smell of the sea it was the fragrance of the carnation border that brought a flood of memory. Yet, for a moment, at the first sight of tidal water, panic had filled Jennifer. Had her coming been a mistake after all?
>
> If she had been able to get here earlier, of course, it would have been different, but bad weather had grounded all planes and flying had been impossible. (16)

This opening passage assumes that domestic flights are now part of the ordinary travel arrangements of middle-class Canadians, yet it simultaneously undermines Margaret Thornton's claims about the straightforwardness and comfort of air travel. The story does not explicitly continue the travel theme: it is a conventional romance centred on an old family home and illustrated with a full-page drawing of a generalised, misty seaside landscape. Yet, as so often in these magazines, the illustrations for stories and articles are related in complex ways to the iconography of advertising. The picture accompanying Barnard's story echoes a Chevrolet advert on page 8 of the issue, which the reader might have seen moments earlier. The full-page ad has a drawing showing a car travelling along a coastal road; the bay is positioned in the same orientation as the one in the story illustration, and in both, a lighthouse stands on the cliff, with several houses at its foot. The advertisement seems like a cheerful, full-colour version of the gloomy yet romantic image drawn for 'Successor to Laura,' and it transforms the Maritime landscape from a backdrop for turbulent passions to a desirable holiday destination. Car advertisements often use location as a fantasy: this ad, like the 'Fashions Right for Flight' spread, locates its wares as separate from ordinary life. In both types of promotion, holiday fantasies are used to suggest an aspect of experience which falls outside of the everyday, but is still considered attainable.

Presenting another facet of domestic travel, an article entitled 'They're off to camp' focuses on the 'healthful mental and physical development of our Canadian children' (Flynn 60). One of its continuation pages contains a large advertisement for Canadian Pacific tours in the Rockies. There is perhaps a suggestion, in this juxtaposition, that parents will be able to take such holidays while their children are away at camp. The drawings in the advertisement show couples taking part in activities similar to those offered to children at camp: swimming, tennis, hiking, canoeing, and riding are mentioned. The advertisement relies on a notion of Canada as a healthy, outdoor paradise, and this is made explicit in the summer camp article: 'We occupy one of the few spots in the world where opportunities for outdoor living are limitless' (Flynn 60). Indeed, outdoor leisure was emphasised particularly strongly in Canadian magazines during the 1950s. Several of the columns and advertisements in the June 1951 *Canadian Home Journal* address an audience of urban dwellers who have access to lakeside or country retreats—a piece on 'Cottage Crafts,' for instance, recommends 'rainy-day projects while you're at the lake this season' and talks about 'the home-mades and the hand-mades at the cottage' (Aliman). Even the article on 'the annual man-hunt, vacation style' is titled: 'Don't be a Babe in the Woods,' and advises girls on how to behave when out in a motor boat with a man, whether to help gather wood for a fire, and what to do when rain or spray threatens to spoil a hairstyle (Cameron). This piece assumes that young unmarried people will be going on lakeside holiday in groups. Indeed, the travel experiences of young Canadian adults during this decade were increasingly focused on backwoods adventure, hostelling, camping, or even hitchhiking across the country. As we discuss in our 'Consumers' chapter, the conservation movement also became linked—in complex ways—to notions of ecological travel, wilderness tourism, and antimodernism.

A further set of features in this issue of the *Journal* centre on foreign travel. 'You cawn't miss it!' by Judith Robinson is a semi-mocking, semi-affectionate account of getting lost in England, specifically in King's Lynn. This provides the occasion for assorted descriptions of English fictional characters, medieval history, and the royal family. A rambling and rather charming piece, it seems to embody the English characteristics it describes, and is illustrated with cartoons by Harold Town showing castles, London buildings, policemen, and perplexed characters all pointing in different directions. While the piece celebrates English traditions and eccentricities, and admires the way the Queen moves 'companionably' among her people (67), it also implicitly contrasts the cosmopolitan Canadian traveller with the insular people she encounters in rural England:

> Not that the English at home are uninterested in far-off places. They are interested. They are as interested as anything. They like to talk about them. Tierra del Fuego or Toronto, London or Manchester or Little Missenden two parishes away: they like to talk about them all and about how to get to them. But do not take the talk for a guide. The English at home haven't the least idea where or how far off far-off places really are. (65)

Judith Robinson was a prominent political journalist with a strong commitment to Canadian parliamentary traditions as well as to the monarchy. An opinion columnist for the *Globe and Mail* during the 1930s and the war years, and Ottawa political columnist for the Toronto *Telegram* during the later 1940s, she also contributed at various times to other periodicals, such as the *Nation*, and started her own weekly paper in Toronto, the *News*.[16] But in the editorial for the issue of the *Canadian Home Journal* in which 'You cawn't miss it!' appears, she is described not as a journalist but as 'the brilliant Toronto author of the distinguished and widely read biography, *Tom Cullen of Baltimore*' ('Among Those'). This is consistent with the magazines' tendency to characterise their contributors as 'authors' and 'artists,' rather than 'journalists' and 'illustrators.' These terms, suggesting originality and artistry rather than

---

[16] See Lang 77, 83, 102; Robinson, *As We Came By*; Taylor 40.

technique or craftsmanship, indicate an aspiration towards high culture which is typical of the middlebrow.

Robinson's contribution is not the only article in the June 1951 *Canadian Home Journal* to present an image of an adventurous Canadian woman travelling abroad independently. Margaret Vollmer's 'A Slow Boat to Fun' is addressed to women who dream of 'faraway places' (82), and recommends that they take one of the handful of passenger berths available on freighter ships. Rather than an impressionistic piece (like Robinson's), this is a practical article, full of detailed advice about cost, routes, and shipboard etiquette. Indeed, Vollmer's rationale for freighter travel is that it enables travellers to avoid the expense, social demands, and predictable itineraries of a cruise ship, substituting independently organised visits to unusual destinations in the Pacific, Caribbean, South America, or Scandinavia. Embodying the paradox of these magazines, which were addressed to a mass audience yet continually emphasised individuality and distinction, Vollmer's article strongly resists models of mass tourism. For shore excursions, she recommends avoiding the guides who will turn up on the waterfront. Instead, she suggests, 'meander on your own speed, and if you have faith in St Christopher try exploring by native buses' (83). Equally, she resists the magazines' dominant construction of travel as a mode of upward mobility:

> Social life on a freighter has few of the peripatetics of a social-director-organized shipboard. No shuffleboard, no deck tennis, no swimming pool, no bingo, no formal dances; but, before you cry out in dismay, also consider: no expensive, extensive wardrobe, no wallet-scraping bar bill from gaily signing chits, no waving palm-grove of tips, no 'must-join-ins,' none of those over-glossed, world gadabouts trying to impress you. Instead you relax in that old-shoe comfort of unplanned days, of unhurried reading or cribbage or just sitting in the sunshine. In this jet-speed age, a slow boat is perhaps the last refuge of time, time without urgency but with good company. In addition to your fellow passengers you will meet probably a dozen thoroughly experienced travellers in the ship's officers, for you eat in their mess. (82–83)

Vollmer redefines 'good company' so that it suggests interesting conversation rather than breeding and elite status, and explicitly appeals to travellers with more intrepidity than wealth. Yet her dislike of the 'overglossed' social climbers is articulated from a position of implicit superiority, since her description of the pleasures of slow travel nostalgically invokes the practices of a disappearing leisure class.

In this respect, her article is aligned with Judith Robinson's, which—as the editorial for this issue notes—records the author's 'pleasant impressions on her return from fourteen months of sauntering around Britain, France et al' ('Among Those'). Both pieces are therefore in tension with the 'Fashions Right for Flight' article, with its insistence on efficient and profitable travelling and its address to a reader who has time only for a short vacation. The 'Fashions' feature is on the whole more representative of the *Journal*'s approach to travel, but the incompatibility of these different perspectives, offered within the same issue, should not surprise us too much. As scholars of modern print culture have long recognised, contradictory discourses frequently co-exist within a single periodical. According to Margaret Beetham: 'The magazine has developed in the two centuries of its history as a miscellany, that is a form marked by a variety of tone and constituent parts' and which is 'fractured and heterogeneous' (1). Ideological inconsistencies as well as continuities may be detected when editorial components are read alongside ads. Indeed, Vollmer's article directly counteracts some of the commercial material surrounding it. An advertisement for the Italian State Tourist Office depicts a five-piece set of luxury luggage and, in a smaller image, a picture of Venice surrounded by a frame as if hanging on a wall. The text reads: 'Italy ... awaits you for your holidays ... There are considerable reductions in the price of gasoline for tourists visiting Italy. Hotels and pensions of all classes at reasonable prices.' This advertisement appeals to upwardly mobile readers who wish to appear prosperous whilst actually saving money, and the framed image of Venice prioritises the souvenirs which may be displayed after the trip over the experience of the trip itself.

Year: *Mayfair* 1935

Neither the *Canadian Home Journal* nor *Chatelaine* ever attracted extensive advertising from travel companies, and *Maclean's* did only a little better. These magazines' coverage of holidays and distant destinations, though gradually increasing during the postwar years, was perhaps not sufficiently marked to lure many advertisers in this area; in many issues, travel advertising was limited to Canadian Pacific or Canadian National rail and hotel promotions. *Mayfair*, by contrast, focused on foreign travel from its inception, and ran many ads for tourist destinations, tour services, and travel-related products. It usually contained a special travel section, and a whole issue would often be devoted to this theme. 'Travel' was sometimes listed on the cover as one of the magazine's specialisms, along with 'society,' 'fashion,' and 'sports.' More broadly, representations of foreign cultures were crucial to the discourses of worldliness, sophistication, and high style through which the magazine articulated its core values. And in contrast to the women's magazines, *Mayfair*'s nationalism consisted more in celebrating the general prominence of 'globetrotting Canadians' than in constructing ideals of the Canadian family.

In 1935, the ninth year of its publication, *Mayfair* continued to be edited by J. Herbert Hodgins, who had led the magazine from the start, with Mary-Etta Macpherson as associate editor. Although it was owned by the Maclean Publishing Company, it wasn't usually promoted alongside the company's nationally oriented titles (notably *Maclean's* and *Chatelaine*), because of its more restricted focus on the urban centres of central Canada. The magazine documented the social lives of the elite families of Toronto, Ottawa, and, to a lesser extent, Anglophone Montreal, together with smaller cities nearby, and this gives it a certain provincial quality. At the same time, its extensive coverage of events in London and Paris, and attention to the activities of Canadians abroad, reveal an aspiration towards cosmopolitan worldliness on the part of the magazine itself as well as the people mentioned in its pages. This dynamic was crucial to the magazine's success, which was maintained until the Canadian elite began to lose its cohesiveness and social dominance. The cover price at this time was relatively high at 25 cents (or $2 for a year's subscription), and a British price of 1/6 was also given, indicating the magazine's importance to the Canadian expatriate community in London and to Canadians travelling in Europe. *Mayfair* was expensively produced, in the same 10 x 14 inch format as the other titles, but on higher quality paper. This was a sign of its specific aspirations, which were social and material rather than intellectual. Virginia Woolf remarked in 1930 that her friend, the artist Roger Fry, was disturbed by a suggestion that the new magazine he was planning to launch might be printed on shiny paper. She commented: 'You know where shiny paper leads— to fashion, rank and Mayfair' (Woolf, Letter). She was talking, of course, about Mayfair in London, but since *Mayfair* magazine was named after that district, Woolf's observation is very pertinent.

The styling of *Mayfair* was distinctive and elegant. It drew heavily on the visual idiom of art deco, with simplified, two-dimensional shapes, stylised block colouring, and bold typefaces. This expresses the magazine's cosmopolitanism and consumerist ethos—art deco was an international style, and was extensively used in commercial art, notably by transatlantic shipping lines. On the one hand, art deco is a form of modern minimalism, yet on the other, its insistently repeating shapes represent a mode of excess. Something similar could be said about *Mayfair*, particularly in relation to its use of blank space. Jeremy Aynsley, in his article on magazine design and typography in the 1920s, notes that a 'spatial airiness, emphasising the whiteness of the page both as unused space and the space taken up, enhances a sense of luxury and extravagance, conventional attributes of fashionable goods' (44). *Mayfair*'s pages were uncluttered: the density of text was far lower than in the other titles and the number of illustrations higher; pictures were larger, with wide borders around them; and a majority of advertisements were of full-page size. Yet *Mayfair* used almost no colour in this era. Colour printing had only ever been used on the covers and inside covers, on a handful of advertisements within the issue, and very occasionally for a society portrait. In any given month from 1935, between 5 and 8% of the pages were printed in colour. (The number of pages per issue ranged from 74 to 140.) The late 1930s saw an increasing number of four-colour advertising pages in *Mayfair*, but editorial content remained entirely in black and white until the end of the magazine's run. In 1935, the black-and-white pages of *Mayfair* already evoked a stylised nostalgia, because other magazines were becoming increasingly multi-coloured and often rather lurid. The restriction to black and white exhibits a restrained sophistication, in contrast to the visual exuberance of titles such as *Chatelaine* and the *Journal*.

Unlike the other five magazines, *Mayfair* generally ran themed issues. The January edition for 1935 was the 'Motor Show Number,' February's was dedicated to winter sports, the 'Spring Shopping and Travel Number' came in March, and the Paris fashions issue (with a special 'British section') in April. May 1935 saw the 'Royal Jubilee London Number,' June's issue was devoted to 'Brides and Bridegrooms' and July's to summer sports and travel, while the 'Vacation Number' appeared in August (see Figure 9). The September edition had no theme, October's was for Paris fashions again, November's was labelled 'The Debutantes,' and December's was of course the Christmas edition. The magazine's departments during this period were titled 'Sports,' 'Variety,' 'Society,' 'Fashion,' and 'Travel' (sometimes called 'British and Travel'), while an 'Every Month' section contained two calendars and several regular columns. The 'Calendar of Events' listed balls, golf fixtures, dog and motor shows, chamber concerts, and shows at Toronto's Eaton Auditorium and Massey Hall, as well as Atlantic, Pacific, and Bermuda sailings from New York and the Canadian ports. The second calendar (present from March to November) listed engagements and weddings. There was a beauty column, 'Boudoir and Powder Puff'; a men's fashion column, 'The Cosmopolite'; and 'Around the Town,' which focused on shopping (mainly in Toronto), and included advice on fashion, beauty, and interior decorating, as well as information on new shops or salons. In the 'Society' department, regular features included 'Toronto High Noon Gossip' by York, 'Montreal High Noon Gossip' by Mollie McGee, and '*Mayfair*'s London Letter' by Kathleen Bowker.

Mayfair was the only one of the magazines to maintain a regular travel section.[17] However, a majority of the 'travel' pieces consist of photographs of prominent Canadians at resorts, or getting on and off ships, together with captions or short texts about society functions, sports, and fashionable hotels. These unsigned pieces were introduced with a reference to a disembodied camera: 'Canadians are a mobile people this year, and *Mayfair*'s camera, which lurks ever ready on shipboard and in far lands, has recorded some interesting comings and goings' ('En Route' 22). *Mayfair*'s camera consolidated the social identities of the Canadian elite, demonstrating that their activities were worthy of being recorded. The magazine policed the boundaries of this group through its continual reference to a small set of prominent families, yet it is in this gesture that the magazine's provincialism is most evident. The same faces and names recur through the photo features and the regular 'Globe-Trotting Canadians' and 'Canadians in New York' columns, which simply list the movements and destinations of upper-class travellers. The extremely repetitive nature of this material forcibly strikes a researcher, reading a whole year's worth of issues in succession, although this aspect of *Mayfair* may have been rather less salient for readers leafing through an occasional copy of the magazine, or even for subscribers receiving issues at spaced intervals. *Mayfair* disguises its own repetitiveness by constructing the everyday as fashionability (what is new this month?) and by its emphasis on movement—arrivals and departures, gatherings and dispersals.

In the 1935 volume, the issues from January to May list only one or two items under 'Travel,' and almost all of them focus on Bermuda, by far the most popular destination for Canadians during the colder months. In general, these pieces are closer to the genre of the society letter than that of the travel article. They offer a combination of gossip, fashion news, hotel recommendations, and accounts of sporting activities. Although the articles often evoke scenery in lyrical, if clichéd, terms, they contain very little information on culture, history, or architecture. Eva Ruberta Bryan's January 1935 piece, 'Bermuda's Lure for Canadians' provides a typical example. She begins: 'Bermuda, cousin to Canada, finds herself hostess to many prominent Canadians again this season. They troop along, these charming cousins: the golf groups; the tennis enthusiasts; and those who come in search of sunshine' (24). She lists the most notable individuals, mentioning their addresses, social circles, clothes, and activities:

---

[17] *Maclean's*, in certain periods, had a section labelled 'travel,' but it usually consisted simply of a set of travel adverts printed at the sides of pages containing unrelated articles.

> Mr and Mrs A. S. Patterson, of Toronto, are again occupying Patterson penthouse, atop the Belmont Manor, with one of the most superb views in all Bermuda. Mrs Patterson is unusually smart this season in warm red and rose dresses that add beauty and background to her wealth of snowy-white hair. Each day at twelve-thirty o'clock, in the grill of the Belmont Manor, Mr and Mrs Patterson entertain a circle of friends at cocktails, calling the function their 'broadcast hour.' Late arrivals are fined 2/6 and Mr Patterson turns his collections over to Lady Cubitt's Compassionate Fund, a charity sponsored by the wife of Sir Thomas Astley Cubitt, Governor of Bermuda. [...]
>
> Mr S. S. Taylor, K.C., and Mrs Taylor, of Vancouver, have taken *Ardley Cottage* for the season, and the Grainger and Hunt families of London, Ontario are others who have joined the cottage colony of Bermuda. (47)

The 'colony' of Canadians in Bermuda reproduces the social relations of the Toronto elite. The group draws in their upper-class compatriots from the Pacific coast, whom they would likely never have met back home, due to the vast distance separating Vancouver and Toronto. In this British overseas territory, the society established by the Canadian visitors echoes the structure of the British colonial elite which had governed at Quebec and, later, Ottawa since the eighteenth century.

There is a clear 'advertorial' quality to articles such as this. Bryan writes of 'the palatial Furness-Bermuda motorships, last word in travel luxury; showboats if you will,' describing their swimming pools, private bathrooms, and 'food evolved by the super chefs that only France can provide' (47). Beside her piece, unsurprisingly, is an advert for the Bermuda Trade Development board, while one for Belmont Manor appears a couple of pages later. Bryan's text emphasises relaxation, sport, and socialising, with stories of fishing, yachting, golf, swimming, drives, and parties. She also makes some gestures towards the arts, noting that among the recent visitors to Bermuda was a painter from New Brunswick, Frank Drummond Allison: 'Incidentally: Mr Allison's water colors have been likened to those of that clever Welshman, Brangwyn. When he had a one-man show in New York recently, the art critic of the N.Y. *Times* gave him this signal credit' (47). This is typical of *Mayfair*'s references to literature and culture, which are evidently designed to be useful for dinner party small-talk. For instance, a piece reporting on the 1935 Jubilee celebrations in London mentions that the correspondent travelled to St Paul's with 'Miss Mazo de la Roche and Miss Caroline Clement' (Bowker, 'London'), while further hints on Canadian literary figures are provided in the September issue, which explains that the Rev. Dr Charles W. Gordon (depicted aboard a liner returning from Australia) is in fact the novelist Ralph Connor ('Mayfair Round-About'). In contrast to the travel pieces in the women's magazines, *Mayfair*'s offerings contain no explicit reference to learning, self-improvement, or the productive use of leisure. This magazine is upwardly mobile in a different way: it offers covert instruction to travellers in the areas of networking, conversation, fashion, and luxury consumption.

In the summer issues of *Mayfair*, coverage of travel expanded and diversified. In 1935, the 'Travel' sections in the numbers from June to September included up to seven items, while additional pieces on foreign destinations appeared in the 'Variety' sections. Each issue contained a feature on the Muskoka region of Ontario, with photographs of wealthy vacationers staying beside the lakes, at Windermere House, or the Royal Muskoka Hotel. Additional domestic travel features covered fashionable destinations in other provinces in the eastern half of Canada, notably St-Andrews-by-the-Sea in New Brunswick and Quebec's Seigniory Club, a log cabin resort on an extremely grand scale which was built during the early 1930s as a wilderness retreat for business and political leaders. Attempting to reinforce the magazine's cosmopolitan image even while reporting on local forest and seaside resorts, the *Mayfair* writers anxiously compared Muskoka to 'the famed English Lakes District' ('Muskoka Interlude' 106) and noted similarities between Le Manoir Richelieu at Murray Bay and 'the old-world beauty of Gleneagles, set amid the moors and lochs of the Scottish Highlands' ('Odyssey of Summer' 106). The Gleneagles reference also seems designed to construct the Canadian elite as a neo-aristocracy, akin to the American Rockefellers or Carnegies.

The Muskoka piece in the July edition opens with a paragraph associating old- and new-world forest environments:

> When the sun beats mercilessly on city asphalt and even cool lilac linen has lost its laundered crispness, there comes a nostalgia for the dim, slumbering shade of green forests and the cool sparkle of rushing water splashing noisily over polished stone. Even the most sophisticated urbanite admits an inherent longing for remote, virgin forests and wooded waters. To the cosmopolite there is an affinity with the beech woods of Germany and the oak forests of England in the tree-clad slopes and silver streams of the Canadian Northland. ('Halcyon Holidays' 74)

'Nostalgia' here operates in more than one sense. It evokes a retreat from the ideal of progress represented by the modern city, and an antimodern desire to return to the unspoiled landscapes of pre-urban Canada. In that sense, the nostalgic escape offered to the *Mayfair* reader takes the form of a brief, temporary respite from the Toronto or Montreal social and business life which constitutes their permanent identity. At the same time, there is a colonial nostalgia for the 'old world' inscribed in this article, and once again, the writer affirms the value of Canadian landscapes by constructing them in terms of the European picturesque. The 'sophistication' of the ideal *Mayfair* reader consists of an ability to modulate between modern urbanity and pastoral simplicity. Indeed, the article itself enacts this, as it moves from the lyrical description of woods and streams to an account of the social pleasures of the Muskoka Lakes Regatta and the Beaumaris Yacht Club.

Occasionally, more distant and unfamiliar destinations were represented in the magazine. In the August 1935 number, Canadian Pacific promoted a 'World Cruise' taking in Egypt, India, Japan, Bali, Java, and China, as well as an 'Africa-South America Cruise,' described as 'the newest travel thrill.' *Mayfair*'s photo features occasionally reinforced the appeal of these advertisements by depicting well-known Canadians as far afield as China or Australia. A small number of articles published during this year ventured beyond the usual destinations: Madge Macbeth wrote a piece on Yugoslavia—though admittedly, it focused primarily on the clothes generally worn there and on Macbeth's luxury sea voyage to Dubrovnik ('Sheep Skin'). Kathleen Bowker, the London correspondent, wrote an article on safaris, but she herself had evidently not journeyed further than the office of the 'Safari' tour agency in St James's Square. In a strategy typical of *Mayfair*, she appealed to the reader's desire to achieve distinction through travel:

> Where did you go last year, when the winter winds blew? A luxury cruise, perhaps. What a marvellous experience! But this year? Do you want to do the same thing over—or would you like a real change— something that will give you tales to tell that other travellers will not find it easy to cap? Something that will give you an adventure in comfort, and comfort in adventure. ('Who Said')

Even safaris, it seems, can offer an experience of luxury—private baths and personal servants are mentioned among the amenities on offer. The superficiality of this piece, its advertorial quality, and its emphasis on display, are all consistent with *Mayfair*'s general approach to travel journalism. The magazine declined to engage seriously with the world beyond Canadian high society; instead, it constructed an artificial realm in which only money, style, and social capital counted. This restricted worldview is particularly evident in a photo feature in the July 1935 issue, offering the following 'sightings' of holidaying Canadians:

During a recent European tour, Mr B. W. Keightley, of Montreal, included an interesting visit to Germany, where he discussed the situation with many citizens—including a smartly turned-out Nazi Storm Trooper. On the other side of the world—in the peaceful gardens of the Empress Hotel in Victoria, B.C., to be exact—Mrs Edith Rogers, of Winnipeg, enjoys a pleasant afternoon in the warm Pacific sunshine. ('En Route' 22)

Of course, general attitudes to National Socialism in Britain and the Dominions were very different, in 1935, from what they would become in a few years' time. Yet the glibness of tone here, and the flattening out of European politics and domestic summer travel into one smooth paragraph, reveals a startling lack of perspective.

Mayfair's limitations, when compared—for instance—to American magazines such as *Vanity Fair* or *Esquire*, reduce its interest for literary scholars. Yet its value for Canadian periodical studies is high, since there is no comparable title in either English or French: *Mayfair* is distinctive in its visual styling and its mix of content, as well as in terms of the audience sector it addresses and the ways in which it constructs that audience. For social historians, the magazine provides an extremely rich resource, and an important insight into the lives of an Anglophone elite which almost amounted to a Canadian leisure class. Certainly, this was not a class founded primarily on inherited wealth—most of the families whose activities were reported in *Mayfair* were headed by businessmen, politicians, diplomats, or other professionals, but their wives were leisured, their daughters were debutantes, and their lives were structured around a ritualised, seasonally organised social scene. At the same time, *Mayfair* was an overtly commercial product, almost amounting to a promotional magazine for the high-end resorts and retailers of eastern and central Canada. Richard Ohmann's comment on American golden-age magazines could equally be applied to *Mayfair*: 'The mass magazines were a hybrid. They offered their contents as surrounded by the aura of elite culture, yet simultaneously proclaimed their commodity status' (224). In addition to the 'advertorial' columns and features, a large proportion of the magazine's space was devoted to paid advertising.

As discussed in our 'Consumers' chapter, the commercial content of *Mayfair* is noticeably different from that of the other magazines. *Mayfair*'s advertising centres on driving, sports, travel, local services, tailoring, and ready-to-wear fashion, while the women's and family magazines advertise mostly household and food products. *Maclean's* came somewhere in between, running adverts from many of these categories, and addressing both male and female consumers. In order to get a sense of the type of commercial material which predominated in *Mayfair* in 1935 specifically, it is worthwhile to take a detailed survey of two issues published in different seasons.

The January 1935 number is 74 pages long, and contains 55 advertisements, of which only one is in colour. A large majority feature artwork or a logo, although about 20% are illustrated with a photograph, and 10% unillustrated. Fifteen full-page or double-page adverts appear, 11 at the front of the issue and four towards the back. These are for national or foreign brands (cars, cigarettes, yachts, silk hosiery, diamonds, sports and formal wear, electric ranges) and for Canadian department stores. The remaining 40 adverts are grouped in appropriate back sections of the magazine. Many of them promoted Toronto shops and services, including salons, photographers, and milliners, and were arranged beside the 'Around the Town' column in the back pages. Occasional advertisements for Montreal-based retailers appear. Travel advertising encompasses shipping lines and hotels or resorts in Bermuda, New York, Montreal, and the Laurentians, while several of the clothing advertisements are for 'cruise fashions.' One advert in this issue picks up the cosmopolitan theme in a different way. Promoting the Paris magazine *L'Illustration*, it claims: 'If you read French, if your friends read French, your knowledge of world affairs will be richer by following "L'Illustration" each week. If you do not read French you will enjoy the superb illustrations which convey much about Travel.' The placing of this advert in *Mayfair* indicates a certain expected level of foreign-language ability amongst Anglophone Canadians, yet the appeal to those who do not understand French is even more interesting, in terms of what it reveals about the aspirations of this audience. Evidently, the cachet of a smart Paris magazine made it sufficiently desirable, as an item for the coffee table or something to be seen reading, even if its textual content remained unintelligible.

The June 1935 *Mayfair* is much longer, at 109 pages, and contains 126 advertisements. Twenty-eight are full-page, and four of these are in colour. About 85% of the adverts in this issue are illustrated in some way, about two-thirds of them with artwork and one-third with photographs. Since the issue has a special section on shopping in London, England, a high proportion of the small ads are for London tailors and fashion retailers, though Canadian department stores are also well represented. This edition appeared near the start of the summer holiday season, and therefore contains a very large amount of travel advertising, covering hotels in Paris, Le Touquet, Aix-les-Bains, Scotland, London, New York, Muskoka, and Murray Bay (Malbaie) on the St Lawrence, as well as cruises, railways, and the tourist boards in Quebec, Newfoundland, and Bermuda. Many adverts for travel-related products such as luggage, cameras, binoculars, car tyres, and petrol also appear, indicating *Mayfair*'s cross-gender appeal. There is even an advert explaining the health benefits of drinking tea during a journey. At the same time, the start of the next academic year was not far distant, and seven advertisements for prestigious Canadian schools and colleges appeared. In the 1935 advertising, then, we can see *Mayfair*'s explicit address to a wealthy, mobile, educated elite who had maintained their comfortable lifestyle during the Depression years. Legible between the lines is an implicit address to a larger group of readers who aspired towards this lifestyle.

Run: *La Revue Moderne* (1919–60)

La Revue Moderne defined its target audience very differently from *Mayfair*— that is, in terms of literary tastes and political orientation, rather than wealth or social status. The editorial in the first issue of *La Revue Moderne*, by founding editor Madeleine, sets out her ambition to create a liberal intellectual magazine for the French-speaking citizens of a united Canada:

> Elle attestera brillamment de la valeur de nos poètes, de nos prosateurs, et elle offrira une lecture abondante et salutaire à tous ceux qui la rechercheront. Là ne devra pas s'arrêter son action. Il lui faudra trouver d'autres moyens de développer le goût des arts et de la littérature. [...] Elle devra remplacer, dans les familles, les magazines extravagants qui enseignent le mauvais goût, et déforment trop souvent la mentalité de nos femmes et de nos jeunes filles. [...] Nous l'avons voulue jolie pour qu'elle enchante tous les yeux et attire toutes les admirations. Ainsi son rôle d'éducatrice lui sera plus facile et plus doux. [...] Il faut aimer cette Revue, créée pour vous, pour faire meilleures vos idées, plus justes vos principes, plus meublés vos cerveaux. Elle sera l'œuvre de talents profonds et sincères, de talents de chez-nous, triés dans toutes nos classes, dans tous nos groupes, talents canadiens-anglais, comme canadiens-français, tous conquis au 'motto' qui doit dorénavant présider à nos actes: '*S'unir pour grandir*,' afin de donner à la patrie canadienne la pleine mesure de nos énergies et de nos vaillances. ('S'unir' 9)

Madeleine emphasises that *La Revue Moderne* will contribute to readers' mental and cultural development, equipping them to be better citizens of Quebec and of Canada. Invoking contemporary discourses of self-improvement, she focuses on education and the development of taste and identifies a need for healthy reading material. A desire for cultural products which were both attractive and improving, both educational and accessible, was characteristic of the middlebrow project at this period, so it is unsurprising that *La Revue Moderne* aspires to be 'jolie' as well as 'salutaire.' Certainly, attention was paid to design, particularly in terms of its unusual covers. As the authors of the collaborative history *La Vie Littéraire au Québec* write:

> Cette publication mensuelle illustrée s'impose rapidement comme une revue à la fois intellectuelle et populaire. Cette double orientation assure son succès; d'une part, elle est « littéraire, politique, artistique », comme l'indique son sous-titre; d'autre part, sa présentation moderne (couverture illustrée, papier glacé, photographies, grand format) l'apparente aux magazines à grand tirage. (Saint-Jacques and Robert 210)

Yet, in its earlier decades particularly, *La Revue Moderne* had rather less visual appeal than some of the other titles included in this study. It was always the most intellectually serious among them, and during the interwar years, its pages were dense with text, with relatively few illustrations. It did not attract as much advertising as the Anglophone women's magazines: for example, in volume 19 of *La Revue Moderne*, running from November 1937 to October 1938, the average number of firms advertising in each number was 40, while in a volume of *Chatelaine* from the same period, the average was 119. This is important because, since advertisements tended to contain both more white space and more colour than editorial material, they contributed substantially to the 'visual enrichment' (Ohmann 235) of these periodicals.

In its design, editorial remit, and mix of content, *La Revue Moderne* exhibits both marked shifts and strong continuities over the period of its publication, from November 1919 until June 1960. The physical format remained consistent, with all issues published in the 10 x 14 inch size, aligning the magazine with the leading Anglo-Canadian and American monthlies rather than with the smaller-format *La Revue Populaire*. Due to its rather dense page design and low volume of advertising, *La Revue Moderne* was thinner than other magazines, with each issue across the whole run comprising around 50 pages. For the first ten years of its existence, *La Revue Moderne* cost 25 cents or 'sous.' In common with other magazines, it dropped its price at the end of the 1920s, and remained at 15 cents from 1929 through to 1947. This still placed it at the more expensive end of the market: *Chatelaine* cost only 10 cents for much of the 1930s and 1940s, probably because it was better capitalised due to selling more advertising space. In January 1948, *La Revue Moderne* moved to 20 cents per issue, remaining at this price point for the rest of its run. From 1932 to 1954, the *La Revue Moderne* company also published *La Petite Revue*, in a smaller quarto format, with a similar mix of content but more pages of fiction (Beaulieu and Hamelin VI: 250).

Cover design at *La Revue Moderne* went through several distinct epochs.

Early covers featured original artwork, occupying the whole page, and usually in black and white (see Figure 16). A majority of the pictures were in a distinctly sentimental or nostalgic idiom; there were many drawings of children and several of mythological feminine figures or women in historical costumes. This visual styling counteracted the emphasis on the 'modern' in the title of the magazine, but from November 1927 onwards, a closer match was achieved through a drastic design change. The new covers were printed as a solid block of colour (a different colour each month), with a 7 x 4 inch oblong illustration towards the bottom right hand corner (see Figure 17). These illustrations usually took the form of black and white photographs, most of them showing Quebec landscapes. Occasionally, drawings, paintings, or a block of cover lines, might be substituted. The title was set in a new, art deco font, with a very long initial 'L' reaching down the left-hand side of the cover and—from November 1931 onwards—joining with an 'L' shaped set of black gridlines running down the bottom left side and along the lower edge of the cover: this was the era when the magazine drew most overtly on the visual repertoire of modernism. In 1933, the cover pictures were enlarged again, and from 1934 until the end of the decade, all covers featured large drawings printed in four colours. Children and landscapes were now infrequent subjects; most cover images showed modern female figures, and images of mobility (cars, boats, and horses) sometimes appeared. The later 1930s was a period of uncertainty for the magazine (as is explained below), and this is discernible in the inconsistent presentation at this time. The title font changed quite frequently, and the designers experimented with frames, using a wide white border throughout 1938. Following a five-month hiatus, *La Revue Moderne* was relaunched in May 1939, with a striking new cover design in royal blue (see Figure 18). In the early 1940s, photographs—now in colour—permanently replaced artwork on the covers.

In the 1919–33 volume of *La Vie Littéraire au Québec*, Saint-Jacques, Robert, and their co-authors note *La Revue Moderne*'s remarkable feat of selling 25,000 copies as early as the second issue (211). However, they argue that Madeleine's initial vision of a liberal intellectual review held sway only during the earliest years of publication, and that the magazine was soon absorbed into the mainstream:

> *La Revue moderne* cherche également à opposer un discours libéral aux thèses régionalistes et au nationalisme étroit défendus par [Lionel] Groulx et ses collègues. Si sa force d'attraction est grande auprès des écrivains libéraux de l'époque, son influence, déclinante après 1922, ne parvient pas à contrebalancer le poids de *L'Action française* et l'entreprise

ne remporte pas le succès escompté. Elle perd peu à peu son lectorat, puis elle se transforme pour devenir une revue féminine. (278)

These critics narrate the magazine's history in terms of a rapid decline in political influence, a drastic transformation from an intellectual review into a women's magazine, and a move from the highbrow down to the popular end of the periodical marketplace. This account is worth pausing over, since it is not the only possible version. *La Revue Moderne*'s history might, instead, be viewed as the success story of a versatile magazine, which survived a severe depression, continued publishing over a remarkably long period, and, even at the crisis point in the early 1960s, when so many general magazines closed, was a sufficiently valuable property to be purchased by Maclean-Hunter and transformed into *Châtelaine*. Its readership certainly fluctuated in size, but the general trend was upwards.[18]

The legend 'LITTERATURE, POLITIQUE, ARTS' appeared on early covers of *La Revue Moderne*; it soon moved to the masthead (recast as 'Littéraire, Politique, Artistique'), and in June 1928 was dropped altogether. Indeed, the contents of the magazine were always more eclectic than this description implied. Topics including travel, gastronomy, religion, history, sport, and popular psychology received frequent coverage; each issue contained a complete romantic story or novella, as well as an episode of a serial; and from the very start, there was a 'Fémina' section, including domestic and beauty articles, dress patterns, and advice pages. Even though *La Revue Moderne* sought, for most of its run, to attract male readers and contributors, it was its appeal to women which allowed it to adapt and survive in the more commercialised market of the mid-twentieth century. In its early years, if the magazine had a feminist dimension, it was in the figure of Madeleine herself—a career woman whose personality and achievements were foregrounded. In one of the few academic discussions devoted to this magazine, Jean-Christian Pleau says of her role as editor: 'Dans cette position, déjà inhabituelle à l'époque pour une femme, Madeleine, par ses éditoriaux, s'aventurait très loin de l'espace féminin et n'hésitait pas, par exemple, à prendre parti sur des questions politiques' (209). Yet the rest of the magazine's contents continued to define women's sphere of activities in very traditional terms. The women's pages focused on cookery,

---

[18] Beaulieu and Hamelin give circulation figures of 23,120 in 1922 and 31,343 in 1940 (5: 294–295). In 1935, a circulation of 25,000 was claimed ('Ce que l'on pense'). An advertisement in the December 1936 issue claimed: 'En moins d'un an, le tirage de *La Revue Moderne* a marqué une progression de près de 60%' (*Revue Moderne*); this figure may have been exaggerated.

fashion, and sewing, and the fiction consisted principally of stories of romance. The articles rarely expressed any opinion on the role and status of women, and where they did, these opinions were largely conservative.[19]

Madeleine continued as editor or co-editor until 1930 (except for a one-year break), but her magazine did not retain the focused political agenda of its earliest years. Indeed, by 1935, *La Revue Moderne* was calling on those establishment figures whom it had initially opposed to provide endorsements of its value. Lionel Groulx, formerly editor of *L'Action française* (1917–28), a monthly magazine published by a group of priests and nationalists committed to protecting the French language in Canada, was among those contacted by *La Revue Moderne* for an opinion survey in 1935. The magazine printed six of the letters sent in reply to the editor, Jean Bruchési. They were from male leaders in business, government, and the universities. Four of them mention, in almost identical terms, the wholesome and enjoyable reading material provided in the magazine ('l'agréable et saine littérature'), and comment on its role in improving the literary taste of its readers (see 'Ce que l'on pense'). There are certainly echoes here of Madeleine's aim, as stated in her first editorial in 1919, to offer 'une lecture abondante et salutaire' and develop 'le goût des arts et de la littérature' ('S'unir' 9). Yet, her focus on the future, her vision of 'une vie nationale, inspirée uniquement des intérêts canadiens, des progrès canadiens, des demains canadiens' (8), is missing from the letters of congratulation received in 1935. Instead, they present the goal of *La Revue Moderne* as, in the words of M. Raoul Grothe, a prominent businessman, 'la sauvegarde de nos traditions et de notre langue.' Similarly, Groulx wrote: 'Vous pouvez, vous devez même combattre chez nous l'influence du magazine américain, et vous faire les défenseurs des meilleures traditions de notre petite peuple' ('Ce que l'on pense'). There is nothing about the modernity of *La Revue Moderne* in any of the letters.

Even if *La Revue Moderne*'s influence on liberal thought in Quebec may have lessened after a few years of publication, the magazine certainly remained powerful in the broader sphere of culture. Pleau offers an illuminating account of its hybridity and cross-class appeal:

---

[19] One example is the series on 'la jeune fille moderne,' which ran for several issues beginning in 1925. An initial article by Luc Aubry quoted from various contemporary thinkers, and solicited the views of readers on the modern girl, 'ses défauts et ses qualités' (12). Although some of the responses selected to be printed in the succeeding issues celebrated the new freedoms allowed to girls, most of them reinforced the importance of motherhood as a woman's primary calling, and berated girls for their self-absorption and frivolity.

> La relative longévité de ce périodique—et l'apparente stabilité à laquelle celle-ci pourrait faire croire—ne doit pas dissimuler le fait que la revue subit des transformations au cours de son histoire: devenue une revue populaire à fort tirage dans les années quarante, elle eut au départ de hautes ambitions littéraires et intellectuelles. À en croire son sous-titre (« Littérature. Politique. Arts »), la revue entendait concurrencer les périodiques littéraires ou politiques les plus sérieux, tel l'austère *Canada français* de l'Université Laval. Mais par la présentation soignée des livraisons, par le luxe affiché dans la publicité ou dans les pages féminines—qui sont en soi un témoignage fascinant sur une certaine prospérité d'après-guerre—, par la place accordée à la littérature romanesque, il est clair que la revue cherchait surtout à séduire un lectorat bourgeois. Jusque vers 1924, on peut dire que *La Revue moderne* a rempli avec succès ce double mandat intellectuel et mondain—à tout le moins, autant qu'il pouvait l'être dans le contexte de l'époque. (206)

Arguably, then, among the six magazines covered by our research, *La Revue Moderne* is the most clearly exemplary of the middlebrow as we defined it in our introduction. In its early years, especially, it combined intellectual with material aspiration, and promoted consumer literacy alongside knowledge of culture and the arts. In its later decades, it moved closer to the more straightforwardly mass-market women's magazines, yet it retained a relatively high proportion of text and continued to run in-depth articles on current topics. Even today, traces of *La Revue Moderne*'s legacy can be discerned in the French-language *Châtelaine*, which has a somewhat more substantial character than its English-language sister magazine. For instance, it has a 'Société' section, which features reportage, photojournalism, and discussion of current affairs and gender issues; there is no equivalent in the Anglophone magazine. *Châtelaine* also gives more prominence to its book club, and substitutes a 'culture' section for *Chatelaine*'s 'entertainment' department.

La Revue Moderne's shifts in appearance and content, and the development over time of its travel coverage, can be productively explored through an account of the character of the magazine during the different decades of its publication. In the 1920s, although it was attractively produced, text dominated many pages. Editorial illustration was limited during the early part of the decade, though more photographs began to appear as the twenties progressed. Much greater visual variety could be found in the 'Fémina' section towards the back, where drawings accompanied the embroidery and fashion columns, and photographs illustrated the beauty articles. In the front section, alongside the fiction and poetry, numerous substantial and serious articles appeared.

These included, for instance, pieces on Quebec current affairs, accounts of particular ethnic communities in Canada or abroad (for example, the Russians in Constantinople) and essays on religious themes such as the Christian dignity of work (also a favourite topic of the *Canadian Home Journal*). There were, in addition, detailed notes on the literary and theatrical scenes. Direct engagement with readers was at its highest level during this decade. Women were invited to write in with their views on topics designated for discussion—the ideal husband, for example, while the lengthy 'Le courrier de Madeleine' column printed responses to readers' requests for advice. Further pages were devoted to graphological analysis of handwriting samples sent in by readers.

An advertisement in April 1928 claimed that '*La Revue Moderne* contient chaque mois: Romans—Nouvelles—Critiques—Voyages—Décors de la Table—Embellisement de l'Intérieur—Recettes de Cuisine—Soins du Bébé—Secrets de Beauté—Culture Physique—Modes—Broderie' (*Revue Moderne*). The item 'Voyages' is a little misleading, since coverage of travel during this era was minimal. Certainly, Canadian Pacific and Canadian National railway advertisements appeared in many issues, promoting domestic and overseas travel. There was also a considerable amount of reporting on cultural and political developments in Paris, as well as features describing different regions of France. But actual travel articles, focusing on foreign destinations or on holidaying within Canada, were rare, and were not in the same style as those found in the Anglophone magazines. A 1928 article on Bermuda, for instance, concentrated almost entirely on the geological and colonial history of the islands, rather than giving the kind of information on liner sailings, hotels, and social life found in *Mayfair*'s Bermuda pieces. *La Revue Moderne* presents Bermuda as a fantasy space, which readers from Quebec are much more likely to dream of than actually see ('Les Bermudes'). The middlebrow emphasis on travel as a learning experience is occasionally discernible—a short 1929 piece entitled 'Impressions de New-York' begins: 'On reconnaît de plus en plus la valeur éducative du voyage' (Mayrand). Again, though, this piece explores the multicultural population, financial power, and political character of the city, rather than the opportunities for enjoyment and luxury consumption which would have been highlighted by *Mayfair*.

In February 1928, Madeleine left to start a new magazine, *La Vie Canadienne*. Robert Choquette, taking over as literary editor, actually became largely responsible for *La Revue Moderne*'s whole content, and signed the editorials. In October 1929, the two titles were merged, with Madeleine and Choquette as co-editors. An editorial titled 'Je reviens ...' appeared, in which Madeleine wrote:

dans la REVUE MODERNE, nous insérons une section qui s'appellera 'la vie canadienne,' et où nous classerons les faits les plus saillants de notre vie nationale et que nous illustrerons de choses du pays, de façon à donner à notre publication une personnalité qui permettra à tous ceux qui la liront de savoir de quel pays elle émane.

The first 'Vie Canadienne' section is a gloomy affair, with three obituaries, some paragraphs on the deaths of children, a charitable appeal on behalf of a seriously ill priest, and an anguished poem entitled 'Partir.' Later examples were more varied, with short reports and opinion pieces on sports, new books and magazines, agricultural topics, and so on. When Madeleine left the magazine in November 1930, Jean Bruchési (who had taken over from Choquette as co-editor, and now became editor-in-chief), wrote in tribute: 'Madeleine a fait *La Revue Moderne*, elle lui a gagné des amitiés fidèles, elle a détourné des magazines américains une partie au moins de notre jeunesse et fourni à nombre de nos jeunes écrivains l'occasion d'exercer leur plume' (Bruchési). Indeed, *La Revue Moderne* did foreground essays and journalism by French-Canadian writers, yet virtually all the fiction it published was foreign. The vast majority was by popular French romance writers, although—in spite of the magazine's initial anti-Americanism—there were also occasional translations of bestselling US novels.

In 1930, Marjolaine (Justa Leclerc) took over the 'pages féminines,' which included sections on fashion, beauty, interiors, cookery, and childcare, as well as a correspondence column. Her name was now listed below Bruchési's in the masthead, indicating the increasing importance of the women's pages to the magazine. The columns on literature, music, and so on were still present, and there was still a good deal of anonymous text, with only a limited number of articles by freelance authors. This era saw a modest increase in attention to travel and foreign cultures. Articles on Alaska, Algeria, Australia, California, Colombia, England, Russia, Spain, and various regions of France appeared in the 1930s, though only some of these were conventional travel articles. In addition, a growing number of features encouraged readers to visit different regions of Canada itself, and several covers depicted the Rockies, the CP hotels, northern Quebec, Ottawa and other potential destinations. There was a continuing attention to the educational benefits of travel: in the July 1932 issue, an anonymous columnist remarks: 'En vacances, il faut savoir *flâner* sans perdre son temps ... il faut savoir profiter de ces journas [sic] *physiquement et moralement*' ('Simples'). This piece anticipates the 'Holiday Dividends' editorial in *Chatelaine* discussed above. Travel advertising in *La Revue Moderne* became increasingly visible and eye-catching during this period: for instance, the CP adverts were especially lavish in the mid-1930s, while the French Lines ran an extensive promotional campaign for their 'Normandie' liner, launched in 1935. Several New York hotels placed small advertisements, as did the Quebec winter sport resorts, and the Bermuda Trade Development Board. Nevertheless, travel remained a minor concern for this magazine, and the volume of advertising in this area was far lower than it was in *Maclean's* or *Mayfair*.

Restricted advertising revenues may have partly explained why the magazine nearly came to grief at the end of the thirties. Following the November 1938 issue, there was a five-month gap in publication, but a new company, La Revue Moderne, Limitée, was set up to take ownership of the magazine.[20] In May 1939, it was relaunched with a new staff, led by a vice-president and director, Roland Beaudry. He was supported by Henri Girard, who had been a contributor since 1928 and would be an influential literary editor of the new-look *Revue Moderne*, and by Roger Frigon as artistic director, and Madame Claude André, who took over the women's pages from Marjolaine. The unsigned editorial for this issue begins:

> Ayant élevé comme elle l'a fait le niveau intellectuel du magazine canadien-français, la Revue Moderne ne pouvait pas disparaître en sa vingtième année d'existence. Après une absence de cinq mois, la voici de nouveau dans votre foyer, rajeunie, vivante et assurée de vivre, aussi riche de couleurs et d'images que les meilleurs magazines du continent. ('Renaissance')

The editors went on to enumerate the typical contents of the relaunched magazine: not only the complete novella and the serial which had always appeared each month, but also several short stories, together with 'des articles d'intérêt général; des chroniques de l'actualité, du sport, de la musique, du théâtre, des livres, des beaux-arts, du cinéma et de la radio; des pages consacrées à la culture physique, à la mode, aux soins de beauté, à l'entretien ménager, au tissage, au tricot, à la cuisine.' The editorial team proposed that readers should write in with their suggestions, in order to 'rendre ce magazine de plus en plus conforme aux souhaits de la majorité. Nous ne pourrons satisfaire tout le

---

[20] This gap further complicates the already eccentric volume and numbering system. The first issue was dated 15 November 1919, but this unusual practice of specifying a day of the month was soon discontinued. Since the first issue had appeared in November, the numbering of the January issue was '3,' through to October, '12.' This continued until November 1938 (volume 20, no 1). After the hiatus, the May 1939 issue was 'volume 21, no 1,' and volumes thereafter started each May.

monde à la fois, mais il nous sera toujours possible de répondre aux désirs du plus grand nombre.' This ambition to cater to popular taste is far removed from Madeleine's initial notion of an improving publication, 'créée pour vous, pour faire meilleures vos idées, plus justes vos principes, plus meublés vos cerveaux' ('S'unir' 9).

During the earlier 1940s, the magazine thrived. In this period, of course, nearly all travel-related material focused on North America, and the quantity did not increase relative to the 1930s. The general expansion of the tourist industry did, however, evoke a response in articles such as the February 1942 feature on the work of air hostesses, or the May 1941 editorial on the significance of tourist income to Quebec's economy. This piece, which emphasised the importance of politeness and care towards visitors, is strongly reminiscent of J. Herbert Hodgins's 'Revenue from Tourist Traffic' article, discussed above. In the later part of the decade, photo essays on foreign countries began to appear, and some of these locations were quite far-flung—one on Tibet, for instance, appeared in April 1949. In the forties, *La Revue Moderne* also published some travel-themed fiction that picked up on the surrounding commercial material—for example, the complete novella by Lise de Cère in the April 1941 issue is illustrated with an ocean liner drawn in the style of advertisements for the Normandie. At this time, the amount of unsigned text decreased. Some major Canadian writers such as Gabrielle Roy published in *La Revue Moderne* during this decade, but the magazine also printed translations of classic or contemporary English-language novels, including *Wuthering Heights*, *Gone with the Wind*, and *Rebecca*.

The 1940s was the period when *La Revue Moderne* placed its strongest accent on fashion and beauty. In the 1950s, this gave way to a greater emphasis on domesticity. The 'chroniques féminines' during this era focused principally on cookery, and provided advice for middle-class housewives who were now obliged to feed their family without the support of a 'bonne.' Advertising during this era was principally for household and food products, but some of it was apparently directed at the husbands and sons of subscribers. For example, the issue for June 1952 contains a full-page colour advert for the RCMP ('Gendarmerie Royale') recruitment. This particular number also advertised products targeted at men, such as whisky and hedge trimmers, as well as a page of DIY tips sponsored by the Molson brewing company. In this decade, coverage of travel increased dramatically. Articles appeared on foreign destinations including Mexico, Las Vegas, Disneyland, Japan, Morocco, Spain, England, France, the Arctic, Bermuda, Gibraltar, Hong Kong, Baghdad, and Australia. Canadian travel was also promoted in many articles and advertisements: the Iles de France, Nova Scotia, Saguenay, and British Columbia were evidently popular. There was a clear overlap with the destinations favoured by the

Anglophone magazines, but, as might be expected, *La Revue Moderne* paid greater attention to France, rural Quebec, and North Africa. In this decade, the magazine became much more colourful and vivid in its presentation, with many four-colour advertisements. This intensified a process of glamorisation which had begun with the 1939 relaunch. The 'Renaissance' editorial proclaimed:

> La Revue Moderne renaît grâce à l'esprit patriotique du président de la nouvelle compagnie qui l'édite. Celui-ci n'a pas voulu laisser cette belle entreprise canadienne-française disparaître ou passer aux mains d'une maison d'édition anglaise. […] On juge d'un coup d'œil que la Revue Moderne ne se contente pas de renaître. Elle s'est transformée: meilleur papier, belle typographie, nombreuses illustrations en noire et en couleurs, dessins et titres de goût moderne.

Ironically, it was precisely the visual appeal of *La Revue Moderne* which eventually attracted Maclean-Hunter as a purchaser, so that the magazine did pass into the hands of an Anglophone publishing company after all.

Conclusion

In the introduction to their collection of essays in the field of book history, *The Future of the Page* (2004), Peter Stoicheff and Andrew Taylor write that 'page layout and design' have 'always had a significant relationship with the semantics of a text' (9). In the case of magazines, page layout is often particularly intricate, forming a sort of collage of headings, subheadings, images, logos, columns and blocks of text, and perhaps also divisions such as lines and boxes. And as a print object, the serial publication is of course complex, due to its repeating (but occasionally disrupted) structure of issues and volumes. The material dimensions of the printed magazine certainly impact on the meanings which it circulates. The research for this book was carried out, in the first instance, in library special collections, using hard copies of the magazines. We became familiar with the textures of the paper and the different formats in which the magazines were printed. We also became aware of their fragility, as well as of some of the ways in which readers had interacted with them—tearing out articles, marking items of interest, filling in crosswords and even colouring in pictures. Back at our desks, writing up our research, we had access only to the digital photographs we had taken in the libraries. The jpeg files retain all of the linguistic code, but only a part of the bibliographic code. We can no longer discern the size of the pages, the quality of the paper, or much information about the trajectory of the physical copies of the magazine from the point of publication to the point at which we consulted them. Their state of completeness, the damage they have endured, and the ways in which they have been bound may often be deduced from the digital reproduction, but we cannot always be absolutely sure that a missing page or issue was absent from the paper collection, rather than having been omitted by us as we photographed. In addition, the double-page spreads are split into single pages for storage in our digital archive, so in viewing the images on screen, we miss a part of the experience of reading the paper copy, in which the opposite page is always visible and always liable to modify our response to the page we are looking at directly.

'Simultaneity is the form of the press in dealing with Earth City' wrote the Canadian media theorist Marshall McLuhan in his 1954 polemic *Counterblast* (n.p.). This enigmatic remark could be applied in many ways, but it seems especially apt for a study of magazines and travel. Magazines, of course, do not have quite the immediacy, the almost instant coverage of contemporary events which was available in the broadcast media or the daily press of the earlier twentieth century. Yet they do operate in a similar way in that they sell novelty, fashionability, and current knowledge. Magazines present simultaneous reports from different places in the world—*Mayfair*, for instance, brings society news from the Bermuda resorts, sports reports from the Seigniory Club, and fashions from Paris. Whilst the reader can only focus on one item at a time, s/he is aware of all the surrounding items on the page and in the issue, and of the shadowy presence of similar items seen in previous numbers of the magazine. For a historian of Canadian print culture, reading 'simultaneously' entails comparing different items which were published at the same moment—reading across several different magazines, for instance. It is also necessary to read 'longitudinally'—across several years or decades of a single title, in order to discern patterns and shifts in both design and content. In addition, there is an 'accidental' way of reading, which led us, as we searched through our material, to serendipitous discoveries—articles or images which shed a sudden light on one of our themes, or answered a question which had been puzzling us. None of these modes of reading allows us to reproduce the experience of contemporary subscribers, encountering each edition of the magazine in the month of its publication. Yet all the methods we have modelled in this chapter allow researchers to generate new meanings from these periodicals. The comparison of individual pages from different titles, the close analysis of a single issue, the survey of an entire volume, or the overview of a magazine's whole history—each of these approaches enables fresh insights into the development of Canadian middlebrow print culture.

Chapter Three

FASHIONS

Bienvenu—an entertaining, informative letter from Soiffield of Paris—gives you a periscopic view of that gay world to the life [sic], *with cursory glimpses of the Riviera—Deauville—Lidol. Fashion is such a serious business these days. No longer is the mode a matter of frivolity—a means of coquetry—a subject in which only the light and frivolous are interested. No longer is there anything virtuous in being frumpy.*

You will be a veritable fashion oracle, after reading our Paris letter. With Soiffield you will gad about among the smart people who trail all over the fashionable resorts of Europe. You will be in the know regarding the exclusive modish ideas—and what is more to the point, you will behold the flower of Paris fashions adapted to that elusive personality—the Canadian woman.

October Mayfair is the big autumn fashion number. There is, for example, authentic news of the much-talked-of waistline—the silhouette—the—but do read it. Above all things, read Bienvenu with its fascinating sketches of the fashionable elect.
—J. Herbert Hodgins, Editorial for *Mayfair*, October 1927

FASHION and travel are intimately connected in the Canadian periodical discourse of the early to mid-twentieth century. This October 1927 editorial, introducing *Mayfair*'s new Paris correspondent, constructs well-dressed, 'smart people' as travellers and, conversely, presents travel itself as a fashionable practice. More broadly, the editorial reinforces the connection between fashion and cosmopolitanism. A familiarity with the latest silhouettes implies familiarity with Paris, the French Riviera, and other European resorts. Those readers who could not, in reality, hope to travel to these places might at least acquire knowledge of them—at the same time as they learned what was mostly worn there—through the pages of the magazines themselves. Indeed, specialist *knowledge* is exactly what *Mayfair* is selling: it presents not only images but also 'modish ideas' and authenticated information, enabling readers to become experts in the 'serious business' of dress.

Fashions, in Canadian magazines, almost always come from elsewhere. Paris dominated; London was an influence (particularly for menswear, and during wartime) and New York became increasingly important, while a Canadian fashion industry did not begin to develop until the 1950s. In the realm of dress, as in other areas, mainstream Canadian magazines became both exhibition spaces and marketplaces for imported foreign styles. Covers and stylised illustrations presented fashion as an art form, often using theatrical or fairytale motifs to exhibit haute couture as something to be admired from afar, as modelled by the 'elect' members of an international leisure class (see Figures 8 and 19). By contrast, in the shopping guides, pattern services, and advertising sections, dresses and tailoring from London, New York, and especially Paris are made available to ordinary Canadians, and specially adapted to suit their tastes and environment. This chapter asks: what happens to Parisian taste when it travels across the Atlantic? How do the discourses of fashion relate to those of nationalism and cultural aspiration at different points in Canadian history? How does fashion reporting in the magazines relate to their construction of certain destinations or modes of travel as fashionable? These questions will be explored through close reading of the fashion reports and advertisements which appeared in the magazines. In the course of the discussion, the rhetoric of fashion writing and its relation to the rhetoric of modernism will be brought into focus, and explored in the frame of current theoretical work on eccentricity, difficulty, and the authentic.

Adverts, features, patterns

Fashion coverage in Canadian magazines took a variety of forms, including feature articles, regular columns (signed or unsigned), letters and dispatches from Paris, London, or New York, captioned photographs of couture models,[1] annotated illustrations from commercial patterns, and even fashion-themed fiction. Editors sometimes drew attention to the authenticity and exclusivity

---

[1] We follow Palmer's usage of this term: 'The strictest definition of "haute couture" refers only to designs produced by accredited Paris haute couture houses that meet standards set out by the Chambre syndicale de la couture parisienne. In this book, the more informal word "couture" is used to embrace all very high-end European dressmaking' (*Couture* 4). In our book, likewise, 'couture' refers to made-to-measure rather than machine-made clothes.

of their illustrations,[2] and sometimes to the authority and originality of their fashion writers, while the balance between visual and textual representation shifted across the different magazines, and over time. Advertisements could also be understood as a form of fashion reporting. As with today's glossy magazines, there was no clear dividing line between editorial and commercial content; rather, there was a spectrum, with paid adverts at one end and signed features at the other. In between came 'advertorial' texts and pattern-based fashion spreads, which functioned to promote mail-order pattern services as well as to provide news of the latest silhouettes. The extent and type of fashion coverage was, of course, different in each periodical. To summarise, the women's and French-language magazines concentrated on home dressmaking while *Mayfair* focused on shopping for clothes, thereby attracting far more fashion advertising than the other titles. *Maclean's* rarely covered fashion, and is therefore excluded from this chapter.[3] In the interwar decades, *Chatelaine* and *Mayfair* are the most worthy of analysis in relation to fashionability, while in the 1940s and 1950s, the fashion writing in the *Canadian Home Journal*, *La Revue Populaire*, and, to some extent, *La Revue Moderne* became more imaginative. The following paragraphs give a brief overview, first, of clothing and beauty advertising across the five titles, and then of fashion coverage in each individual magazine.

In *Chatelaine*, the *Journal*, *La Revue Moderne*, and *La Revue Populaire*, beauty preparations (mostly American, British, and French brands) were heavily promoted. However, these titles attracted very little fashion advertising, except for the ubiquitous ads for Canadian Celanese, a firm that produced synthetic fibres and finished fabrics. The French-language magazines also included small adverts for Montreal retailers of furs, gloves, shoes, and other items that could not easily be made at home. In *Mayfair*, commercial material was divided into two types. Full-page adverts for international brands appeared in the front pages; during the 1920s and 1930s, many of these were for clothing or cosmetics. Towards the back, a shopping guide featured local adverts directed at *Mayfair*'s primary readership in Ontario and Anglophone Quebec. As it expanded, the

---

[2] For example, in *La Revue Moderne* in 1934, a set of photographs was labelled: 'Ce modèle de la collection de Worth est publié en exclusivité par LA REVUE MODERNE. Reproduction interdite' ('Modes parisiennes'). A 1936 millinery feature emphasised: 'The hats on this page were especially posed for *Canadian Home Journal*' ('High Hat and Low Brow').

[3] Not even *Maclean's* women's section covered fashion, beyond an occasional page with photographs of holiday dresses or gift ideas. Commercial material was restricted to infrequent adverts for men's tailoring or hosiery.

'Shops of Mayfair' section began to devote separate pages to Montreal, Toronto, Hamilton, and, occasionally, Ottawa, London, or Sherbrooke (see Figure 20). The advertisers were primarily high-end clothing boutiques, although hair salons, gift shops, tea rooms, and furniture retailers also purchased space. A short advertorial text appeared on each page; in 1932, this was replaced by an anonymous editorial column (now titled 'Smart Shops of Mayfair') and in 1934 by a signed feature, 'Around the Town with Mayfair.' These shifts demonstrate the developing emphasis on achieving individuality and distinction through consumer goods, and the growing attention to shopping as part of the experience of smart, urban modernity. By 1949, travel companies had come to dominate *Mayfair*'s advertising space, and the shopping section disappeared.

In its early years, *Mayfair* employed a particularly idiosyncratic fashion writer, 'Soiffield of Paris,' whose monthly letters ran from 1927 until 1930. Soiffield's persona was extravagant and frivolous, and the letters ranged beyond clothes to comment on society gossip, the arts, and the Paris scene. Each issue also featured one or two more sober, informative fashion features. From February 1931, *Mayfair*'s contents were organised into sections; their headings varied slightly, but a representative list runs: 'Sports,' 'Society,' 'Fashions,' 'Variety,' 'Travel,' 'General.'[4] The fashion coverage became gradually more extensive, with up to six individual items per issue in the thirties, and ten or 12 in the immediate postwar years. But during the 1950s, these articles were cut to an average of two per issue, while an expanding space was devoted to food and interiors. *Mayfair* was the only magazine to offer regular discussion of menswear. In the early 1930s, it ran a 'London fashions for men' column; in July 1934, its title changed to 'The Cosmopolite,' explicitly yoking fashion sense with mobility and an awareness of foreign styles. This column, contributed by a series of authors, lasted until 1941, and was followed by similar features titled 'Men and their Apparel' and 'Men About Town.'

The closest magazine to *Mayfair*, in terms of fashion coverage, was *Chatelaine*. Since both were owned by Maclean Publishing, and several fashion writers and editors, such as Mary Wyndham, Eustella Burke, and Ellen Mackie, worked across the two titles.[5] During the 1920s, *Chatelaine* published a lengthy Paris fashion letter in most issues, while the earliest evidence of its attention

---

[4] The 'General' section included regular departments such as 'Mayfair's Hostess,' 'Boudoir and Powder Puff,' and various calendars. In March 1940, *Mayfair* dropped the section divisions, but reinstated them in September 1945.

[5] Wyndham contributed Paris letters to both magazines. Burke and Mackie wrote fashion letters for *Chatelaine* and served as associate editors for *Mayfair* during its early years.

to New York fashion comes in March 1930, with a special letter from Mackie. But it would be three more years before a regular New York column was launched. This was Kay—or Kathleen—Murphy's 'Fashion Shorts,' a series of brief paragraphs in a colloquial idiom, which soon superseded the Paris Letters. Her reports were located in the beauty culture section, which was frequently renamed and reorganised. Subtitles such as 'A department for style, health and personality' pointed to the magazine's insistent construction of personal appearance as an aspect of character. In 1943, *Chatelaine* launched a separate 'Fashion' department, greatly expanding its coverage, but in the fifties, this change was reversed. The fashion and beauty sections were recombined and cut back, making way for a renewed focus on homecraft and needlework.

The *Canadian Home Journal*, *La Revue Populaire*, and *La Revue Moderne* were aimed at women who made their own and their children's clothes. Their attention to couture was never extensive, although their dress patterns were frequently identified as being based on Paris models. For most of the *Journal*'s publication run, the fashion pages were largely taken up with pattern illustrations, with bland—and often coy—annotations. Here is an example from 1935:

> 'Stiffness' is synonymous with 'smartness' in evening clothes—which makes slipper satin one of the best fabrics of the season. It makes this enchanting dress 6011, almost able to stand by itself. The décolletage goes down to *there* in back. Junior Miss 12 to 20; 30 to 38. 65 Cents. ('Night Life')

In the 1930s, the *Journal* had quite a large fashion section, but it was located near the back, subordinated to the health, family, and needlework departments. Many items were anonymous, though occasional signed contributions appeared. During the war years, the fashion pages were subsumed under the 'needlework and handicraft' section, and the *Journal* was a little slow in resuming its coverage of the new styles after the war. A separate fashion section was not re-introduced until 1948. In the early 1950s, the magazine had a fashion editor, Margaret Thornton, and a beauty editor, Peggy Benjamin, but these roles disappeared later in the decade, as an increasing focus on food and, especially, interiors largely displaced the fashion journalism.

Fashion was not a dominant preoccupation of *La Revue Populaire* in its earlier decades. From the 1920s onwards, there was an irregular feature, 'La Mode,' consisting of one or two pages of drawings taken from Butterick or Simplicity patterns, with very brief captions—for example, in April 1932: 'Remarquez le collet carré'; 'Robe charmante' and so on. From 1933, photographs of Paris models were also used, and from the late 1930s, the magazine began to comment occasionally on American fashion. Signed fashion reports were rare in *La Revue Populaire*, although 'Francine' (Thérèse Surveyer), who contributed the magazine's women's column from the 1920s through until the 1940s, sometimes wrote about clothes. Her style of reporting was extremely factual, making no reference to individual designers, and never including illustrations. During the war years, the focus in *La Revue Populaire* was, even more than usual, on sewing and embroidery, rather than shopping, but the magazine was particularly prompt in resuming attention to French couture after the liberation of Paris. In the more competitive postwar market, *La Revue Populaire* attempted to convert itself from a family title into a women's magazine. With the advent of the experienced journalist and novelist Odette Oligny[6] as fashion editor in 1957, coverage of clothes increased, and began to include more signed editorial content. In all the other magazines, attention to fashion was declining during this period, so *La Revue Populaire* may have been trying to establish itself as distinctive. This could not, ultimately, ensure its survival.

La Revue Moderne differed from its competitor more in the extent than in the type of its fashion features. Most interwar issues devoted at least five pages to Butterick patterns, and from the mid-1930s, they were supplemented by photographs of Paris models, and by occasional written commentaries. Regular features on skincare and hairdressing appeared from the late 1920s onwards, and, in general, *La Revue Moderne*'s fashion and beauty coverage expanded over the course of the 1930s and 1940s. Signed fashion articles, contributed by writers including Michèle Lemaître, Lucienne Boucher, Paule Benoit, and Raymond St-Georges, became more frequent during the wartime and postwar years. In the 1950s, a growing attention to housekeeping and cookery displaced some of the fashion coverage, as happened with the Anglophone magazines. Yet at the same time, there was a large increase in beauty and clothing advertisements, mostly for Montreal – or Toronto-based firms. *La Revue Moderne*'s more successful commercial model in this period may have been the reason why it, and not *La Revue Populaire*, was bought by Maclean Hunter and turned into *Châtelaine*.

---

[6] Oligny (1900–62) wrote a 'chronique libre' (a regular letter) for the daily newspaper *La Presse*, and had a long career as a fiction writer, sometimes using the pseudonym Michelle de Vaubert. An early magazine fiction publication was 'L'accident' in *La Revue Moderne* for August 1928; a late example was her novel *L'amour du clair matin*, published complete in *La Revue Populaire* for April 1958.

Authorship, gossip, masquerade

'Do read it,' urges the editor of *Mayfair* in the passage quoted at the start of this chapter and, indeed, Soiffield's Paris letters are designed to be read, not merely looked at. Certainly, they are beautifully illustrated with line drawings in a style somewhere between Erté of *Harper's Bazaar* and Anne Harriet Fish of *Vanity Fair*. But they are also carefully crafted and highly entertaining pieces of writing. The monthly letter was contributed by Soiffield over an extended period, and this consistent signature, together with the idiosyncratic personality projected through the texts, lays a special emphasis on original writing and individual authorship. While this privileging of written fashion reporting was particularly strong in *Mayfair*, it was also evident at different points in the other magazines. *Chatelaine*, from its earliest years, promoted itself on the basis of the high quality of its contributors, including fiction writers, artists, and journalists. In the September 1931 issue, a small insert advertisement states: 'You'll enjoy these Canadian writers in early issues of *The Chatelaine*.' The list includes Ellen Mackie, alongside L. M. Montgomery, Nellie McClung, and Florence Randall Livesay (*Chatelaine*). An April 1931 headline ran: 'Eustella Burke, the Canadian writer, visits the Paris Openings, for *The Chatelaine* ... and in this letter, reports the absorbing story of the new fashions' (Burke, 'Paris Letter' 9). The emphasis here is not only on Burke's Canadian perspective, but also on her status as an established 'writer,' and her ability to make clothes into a narrative.

Gossip, the main currency of the society columnists, was also important to the fashion reporters. Soiffield remarks, after identifying some well-dressed Canadians seen on the Paris streets: 'however, I am drifting into social chatter ... but after all, what are clothes and fashions without it?' ('Bienvenu' 20). In other examples, gossip was seen as a kind of transcription of the social and architectural topographies of the city: *Chatelaine*'s fashion report for February 1929 was headlined 'Paris Patter: As Taken Down by Mary Wyndham.' Both fashion news and society gossip are forms of representation of the foreign city: as Aaron Jaffe and Jonathan Goldman observe in their work on celebrity, the street is 'governed by the most chatty, dispossessed, and transient of creative practices, namely, fashion and gossip' (12). Gossip has been theorised, on the one hand, as a mode of social control and moral policing, and, on the other, as a subversive form, espoused by marginalised groups seeking to protect their own interests and critique the dominant culture (see Phillips 3–5). The second theory emphasises the valuable work performed by gossip in shaping communities, particularly among women, and this partly explains its importance to the magazine fashion reports, which seek to replicate the model of private feminine correspondence. In *Chatelaine*, the first Paris report to be formulated as a letter appeared in August 1929, and opened: '*Paris, ce mois de mai, 1929, Mes Chères* ...,' before relapsing into English (Einna, 'News' 20). The same journalist, signing herself 'Einna,' comments in her January 1930 dispatch: 'I feel this letter is becoming more of an intimate prattle than anything else' (12–13). As Patricia Meyer Spacks points out, gossip is feared because of its potential to propagate itself by exceeding the bounds of the intimate exchange (263). Magazines dramatically expand this process, making their profit by circulating news and gossip publicly, and aiming to present content which is so new and exciting that it will be reported still more widely through word-of-mouth and in other periodicals. At the same time, the appeal of items such as advice columns and society reports depends on the fake intimacy created through a personal mode of address, something which is most easily achieved through the letter form.

While Einna and her colleagues Wyndham and Burke used the letter form in a fairly straightforward way, Soiffield both exploits and mocks the notion of gossip as a mode of feminine creativity—'*mon dieu*, I am an old gossiper and feel that the world in general might like to share my opinions' ('Paris! ... The Tea Hour' 24). Soiffield cultivates a rather breathless way of writing: 'What a month I have had since last I took up pen to write to you! [...] But, pause, *mes chères*, and bear with your devoted French correspondent, while she summons her distracted thoughts, and attempts to give you a picture of this Paris, *en hiver*' ('In Paris' 19). The style suggests unedited, authentic, 'hot off the press' prose, yet, at the same time, it is highly artificial. Indeed, as may be guessed from the campiness of the writing, Soiffield was not really a Frenchwoman, or indeed any kind of woman. Editorials in the issues containing the early Soiffield letters carefully avoid attributing a gender to the correspondent, but in April 1928 the editor declared that Soiffield: 'knows his Paris as you know your *Mayfair*. He has the entrée into the most inaccessible ateliers ... so you know what to expect of Soiffield' (Editorial). A survey of the back pages yields the correspondent's real name: the May 1928 issue printed a small advertisement headed 'Mayfair's Paris Representative' and offering the services of 'Richard Geoffrey Swaffield, 47 Rue Washington, Paris,' who 'undertakes and arranges exclusive shopping and sightseeing tours,' deals in real estate and antiques, and will meet steamers or steamer trains by appointment (Mayfair's Paris).[7] Whilst he does report in detail on current fashions, Soiffield seeks more to seduce than to instruct. Eschewing the warm, sisterly tone of the correspondents for the women's magazines, he is deliberately artificial in his use of phrases of intimacy, and sometimes pokes fun

---

[7] In the issue containing his last *Mayfair* letter, in July 1930, 'Richard G. Swaffield, Paris correspondent' is listed in the masthead, indicating the importance he had acquired.

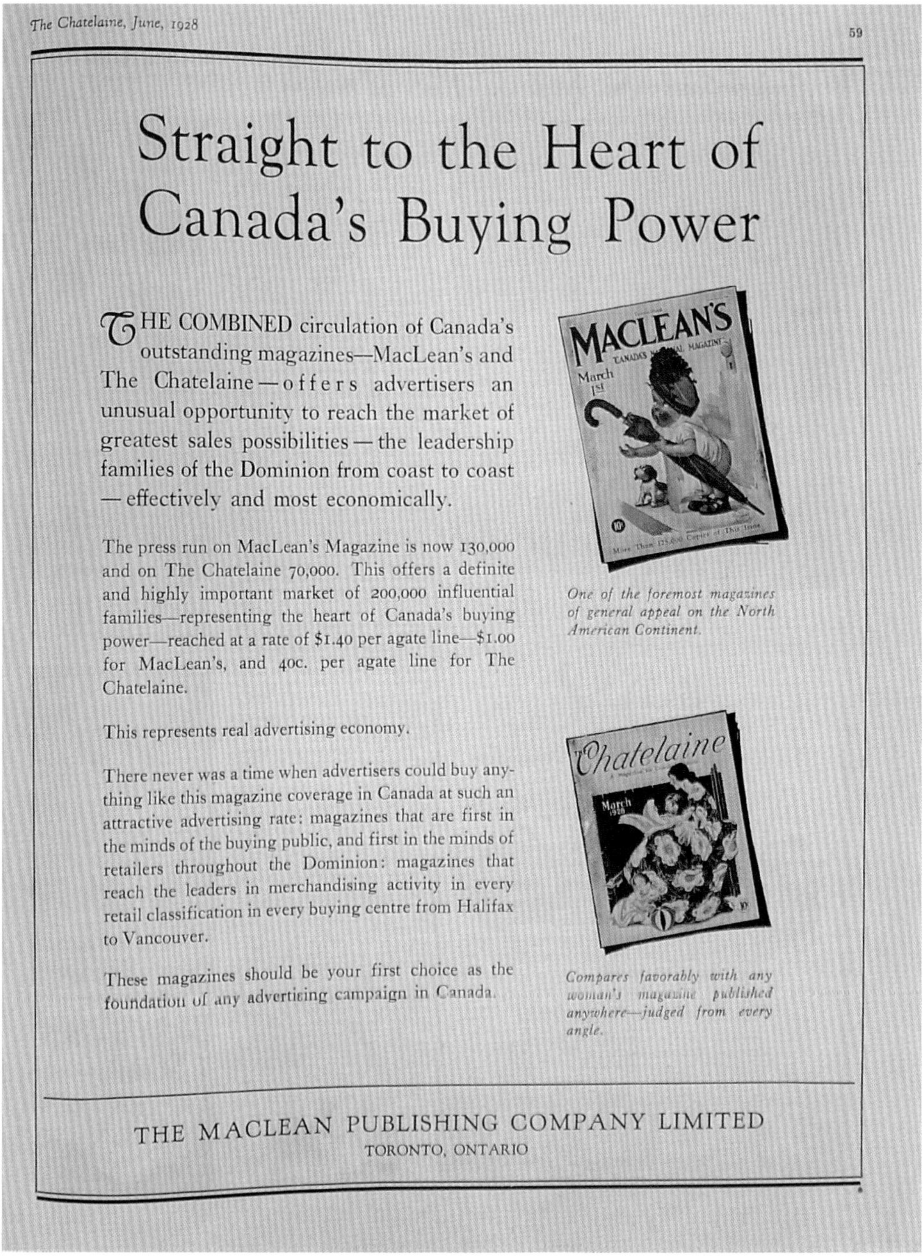

Straight to the Heart of Canada's Buying Power

THE COMBINED circulation of Canada's outstanding magazines—MacLean's and The Chatelaine—offers advertisers an unusual opportunity to reach the market of greatest sales possibilities — the leadership families of the Dominion from coast to coast — effectively and most economically.

The press run on MacLean's Magazine is now 130,000 and on The Chatelaine 70,000. This offers a definite and highly important market of 200,000 influential families—representing the heart of Canada's buying power—reached at a rate of $1.40 per agate line—$1.00 for MacLean's, and 40c. per agate line for The Chatelaine.

One of the foremost magazines of general appeal on the North American Continent.

This represents real advertising economy.

There never was a time when advertisers could buy anything like this magazine coverage in Canada at such an attractive advertising rate: magazines that are first in the minds of the buying public, and first in the minds of retailers throughout the Dominion: magazines that reach the leaders in merchandising activity in every retail classification in every buying centre from Halifax to Vancouver.

These magazines should be your first choice as the foundation of any advertising campaign in Canada.

Compares favorably with any woman's magazine published anywhere—judged from every angle.

THE MACLEAN PUBLISHING COMPANY LIMITED
TORONTO, ONTARIO

Figure 1   Maclean Publishing advert. *Chatelaine* June 1928

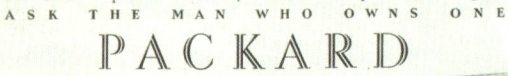

Figure 2   Packard Cars advert. *Maclean's* 1 Jan. 1930

Figure 3   Ford advert. *Chatelaine* Aug. 1930

Figure 4   Cover image. *Canadian Home Journal* Aug. 1939

Figure 5   Cover image. *La Revue Populaire* Aug. 1939

Figure 6   Cover image. *Maclean's* 15 June 1930

EVE AU MIROIR

OÙ ALLONS-NOUS ?

Par Celia Caroline COLE

Nous sommes tous des voyageurs. Poursuivons-nous notre voyage en de bonnes conditions ? Nous munissons-nous de tout ce qui est nécessaire ?

UN vieux dicton dit que personne ne s'arrête en cours de route. Si vous n'avancez pas, vous reculez.

Cela peut être vrai. Souvent, il semble que nous nous arrêtons lassés — quand nous ne paraissons pas grandir en taille, en bonté, en sagesse ou en beauté — et que nous restons là, attendant nonchalamment la poussée d'une nouvelle vague. C'est comme une halte de paresse qui nous immobilise, un engourdissement qui nous paralyse, qui ronge le courage et opère une lente détérioration. Nous restons stationnaires. Ne pas avancer, n'est-ce-pas reculer ?

L'arrêt est impossible à toute créature humaine. Si nous ne tentons pas d'atteindre les sommets, du moins nous en rêvons. Mais si nous n'en rêvons pas, nous reculons.

Quel chemin suivons-nous ?

La vie a des exigences. Elle impose le travail et la lutte. Elle crée des obligations et des devoirs, et quelle que soit la situation, les efforts attendent notre bonne volonté. Où en sommes-nous sous ce rapport ? Veillons-nous à nous habiller d'une manière plus attrayante, avec plus de chic, plus de goût ? Notre figure, est-elle plus agréable à regarder que l'année dernière ? Et notre vie, cherchons-nous à la vivre avec plus de compréhension, de profondeur et d'efficacité qu'avant ? Qu'importe l'âge. La vie conserve toujours sa valeur et la marche est la même pour tous les hommes.

Si les années repoussent un peu dans l'ombre les femmes qui savouraient naguère sur leur passage l'exclamation admirative: "Qu'elle est belle" ! Si le temps leur enlève la puissance mystérieuse de la jeunesse, doivent-elles pour cela s'arrêter en route, s'abandonner à la lassitude et aux regrets ? Certainement que non. Si le teint perd son charme et les yeux leur éclat, l'intelligence y supplée largement. Elle alimente le vif intérêt, l'affabilité que l'on porte aux gens et aux choses et aux douceurs mystérieuses qui nous entourent et qui est la vie !

Pour cela, il faut monter, ne pas s'abandonner à la bassesse, cultiver le charme, devenir compréhensive, savoir sourire, devenir meilleure et plus délicieuse à connaître que la veille, posséder plus de bonté et aimer le beau...

Au début de l'existence, le voyage est facile, le bagage léger, et quel que soit ce bagage, d'autres nous l'ont donné. Plus tard, c'est différent. Que nous ayons seize ou soixante ans, le voyage ne se fait plus dans les mêmes conditions, mille choses le compliquent et souvent par notre faute. Et quelles sont ces choses ? Ont-elles la beauté et la bonté que nous devons mettre autour de nous, ou ne sont-elles que des inutilités, des obstacles ?

Janvier est un mois de réflexions et d'examen. Il est comme la mesure de notre valeur. Il nous révèle l'état de notre esprit, la chaleur de notre cœur, notre bonne volonté, la générosité de notre âme. C'est aussi le mois qui rappelle les devoirs d'amitié et de reconnaissance. Il fournit l'occasion de faire plaisir, de donner de la joie, de faire des heureux, de préparer de joyeuses surprises.

Profitons de la circonstance pour offrir à nos amies de ces petites choses utiles, agréables, peu coûteuses, mais qui par ces temps durs, les aideront à maintenir un peu de beauté autour d'elles. Ainsi, pour celles qui voyagent en fin de semaine, il y a de charmants petits nécessaires de toilette pourvus de toutes les préparations qui maintiennent en beauté en en fraîcheur, et d'un prix très raisonnable. Ils sont légers et se glissent facilement dans le sac de voyage où ils ne prennent peu de place. Il y en a des bruns, des rouges, des verts, des noirs, des bleus. Ils sont doublés de couleurs contrastantes et ils contiennent des crèmes astringentes, toniques, stimulantes, des lotions et des poudres. Ce sont évidemment des accessoires de voyage pour entretenir l'élégance en cours de route.

Il y a encore les sels de bain à la lavande ou à la rose, la poudre et le parfum, les compacts qui font la joie de celles qui les reçoivent. Qu'y a-t-il de plus charmant que d'en avoir un pour chaque toilette ? A propos de parfum, il est préférable de choisir une bonne qualité. La douce senteur s'imprègne davantage, se conserve plus longtemps et nous donne l'illusion de respirer une véritable fleur.

Que peut-il y avoir de plus agréable, à l'époque du nouvel an, que de recevoir un cadeau dont on se servira tous les jours, qui nous rappellera constamment l'attention délicate qu'on nous a témoignée ? Et qu'y a-t-il de meilleur que de choisir un article qu'on saura faire plaisir, être utile ? Quel qu'il soit, petit ou considérable, choisissons-le joli, élégant, pour qu'il mette de la beauté où il sera.

C'est de la sagesse que d'aimer le beau, que de le faire aimer, que de le cultiver, pour élever l'esprit et le diriger vers le bien. C'est cette sagesse qui murmure aux femmes qu'il n'y a pas de jour dans la vie où la beauté n'ait sa place.

Allons sûrement vers le but que nous devons poursuivre, à la clarté des étoiles, malgré le vent un peu rude et le bouleversement du monde, avec toute la capacité d'amour et de foi qu'il y a en nous.

(Continué en "Références")

Figure 7   'Où allons-nous?' article. *La Revue Moderne* Jan. 1932

Figure 8   Cover image. *Mayfair* May 1928

Figure 9   Cover image. *Mayfair* Aug. 1935

Figure 10   Cover image. *Mayfair* Mar. 1947

In the Editor's Confidence

IN A letter received from R.H.M. of Montreal, there is quoted a criticism that the Canadian author, in his anxiety to produce something distinctively Canadian, has developed a 'sort of advertising booklet,' paying so much attention to Canadian environment and setting that the literary value is completely submerged. R.H.M. then refers to MacLean's short story contest, in which a requirement is that all stories submitted must be distinctively Canadian, and says:

"You immediately dive right into the centre of this pool of narrow-mindedness ... What is meant by distinctively Canadian? ... Canadian setting — Canadian peculiarities—Canadian physique— Canadian frame of mind (self adulative and provincial) —Canadian food—Canadian bush—Canadian snow—Canadian women—just in what way are these nationally distinctive? ... To find a distinctively Canadian type ... is impossible in a land where people seldom remain in one spot longer than a generation and who, to begin with, are of another country or are of a mongrel race. The solitary possible Canadian type might be found in the back-woods of Quebec. A writer could attribute almost any characteristic or action to a citizen of Canada and would be quite correct. You can put a Canadian citizen in Boston or Florida and he would be recognized simply as an Anglo-Saxon or some other parent stock, or as an American. There is no real difference between him and the common herd of humanity about him ...

"So far as habits, customs, environment, scenery, politics, business, hopes and fears, and reading matter, are concerned, we people in the upper half of North America are just a conglomeration. Thus, if you insist on having a story distinctively Canadian—give it any mark of individuality as to human character and name its setting after some well-known locality, and you've about hit the nail on the head ... I am surprised that you still fancy that hackneyed and fallacious desire to get stories distinctively Canadian. There ain't no such animal.' "

R. H. M. is entitled to his opinion. He asks mine. It is this:—

When he uses the phrase "There ain't no such animal," he uses the words of the farmer who gazed at a giraffe and didn't believe it existed. But the giraffe was there. Those who framed the conditions of MacLean's short story contest believe that there is such a thing as a story that is 'distinctively Canadian.'

Now to analyze that 'distinctively Canadian' in a reasonable way, R. H. M. is correct, of course, in saying that human emotions cannot be classified in terms of nationality. But what objection can any Canadian have to the use of a Canadian setting? With all the wealth of color this Dominion offers, why should a Canadian author go to Moscow, Paris or Timbuktu? Human emotions are akin. But the manner of emotion is affected by environment. Morbidness exists in Russia and, to a lesser degree, in Canada. But its effect on a Russian peasant differs from its effect on a Canadian homesteader, say. Love is common to the people of Spain and to the people of Canada. But, put a Calgary youth in Madrid and call him Don Fandango. Does he become a Spaniard? Pick up any average Montrealer, any average Vancouverite, and put him in New York. Like the New Yorker he eats, brushes his teeth, loves and hates. But is he a typical New Yorker?

Even assuming that conditions in the cities and rural parts of the United States are identical with those of Canada, why need the Canadian write of people and places not his own? But, having lived in both countries, I do not assume that conditions are identical save in the very broadest sense. To take only one phase of life—settlement of the country. The United States West was settled by a different breed to that which settled our own West. The very ingredients of the 'melting pot' are different. Take the Scots and the English who first pioneered in Canada. Consider the life they left and the life they adopted. Consider the influence of Canada on stock such as this. Study the development of character under that influence, the achievements wrought under that influence plus their native and inherited influences. The product, whether it be of themselves or of their progeny, cannot be otherwise than something distinctively Canadian.

It is impossible in a limited space to expand the point. But when R. H. M. states that 'so far as habits, customs, environment, scenery, politics, business, hopes and fears, and reading matter we people in the upper half of North America are just a conglomeration,' I beg to differ. The romance of Canada, whether it be of the days of Port Royal or of the business conquest of the Saguenay; whether it be of the Royal Canadian Mounted or of the wheat pool; whether it be of old Montreal or of Vancouver Island, belongs to Canada. It was not made in the United States.

It would be silly to deny that under given circumstances people might behave in precisely the same manner whether they were born in Le Pas or in Los Angeles. But it is equally futile to deny that anything can be distinctively Canadian.

And if to believe that is to be narrow-minded, I, for one, am glad to be so classed.

H. Napier Moore

MACLEAN'S
PUBLISHED SEMI-MONTHLY
On the First and Fifteenth of Each Month

H. NAPIER MOORE, Editor. GEORGE H. TYNDALL, Business Manager.

CONTENTS

JANUARY 15, 1927

VOLUME XL   NUMBER TWO

Cover painted by Wilma Bruce.

THE SPLENDID SILENCE (Serial: Part One) — *Illustrated by H. Weston Taylor.* Alan Sullivan	3
GOVERNMENT SERVICE—AND YOU. Article Two: Buoys and Beacons....Norman Reilly Raine	8
CABINET PORTRAITS: Hon. James L. Ralston.......H. C. Crowell	10
ABOVE THE LAW (short story)..William Merriam Rouse — *Illustrated by A. C. Valentine.*	11
FOOTNOTES (short story)..........Thomas P. Freney — *Illustrated by E. J. Dinsmore.*	12
GROWING OUR OWN (article)........Douglas MacKay	14
STAGE STRUCK (short story)........Archie McKishnie — *Illustrated by E. J. Dinsmore.*	16
MAKING THE TARIFF SAFE FOR DEMOCRACY (article)..............Grattan O'Leary	18
GHOSTS (short story)................C. F. Lloyd — *Illustrated by Paul Konoff.*	19
EVOLVING THE ARCTIC COW (article)..Alan Longstaff	21
THE DUNCAN PRESCRIPTION.......................	22

Special Departments

REVIEW OF REVIEWS..............................	24
WIT, WISDOM AND WHIMSICALITY...............	26
THE HOME BEAUTIFUL—The One-room Apartment....Anne Elizabeth Wilson	57
BUSINESS AND INVESTMENTS— Revenue From Tourist Traffic.....J. Herbert Hodgins	60
Financial Queries..............................	61
MAYBE ADAM LAUGHED AT THESE................	63
IN THE EDITOR'S CONFIDENCE....................	64

Women and Their Work

MIND PICTURES AND THEIR POWER....Pansy Atkins	53
MACLEAN'S QUESTION BOX............Edwina Seton	59

SUBSCRIPTION PRICE—In Canada, Great Britain, and most British Possessions, $2.00 per year; In United States and possessions, and in Mexico, $2.50 per year; In India, Australia and all foreign countries, Fifteen Shillings per year.
Single copies, in Canada, Ten Cents; in Great Britain, One Shilling.
NOTE—If correct amount not remitted, we will bill for difference so as to avoid delay in filling orders.

Copyright, 1926, by the MacLean Publishing Company, Limited, All rights reserved.

THE MACLEAN PUBLISHING COMPANY LIMITED
143-153 UNIVERSITY AVENUE, TORONTO, 2, CANADA.
JOHN BAYNE MACLEAN, President   H. V. TYRRELL, General Manager.
H. T. HUNTER, Vice-President.
THE MACLEAN COMPANY OF GREAT BRITAIN, LIMITED,
88 FLEET STREET, E.C., LONDON, ENGLAND.

BRANCH OFFICES: Montreal, Southam Bldg., 1070 Bleury St.; Winnipeg, 810 Confederation Life Bldg.; New York, Room 1606, St. James Bldg., 1133 Broadway, (corner 26th St.); Chicago, London Guarantee & Accident Bldg., 360 N. Michigan Blvd.

Figure 11   Table of contents. *Maclean's* 15 Jan. 1927

Chatelaine
"Mistress of her Castle"

This magazine is equipped to serve the chatelaines of Canada with authoritative information on housekeeping, child care, beauty and fashions, and with entertaining fiction and articles of national interest.

TORONTO, ONTARIO

H. NAPIER MOORE, Editorial Director   BYRNE HOPE SANDERS, Editor   GEORGE H. TYNDALL, Business Manager

Holiday Dividends

MONEY spent in travel is a sound investment. Nothing can take from you the returns it guarantees — broadmindedness, pleasant education, relaxation, recreation and lasting memories.

You can render no greater service to your children, derive no greater pleasure yourself, than to enlarge knowledge of your own country.

Have you sailed the inside passage from Vancouver to Skagway; followed the Trail of '98 from the observation platform of the train that climbs over the White Pass and into the Yukon? Or driven over the spectacular highways of Vancouver Island from Victoria the Beautiful?

Have you basked in the Okanagan; followed in retrospect the gold seekers plodding the Cariboo Trail? (You motor over a smooth road now).

Do you know the majesty of the Rockies, the marvels of Banff and Jasper, the loveliness of Waterton Lakes?

Or the freshly revealed beauties of the National Parks of Saskatchewan and Manitoba?

Do you know the peace of the Lake of the Woods, the rugged fascination of Algoma, the pastoral charm of Manitoulin, the cliffs of Georgian Bay and the gem-like waters of Muskoka?

Have you visited your capital, Ottawa, and the glorious background of the Gatineau? Or seen a Laurentian sunset?

Have you sailed the St. Lawrence from Montreal to citadelled Quebec, to Murray Bay, to the Saguenay? Or driven down the North Shore, or round the thrilling Gaspé route?

Have you skirted the shimmering Bras d'Or Lakes, or been tempted to travel the new Cabot Trail binding the tip of Cape Breton?

Have you seen the tide roar up Fundy, or idled in the fishing villages snugly tucked into Nova Scotia's coves; ambled through the Annapolis Valley with its hourly change of historic scene?

Do you know New Brunswick, its valleys, woods, rivers and its picturesque coast? And have you tasted of the calm and rest and loveliness of Prince Edward Island?

Do you know your Canada?

Travel, and you make your holiday an investment as well as a joy.

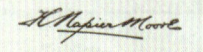

H. Napier Moore

CONTENTS, JULY, 1934
Volume VII. -:- Number 7.

FICTION
Tomorrow We Live (short story) .... Ann Morse   7
Portrait by Mari (short story)
.... Louise M. Comstock   12
Disturbing Age (short story) .. Elizabeth Whiting   14
Each in His Own Time (short story)
.... Margaret E. Barnard   18
Nor' Easter (short story) .... Nancy Barnes   20

GENERAL ARTICLES
Editorial .... H. Napier Moore   2
My Hollywood Diary ..... Madeleine Carroll   10
Fashion Shorts for Summer ...... Kay Murphy   16
Old Folks at Home .... Maud Pettit Hill   24

BEAUTY CULTURE
July Jottings .... Annabelle Lee   35
Mary Pickford on Charm ..... Norah Whitton   36
The Summer's Shoes .... Anne Thompson   37
Your Beauty Problem .... Annabelle Lee   37

THE CHATELAINE INSTITUTE
Cool Drinks for Hot Days .. M. Frances Hucks   54
Salad Days .... Helen G. Campbell   56
Testing Foods .... Helen G. Campbell   58
"Keep Cool" .... Helen G. Campbell   63
CHATELAINE PATTERNS 71

CHILDREN'S FEATURE
The Queen Fish Cat .. By Anne Elizabeth Wilson   69

THE MACLEAN PUBLISHING COMPANY
LIMITED
481 UNIVERSITY AVENUE, TORONTO 2, CANADA
JOHN BAYNE MACLEAN, Chairman of the Board.
H. T. HUNTER, President.
H. V. TYRRELL, Vice-President and General Manager.

Publishers of: Chatelaine, Maclean's Magazine, Canadian Homes and Gardens, Mayfair, The Financial Post, Hardware and Metal, Canadian Paint and Varnish Magazine, Sanitary Engineer, Canadian Grocer, Dry Goods Review, Bookseller and Stationer, The General Merchant of Canada, Canadian Hotel Review and Restaurant, Canadian Machinery and Manufacturing News, Bus and Truck Transport in Canada, Canadian Automotive Trade, Canadian Printer and Publisher, Canadian Advertising Data. BRANCH OFFICES: 1076 Bleury St., Montreal; 420 Lexington Ave., New York; 919 North Michigan Ave., Chicago; 621 Monadnock Bldg., San Francisco; England, The MacLean Company of Great Britain, Limited, Sun Life of Canada Bldg., 2 Cockspur Street, London, S.W.1. Telephone, Whitehall 3663; Telegraph, Atabek, Lesquare, London—SUBSCRIPTION PRICE: in Canada, Great Britain and British Possessions, $1.00 per year; United States, Mexico, Central and South America, France and Spain, $1.50 other countries, $2.00 per year. Single copies 10c. Copyright, 1934, by The MacLean Publishing Company, Limited. Registered in Canadian Patent and Copyright Office. Registered in United States Patent Office.

Manuscripts submitted to Chatelaine must be accompanied by addressed envelopes and sufficient postage for their return. The Publisher will exercise every care in handling material submitted, but will not be responsible for the loss of any manuscript, drawing or photograph. Contributions should send copies of material submitted. Chatelaine is fully protected by copyright and its contents may not be reprinted without permission. Use of its articles, in whole or in part for advertising purposes or in stock selling or promotion is never sanctioned.

Figure 12   Table of contents. *Chatelaine* July 1934

WATCH
THE FORDS
GO BY

"THE EASIEST CAR TO DRIVE"

THE NEW FORD V-8 is a grand car for a woman to drive because it is so safe and dependable—and so easy to handle.... "I used to be afraid of traffic," one woman writes, "but now I go everywhere. I feel safer in my Ford than in any other car I have ever driven."

There are many reasons for the ease of driving the New Ford V-8. The comfortable driving angle of the seat—the wide windshield and windows that give you a clear, unobstructed view of the highway—the ease of steering, of shifting gears and of parking on a crowded street—the powerful, effective brakes—the substantial security of the car on all roads and at all speeds.

The remarkable performance of the Ford V-8 engine is also a factor in driving ease. Its quick acceleration enables you to get out in front and escape the jam at every traffic light—its instant, eager speed helps you to pass other cars with greater safety.... We invite you to ride in the good-looking New Ford V-8 and see for yourself why it is such a grand car for a woman to drive.

Figure 13   Ford advertisement. *Chatelaine* July 1934

Figure 14 'Fashions Right for Flight.' *Canadian Home Journal* June 1951

...Y BAG TO GO TO VANCOUVER, AND IN IT I PUT—!" RE-
...ST MEMORY-TEASING GAME YOU USED TO PLAY IN
...WHEN EVERYTHING FROM A PIN TO A PONY WENT
...YTHICAL BULGING BAG? DISTANCES WERE NOTHING TO
..."MAGIC-CARPET" IMAGINATION. NO PROBLEMS FOR
...ON WHAT TO PACK. ANYTHING AND EVERYTHING COULD
... YOUR BAGGAGE HAD NO DIMENSIONS, NO CONFINES!

west coast holiday

...traveller, however, is a realist in the matters of how
...nd what to take. Suppose it's you—a career girl,
...a student—with a time limit on your holidays: two
...aps, a month if you're lucky. No world gadding for
...want to see our own beautiful West Coast. Perhaps
...relatives or friends there. You want to spend every
...inute with them, amid the unbelievable loveliness of
...st scenery, and so you decide to be air-borne. Trans
...rlines' great forty-passenger "North Star" wings its
...mming way across the 2,237 air miles from Toronto
...ver in ten hours and fifteen minutes (aided by the
...s you gain as you catch up with the sun!). One day—
...! Breakfast in Toronto, and you can have steaks at
...Vancouver the same night. Between them, a vast
...Canada, from lakes to prairies to mountains, rolling
...ath you as swiftly and easily as the turning of the
...our own library!

By Margaret Thornton

Sunshine and the blue waters of Burrard Inlet for background, and nearby the spanking-fresh paint of a lighthouse. The navy pique dress boasts a red stole, by Star Dress. Betty wears the same outfit on a visit to Royal Roads on Vancouver Island, and again in the lounge at Harrison Hot Springs Hotel, famous spa just 80 miles east of Vancouver.

Figure 15   Cover image. *Canadian Home Journal* June 1951

Figure 16   Cover image. *La Revue Moderne* Aug. 1927

Figure 17   Cover image. *La Revue Moderne* Nov. 1927

Figure 18   Cover image. *La Revue Moderne* May 1939

Figure 19   Cover image. *Chatelaine* Aug. 1929

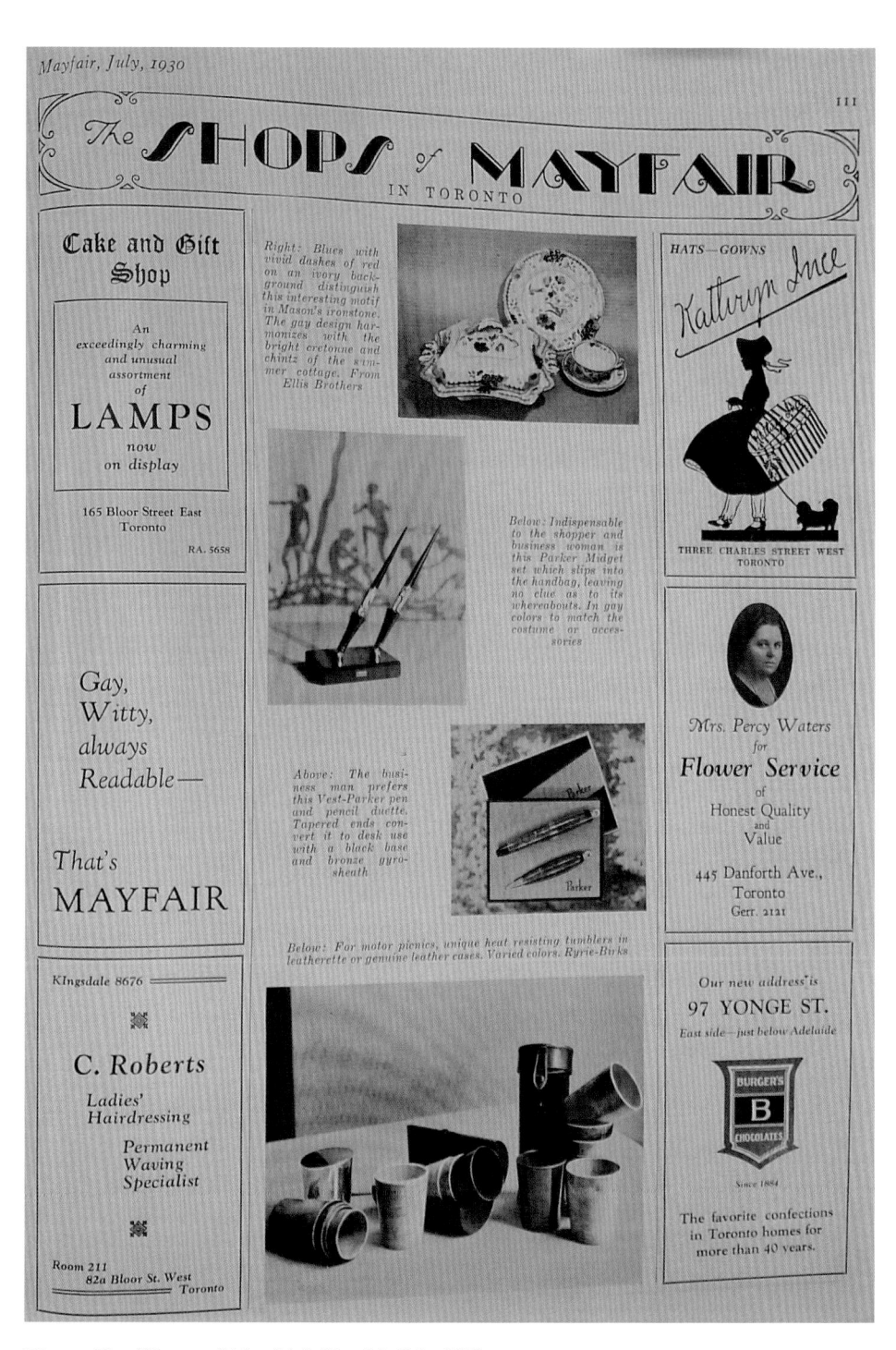

Figure 20   'Shops of Mayfair.' *Mayfair* July 1930

A NEW-YORK...

Nette, soignée, élégante à toute heure, telle est la New-Yorkaise, femme d'affaires qui circule sur Fifth Avenue, sur Park Avenue aussi bien que sur Broadway. Le vêtement sport sied à ravir à sa silhouette élancée et gracieuse, et s'adapte à sa vie active. La robe américaine est simple et du genre fourreau, excentrique et théâtrale quelquefois, mais avant tout pratique. Ingénieux, ses couturiers transforment une petite robe de rue en robe bain de soleil ; avec un ruban de brocard, des perles ou de brillants accessoires, ils en font une robe habillée que l'ouvrière, aussi bien que la femme du monde, peut se procurer. Malheureusement, les créations américaines, taillées rapidement et en grande quantité, ne durent que l'espace d'une saison. La New-Yorkaise est toujours à la recherche d'un arrangement nouveau, d'une décoration différente, d'une fantaisie originale qui mettront en valeur son charme.

Photos Black Star, N.-Y.
Exclusivité La Revue Populaire.

Figure 21   'À New-York …' fashion feature. *La Revue Populaire* July 1946

À PARIS...

Depuis des siècles, Paris est considéré comme le centre de la haute couture. Ce qui fascine dans la mode parisienne, c'est cette ligne du couturier-créateur, c'est un drapé savant qui épouse la taille, c'est un mouvement qui donne une allure royale, c'est la grâce d'une épaule arrondie, c'est un décolleté coquet et indiscret; c'est le charme séduisant du couturier-décorateur qui joue avec les couleurs; c'est l'ingéniosité du sculpteur qui drape et fait jaillir de ses doigts la coiffure idéale; ce sont les doigts patients et habiles des midinettes qui travaillent amoureusement à la réalisation de ces rêves tant caressés. Photos S. I. F.

Figure 22 'Empress of Britain Fashion Story.' *Canadian Home Journal* May 1956

Figure 23   Canadian Pacific *Empress of Britain* advert. *Mayfair* Apr. 1931

Mayfair, May, 192

the Only Paris
by madge

I doubt that all those with widows' weeds have been bereft of a husband...

I gave myself into the hands of an amiable blonde ox of a man

Along the Seine artists continually paint...

Adorable men with faces like movie heroes are chambermaids...

BEFORE Mary Pickford, Paris w the sweetheart of the world, a judging by the 400,000 foreign who live here, not to mention the floo tourists, there are those who have swerved in their allegiance.

No wonder! In Paris adventure is unav able even to the unadventurous. New atrophied emotions are stimulat Smiling becomes a habit; laughter, sponta ous. Politeness is national and leisure inescapable in a l where the busy business man takes two hours for his lunch! (can scarcely imagine a Frenchman complaining that he hadn't ti to eat. A thousand thunders, no! He makes time, meticulou chooses his food and enjoys it. He has little dyspepsia, rare misanthropia, practically no ennui.

This is the life!

I landed at Havre, argued pleasantly (and successfully) about getting typewriter through the customs and made my way by autobus to the train Paris. A merry rogue of a *porteur* attached himself to me, fighting in a flatter manner for the privilege of carrying my luggage. Waiting for the gates to op he confided in picturesque idiom that he felt extremely swanky carrying s beautiful valises. So I prepared for the payment of an extra *pourboire*, wh indeed he demanded. Said he, "You have much luggage and I have much fam and this relationship between us seems to call for excessive generosity on y part" or words to that effect. I only hope he did not go home b drunk on the proceeds of his hold-up. Of course, every English-speaking per is presumed to be an American and sprouting the root of all evil. Legitimate p therefore. The other day, I put one over on my chauffeur by pretending I w Mexican!

Arrived in Paris, I gave myself into the hands of an amiable blonde ox man wearing the picturesque blue smock of the railway porters, and he harnes himself with my three large bags and the wardrobe trunk, to boot! Carried lot distributed all over his body, and put them all into the taxi which bore with incredible rapidity to the hotel. Half a block away on the same st stands the house where Alphonse Daudet was born and died. It has the allu outer gate and courtyard of the best old houses and it is not hard to imagine author bent over the manuscript of *Sapho*, or *Jack* or *Rose et Ninette* when street was a more leisured thoroughfare; where women with a yard of brea their arms and men in flowing capes, and an occasional *voiture* passed the d Now, by conservative estimate, a taxi a minute whizzes through the nar lane filling the air with a confusion of raucous noises.

Figure 24 'The Only Paris.' *Mayfair* May 1927

Paris macbeth

Bearded gentlemen in long black capes like benevolent bolshiviki...

One savors full significance of the phrase "to be on the qui vive"...

I have not so far seen any fish taken...

Busy business men take two hours for lunch...

1 Paris one savors the full significance e phrase "to be on the *qui vive*," espe- if one fares forth afoot. Business and 1 intercourse may be conducted slowly, obody wastes time in transit. Truly, it wonder that any pedestrian *vives* at Even the traffic policemen stand in the shadow) ath all day. There seems to be about five *tax-res* very pedestrian, and no matter how clear the way may be when one starts to cross, motors multiplied like germs by the time one reaches the middle. attitude of the drivers is not to give one any small advantage may arise, but rather are they like sharpshooters determined k off the greatest number of the enemy.

he taxi horns are absurd affairs—little toots and hoots and squawks, ding one of the toy bugles found in those crackers which are indispensable hristmas and New Years' parties. For days I used to run to the window ting to see a company of small children playing soldier in the street.

he variety of motors is bewildering; the contrast immense. Stepping briskly wake of a magnificent Hispano-Suize, one sees a diminutive vehicle that as though it might be an arm-chair mounted on wheels and concealing an e somewhere about its person. How anyone dares drive the things, I simply ot imagine!

long the Seine, which is crossed by thirty-one bridges, artists continually "he Frenchmen look the part—in soft green or blue or rose smocks and t caps—with an engaging unconsciousness rarely achieved by a foreigner. v the level of the street, fisher-folk amuse themselves. I have not, so far, ny fish taken, but it must be pleasant to remain, unmolested, all day, in the air.

he shops along the *Rue de Rivoli* are strongly suggestive of Atlantic City, he shopping section including *Place Vendome*, *Rue de la Paix* and *L'Opera* conceivably be Fifth Avenue . with one or two conspicuous excep- Behind an exquisitely wrought-iron grille, on the far side of a spotless yard, a famous costumer's name steals out; or a furrier's, or an art dealer's. is no gaudy display. That would be second class and vulgar. Indeed, one penetrate, to explore. Then, across a jeweller's window will be boldly d "Imitation." Where else would one see that? Its unique quality is ly tempered by knowing that articles of genuine make—gold and silver— he stamp of the mint.

1 the other hand, a deliciously foreign flavor attaches to most sections e Faubourgs—the old suburbs of Paris. Not merely because of the

See also page 46

Figure 25   TransCanada Airlines advert. *La Revue Populaire* Sept. 1954

Figure 26　Canadian Pacific advert. *Mayfair* Aug. 1929

We Dine and Wine in London

The Cheshire Cheese, loved of Dickens and Dr. Johnson, must be visited (top and right)

By CLAIRE WALLACE

BY JOVE, where shall we eat? Well, by Jove, there are so many places to eat—and drink—in London that it's a pleasure to be hungry—and thirsty.

Of course, you get the habit of good food—if you haven't had it anyway—on the way over. I mean, you don't spend seven days crossing the sea on the *Duchess of Bedford*, for instance, living on the luscious fare of an ocean liner, without feeling you want to keep it up. After consuming sole with mushroom sauce every day or so, who wants plain bread and butter? So, out you go in search of good food, interestingly served.

And, how you get it! You have Sunday supper at the swanky Savoy with an Irish peer (and have an awful time remembering to say m'lord, instead of mister) and at the next table see "June", of London dancing fame; you supper-dance at the Carlton and see Michael Arlen among those present; and you drop into a French restaurant in Soho and find George Bancroft, in a green suit, at a nearby table—all great thrills for a Toronto gal.

But, let's begin at the beginning. If you are planning a trip to London this summer, let this be your guide:

COFFEE STALLS: You stop off at one of these funny little caravan-restaurants on your way home from theatre or dance, lean against a wheel and drink a grand cup of coffee for a penny. On your right you'll probably have a real down-and-outer, on your left a slick gent who has just stepped out of a Rolls-Royce; both are chatty because it is a London night, and London nights are that way.

PUBS: A trip to a pub if you want atmosphere, not the cheapest and best luncheon in London. But, it isn't done if you are a la-a-ady, so you stay away during the day and only go "pub-crawling" in the evening with a party of friends. Then you visit "The Doves", a 500-year old pub in Hammersmith, on the Thames, and on the way there you pass the house in which the first London telephone was installed, and, a little farther on, the house that Nell Gwynne occupied when she and King Charles were buddies. You visit "Charlie Brown's" pub in Limehouse to see his famous curios, gathered from all over the world; the "Running Horse" in Mayfair, to see strange people—and usually a few Canadians; and the "Fitzroy", to have a startled look at London's Bohemia—and how!

SNACK BARS: otherwise known as BUTTERIES. The place for a cocktail at the end of a hard day, a quick snack before the theatre, or a supper after; but always the place to see smart women and handsome men. Day clothes, cocktail suits or evening clothes, okay. The BERKELEY, the SAVOY and the BLUE TRAIN bars, you mustn't miss.

CHOP HOUSES: Eliminate a visit to the famous CHESHIRE CHEESE, in that dark little court just off Fleet Street, and you'll regret it to the end of your days—for this is one of London's most interesting spots. There you can sit in the very seat Dickens occupied when he wrote part of "Tale of Two Cities", or in the favorite corner of Dr. Samuel Johnson 'way back in 1775. There you have that important English dish, steak-and-kidney pudding, or the special dish of cheese moistened with beer and melted to a golden lusciousness. With luck you might see G. K. Chesterton at the next table, or other famous folk. No one knows how old the CHESHIRE CHEESE is. The original place was destroyed in the great London fire, and was rebuilt in 1667.

THE SAVOY: Famous for its smart crowds, its crepe suzettes (yum), and the "rising floor" for cabaret entertainment—the only one in the world of its kind, installed at a cost of $50,000. You go there for luncheon (Costs about $2 a head), for supper *(Continued on page 35)*

A pretty girl from the supper show in the Trocadero Grill (above)

☆

The Berkeley Buttery attracts London's "smart young things" (right)

☆

Coffee stalls, an interesting part of London night life (right, below)

☆

... The Savoy appeals to the sophisticates of every nation (top, right)

CANADIAN HOME JOURNAL [JUNE, 1935]

Figure 27 'We Dine and Wine in London.' *Canadian Home Journal* June 1935

Montréal, septembre 1954

CUISINE FRANÇAISE

LA TOUR D'ARGENT

La *Tour d'Argent* n'est pas seulement l'un des restaurants les plus luxueux de Paris. Sa renommée a depuis longtemps franchi les frontières et il n'est que de voir parmi la clientèle élégante qui s'y presse chaque jour, la proportion d'étrangers venus de tous les continents pour se convaincre que ce temple gastronomique possède une réputation mondiale.

Fondée en 1582, la maison, que dirige maintenant Claude Terrail, n'a toutefois acquis cette « classe internationale » que depuis 1890, sous l'impulsion du plus fameux maître-queux de l'époque, le « grand » Frédéric, inventeur de plats raffinés, et qui perfectionna la recette du *Canard au Sang*, spécialité numéro un de *La Tour d'Argent*. C'est lui qui imagina de numéroter chacun de ces volatiles et c'est ainsi que, si vous venez en déguster un, en 1954, il vous sera remis une carte portant un numéro approchant de... 250,000 !

Actuellement, c'est l'excellent chef Pierre Descreux (à droite) qui règne sur les cuisines de l'établissement, dont les terrasses dominent un magnifique panorama sur Notre-Dame et la Seine.

Oeufs farcis Olga

Faites cuire des oeufs pendant 10 minutes. Épluchez-les et coupez-en les deux extrémités. Évidez-les. Hachez le jaune avec les débris de jambon et des champignons cuits au beurre. Liez le tout avec une sauce béchamel à la crème. Fourrez les oeufs avec cette farce. Dressez-les sur un plat et nappez-les avec le reste de la sauce. Saupoudrez de fromage râpé et passez au four chaud quelques instants.

LE RESTAURANT PRUNIER

Il y a trois restaurants Prunier : la maison-mère qui est située rue Duphot, près de la Madeleine, la succursale parisienne Prunier-Traktir, avenue Victor-Hugo, non loin de l'Etoile, enfin Prunier de Londres, St. James Street.

Ce sont M. et Mme Prunier-Barnagaud, les petits-fils du fondateur Émile Prunier qui depuis plus de vingt-cinq ans, assument la responsabilité d'une maison où toutes les spécialités sont représentées mais qui a surtout acquis sa réputation par ses huîtres, coquillages et autres « fruits de mer » dont l'excellence et la fraîcheur tiennent en grande partie au fait que la maison possède, sur la côte de l'Atlantique, ses propres pêcheries, ses viviers à crustacés et ses parcs à huîtres.

Mais Prunier possède aussi ses caves personnelles et sa réserve de la Halle aux Vins contient de nombreuses et vénérables bouteilles des plus grands crus de France.

Turban de langoustines à l'armoricaine

Passez au beurre 100 gr. d'oignons hachés et 100 gr. de champignons. Versez votre riz bien lavé, dans ce fondu d'oignons et mouillez-le avec trois fois son volume d'eau. Laissez cuire 15 minutes à couvert. Sel, poivre. Tenez-le au chaud.

D'autre part, faites cuire les langoustines sautées au beurre chaud. Assaisonnez avec un demi-litre de vin blanc sec, de la purée de tomates et une cuillerée à café de curry, thym, laurier, persil. 20 minutes de cuisson. Égouttez et décortiquez. Seule la queue garnira le turban.

Faites réduire le tout d'un quart. Incorporez un léger beurre manié et 2 cuillerées de crème fraîche. Liez avec cette sauce le chair des langoustines, que vous disposerez autour du turban, le riz au milieu et une garniture de crevettes roses.

Soucoupe volante

Génoise : Mélangez pendant une dizaine de minutes 4 jaunes d'oeufs avec 250 gr. de sucre. Ajoutez ensuite 200 gr. de beurre, 125 gr. de farine, un petit verre de rhum, un peu de levure, 200 gr. d'amandes émondées, hachées très fin et en dernier lieu 4 blancs battus en neige. Mettez dans un moule beurré et enfournez de suite à four moyen. Lorsque le gâteau est cuit, imbibez-le généreusement de rhum, fourrez-le de crème au beurre pralinée, et recouvrez de crème au chocolat. *Décor :* Sertissez le gâteau de demi-lunes en nougat, disposez des cornets de pâte d'amande fondante fourrés de crème au beurre, et surmontez d'une dragée d'argent. La rosace du milieu est en crème au beurre.

LE CAFE DE LA PAIX

Sur la place de l'Opéra à Paris il y a deux monuments qui sont également célèbres dans le monde entier : l'Opéra, bien sûr, mais aussi le Café de la Paix. Créé vers 1870, il fit s'interpeller d'une table à l'autre, à « la belle époque » (celle qui se termina qu'en 1914) des personnalités telles que Massenet, Zola, Maupassant, puis, entre les deux guerres, Dranem, Paul Poiret, Diaghilev, Victor Boucher.

On pourrait conter cent anecdotes sur cet établissement si parisien. Je n'en retiendrai qu'une, particulièrement typique : en août 1944, après que le Général de Gaulle y eût pris son premier repas parisien, des services américains voulurent le réquisitionner. Alors, levant les bras au ciel, le colonel des U.S.A. chargé des « civil affairs » s'exclama : « Réquisitionner *Le Café de la Paix* ? pourquoi pas Notre-Dame ? »

Mais dira-t-on, si tous les touristes fréquentent sa fameuse terrasse, si de nombreuses réunions privées et même internationales ont pour cadre ses luxueux salons, qu'a donc à faire la Gastronomie dans un café, si renommé soit-il ? Eh bien ! elle y a pourtant sa place. Car en dépit de son nom le *Café de la Paix* est aussi un restaurant dont le chef M. Jousselin (à droite) est un remarquable maître-queux. En présentant à nos lectrices quelques-unes de ces spécialités des grandes maisons parisiennes, c'est à un petit voyage au pays de Vatel et de Brillat-Savarin que je les convie. Peut-être réussiront-elles à confectionner certains de ces plats ? L'idéal, en tout cas, serait plutôt qu'elles puissent, un jour, venir visiter la France et déguster sur place toutes ces excellentes choses.

C'est du moins ce que je leur souhaite.

MARYSE THILL

Figure 28   'Cuisine Française.' *La Revue Populaire* Sept. 1954

Figure 29   Canadian Pacific Banff advert. *La Revue Populaire* July 1930

at the appearance of fashionable women. One example is his report on motoring outfits shown at the Salon d'automobile: 'Some of the things shown were quite sensational. One in particular created much comment and amusement—a gray-green tweed walking suit, which had the skirt divided down the middle' ('Paris! ... The Tea Hour' 74). He adds: 'the girl displaying this amazing novelty certainly looked very nice and "sporting". But so few of us have the right legs these days for such eccentricity' (78). Soiffield represents fashion as a perilous realm, where a woman is as liable to attract ridicule as admiration.

In the mid-1930s, the letter form began to give way to other modes of reporting in the Anglophone magazines, and this coincided with an increased attention to New York style. Kay Murphy's New York 'Fashion Shorts' column, which first appeared in November 1933, radically altered the tone of *Chatelaine*'s fashion reporting. In the February 1934 issue, 'Fashion Shorts' appeared on the lower half of the pages on which Wyndham's 'Paris Letter' was printed, and the adjacent texts exemplify the contrasting tones of the two journalists:

As for colors, I should say you could choose practically any becoming color and be nicely 'in the picture.' All shades of blue, including navy and gendarme blue, which is a shade lighter, greens galore and brown and grey. (Wyndham 34–35)
Saw the most luscious nightie. I thought it was an evening gown. Palest peach, gored to fit the figure, tiny train, high front and low back, just as a décolletage. Absolutely untrimmed. (Murphy 34)

Murphy's column was aimed at the younger end of *Chatelaine*'s readership. The March 1934 instalment, 'Bright news notes from a Canadian on Fifth Avenue,' advises: 'The double-breasted reefer suit is cunning, with enough thick seams and leather buttons to please even the most sophisticated Young Salt.' Murphy refers to smoking, tells that 'the newest shirtwaist blouses have long, split tails just like daddy's,' and recommends getting 'a bang cut' (41). At this period, younger readers might have been more attuned to recent developments in America, such as the flapper style and bobbed hair, while their mothers continued to focus on Paris fashions. And Murphy's telegraphic style is appropriate to the rather abbreviated outfits she often described, just as Wyndham's more flowing, conventional writing suited the types of clothes she was writing about. Perhaps Murphy's style, which was distinctive in the context of the Canadian magazines, might even owe something to the elliptical or pared-down style of some modernist prose.

From July 1934 until May 1937, *Mayfair*'s men's fashion column, 'The Cosmopolite,' was signed 'K. M. Morphy,' and presented as a series of short, gossipy paragraphs on trends observed on the street and in the shops. It is written in an extremely similar idiom to that of Murphy's 'Fashion Shorts':

> The white belt is taking all the belt bows for the summer. It will be worn with practically every color of summer suit. It is often matched up with a white tie. Imagine it on yourself, with a deep blue shirt, and a white or grey flannel outfit. Does things for you ... (Morphy 84)[8]

Clearly, Murphy 'morphed' into Morphy, carefully avoiding self-reference and gendered personal pronouns, but retaining a rather intimate voice which could be read either as that of a female *flâneur* observing well-dressed men, or as that of a male dandy. Murphy, then, offers an intriguing parallel to Soiffield's 'cross dressing,' and their shared masquerade fits with *Mayfair*'s irreverent attitude.

Mobility, fantasy, foreignness

Georg Simmel observed in 1905 that 'there exists a widespread predilection for importing fashions from outside, and such foreign fashions assume a greater value within a particular social circle, simply because they did not originate there' (191). In Canadian magazines, discourses of cosmopolitanism and exoticism were strongly inscribed in the reporting and marketing of fashion. In *Mayfair*'s November 1927 issue, Adele M. Gianelli reported on the 'Great Fashion Show' at the new London Olympia, describing 'Kiosks of black and gold lacquer in futurist design, scarlet Japanese temples, Elizabethan cottages, *Palais de danse*, [...] Moorish balconies, Spanish patios, Egyptian harems' (7). In the issue for April 1928, the advertorial text on the 'Shops of Mayfair in Montreal' page similarly evokes the appeal of the exotic:

> In one brief morning you can shop the world around; buy treasures from the Orient, Paris, London, New York ... every known centre where delightful things abound. And they are just around the corner from your own home. That is the charm and wonder of the Mayfair shops. The hat, the frock, the bag, symphonies of chic, each bearing the magic name of some world-famous designer ... and yet, comparatively inexpensive.
>
> One cannot sail to Paris for every gown ... but proud Paris comes to you through the shops of Mayfair. (95)

---

[8] Murphy worked across the Maclean titles: one of the very few fashion items in *Maclean's* from this era is by her ('Fashions for Autumn').

As shopping is constructed as a foreign tour, *Mayfair* itself takes on the function of a guidebook. The world of fashion is evoked as a space of fantasy ('charm,' 'wonder,' 'magic'), yet it is located *within* Canada, right around the corner, and inexpensive to reach. The passage suggests that, like C. S. Lewis's Narnia, the magic world of Paris can be reached simply by walking into the wardrobe in your own house. The series of ellipses, which appear so often in both fashion and travel writing in these magazines, seem to leave spaces for the reader's imagination to supply images. The ellipses also acknowledge the impossibility of capturing the *je ne sais quoi* of Parisian style in the English language.

In April 1928, Arnaud Renaud, a staff writer for *La Revue Moderne*, contributed a celebratory text entitled 'Variations sur les toilettes de Pâques.' While it does not give any concrete information about the current styles, it is filled with sensuous detail, almost turning fashion into a poem:

> Le printemps est bien là, éclos au cœur de cette effloraison de tissus clairs et délicats, de gazes fluides, de ravissantes lingeries ...
>
> O les coupables vitrines, qui expriment avec une éloquence toute de charme et de séduction le langage des choses! La perpétuelle invite à la bourse! *l'invitation au voyages* des divers et multiples rayons! Elle appelle, elle danse, elle affriole, elle chante, elle capture, la vitrine ...
> (Renaud)

Again, the ellipses, and again, the metaphor of fashion as a leisure trip. This association of new clothes with adventure was, as might be expected, particularly prominent in holiday fashion features. In *Chatelaine*, Mary Wyndham began her February 1929 letter by invoking the idiom of luxury tour brochures: 'If you are setting off for sunny climes, palms that are not in pots, indigo and jade seas, orange trees, spice-laden breezes and all the other lyric what-nots of the travel bureau poets, be sure to pack a goodly number of white frocks.' She adds that she is 'really only quoting Biarritz,' since 'as everyone will tell you Biarritz [...] was really more a white season than it was anything else' (18). 'Everyone,' in this passage, means 'everyone who is anyone': a very restricted group and one to which, in all likelihood, very few of Wyndham's Canadian readers actually belonged. *Mayfair* was mainly preoccupied with identifying those who had achieved membership of the travelling elite: its society pages featured photographs of wealthy Canadians boarding cruise liners, accompanied by informative accounts of their destinations or tips on shipboard fashions and etiquette. Even *La Revue Populaire*, which was less focused on foreign travel than were the English-language magazines, fostered this kind of aspiration. Francine's May 1937 article 'Voyages,' for instance, advises on what to pack for a transatlantic trip, and what type of evening dress to wear in London and Paris. The piece appeared opposite a full-page CP advertisement for the *Empress of Britain*, revealing the shared project of advertisers and editors to promote luxury travel as an ideal. From the 1940s onwards, *Chatelaine*, the *Journal*, and the Francophone magazines began to focus more on practical outfits for family holidays, while *Mayfair* continued to envisage an upper-crust style of travel. Nevertheless, throughout the period from the 1920s to the 1950s, all the magazines, in their different ways, presented tourism as a status symbol, and offered a training in appropriate dressing for would-be travellers.

In addition to being constructed as a journey in itself, fashion was often presented as part of the experience of a destination. On the French Riviera, Wyndham notes in February 1929, 'there were foulards and printed crêpes about in the daytime' but 'there were no sailor-looking, brass-buttoned navy blue reefers in the landscape' (18). In Paris, the fashions were part of the tourist spectacle: they could be viewed on the street, in the shop windows, in the ateliers and salons, and at the couture shows, but they were also—for wealthier visitors—available to be purchased and taken home. This is obviously what differentiates fashion from the other 'exhibits' of Paris: monuments, gardens, hotels, galleries. According to the British novelist Elizabeth Bowen: 'In theory, dress is an art. The architecture of textiles ought to rank only less high than the architecture of stone in so far as textiles are less durable' (112). For those Canadian women who could only dream of visiting Paris, the magazines offered a vicarious experience of both its clothes and its buildings, which were often described together in the same piece of writing.

In *Mayfair*, with its visual repertoire of whimsy and fantasy, fashion was sometimes brought together with mobility in a single image (see Figure 8). The other magazines often yoked travel and fashion in more literal ways, especially in the mid-twentieth century. The Montreal couturier Jane Harris, whose salon operated from the early 1940s until the early 1960s, had her live models photographed on ships and airport runways, or beside trains and highway signs. Harris's work was widely reported in the print and broadcast media—even *Maclean's* magazine published a piece by her (Harris). In 1958, she launched the 'Air France Fashion Tours of Europe' at Dorval airport (Sharman 282), and her promotional images were echoed in several photo features in the women's magazines that year. For example, the *Canadian Home Journal* published an extended feature by the editor-in-chief, Rosemary Boxer, on fashions inspired by Chinese and Japanese textiles and motifs. The outfits were photographed on Japanese models posing on airport runways, and the opening caption reads: 'Canadian fashions shown on the following eight pages were flown to Japan on a

FASHIONS

Canadian Pacific Air Lines DC 6B' ('Fashions' 17). The clothes almost become ambassadors for Canada in the wider world.

The *Journal* also published an automobile-inspired fashion feature, illustrated with photographs of models lying on car bonnets:

> From dazzling new high-power cars comes the flair for colour in this spring fashion collection. These dresses which capture the season's important shades show the high-style colors busy young Canadian sophisticates are wearing. Luminous blues, fiery reds, dazzling greens and brilliant prints are all part of the fashion panorama for spring. This year's futuramic fashions incorporate a hint of the waistless '20s in their modern streamlining. Fashion '58 is a carnival of new strong colour. (Boxer, 'Spring' 17)

The annotations specify the makes and shades of both dresses and cars, connecting them through a discourse of sophistication which balances nostalgia for the 1920s and a longing for the future.[9] Similarly, a May 1956 piece in the *Journal*, 'The Empress of Britain Fashion Story' (see Figure 22) eschews contemporary, fast forms of transport in favour of slow, luxurious liner travel, yet, at the same time, strongly emphasises modernity through the reiteration of ideas of newness and arrival:

> When we first learned that the Empress of Britain was to wind up her maiden voyage at Montreal we wrote to the Canadian Pacific suggesting that their new Canadian liner would make a wonderful stage for new Canadian summer fabrics and fashions and suggested a fashion show to mark the ship's arrival in Canada. They agreed and we next contacted Canadian textile companies who immediately began producing fabrics in exciting new colors copied from the Empress' lush interior decor. These were passed along to Canadian designers who created the clothes. ('Empress' 30)

All three of these 1950s *Canadian Home Journal* features, as well as the 'Fashions Right For Flight' article discussed in Chapter Two (see Figure 14), promote consumer-based nationalism via collaboration between travel

---

[9] 'Sophistication can operate through nostalgia (self-conscious reference to the styles of the past), but it cannot be old-fashioned. Therefore, sophisticated nostalgia is much more likely to focus on the unfamiliar glamour of a long-past era than on the merely outdated fashions of recent generations' (Hammill, *Sophistication* 38; see also 164–70).

companies and the garment industry. This makes explicit the interdependence of fashion and travel (on both discursive and commercial levels) which had long been subtly evident in the pages of the mainstream magazines.

Nation, war, exchange

The assumption that new styles came exclusively from Paris, or at least from Europe, and travelled westwards across the Atlantic, undergoing some adaptation on the way, became deeply ingrained during the nineteenth century, and was still dominant in the 1920s and 1930s. Yet the international trajectories of fashion were becoming more complex during this era. The New York fashion industry was developing rapidly, and transatlantic exchange was increasingly evident in the couture world. In November 1938, 'Paris Opening,' a novella by the American author Anne Green, was published in full in the *Canadian Home Journal*. It centres on a young designer, Alicia, who moves from New York to Paris to work with an established French couturier, Madame Regnier. Their styles are so different that Madame Regnier asks Alicia to prepare a solo show instead of contributing to her own collection, commenting: 'you are the exponent of youth, you could never design for me' (14). At the end of the story, she reveals her vision for her protégée's future:

> 'I intend you to be the best dressmaker in the world for the American market.'
> 'But I thought you were that yourself.'
> 'No, I design unusual fashions, the ones which are worn by the elite, two leaps ahead of the common trend, but the elite has no preoccupations beyond parading about in new clothes. It has often occurred to me that there are thousands of smart, busy women in America who need models specially fitted to their active lives, gowns that are original, chic, yet adapted to their requirements. [...] One has to be American to have intimate knowledge of its intricacies of life. And that is not to be acquired by a foreigner.' (35)

There is a tendency here to associate the 'elite' solely with European women, but also an acknowledgement that the market for Parisian couture was now largely found in North America. National difference is reinscribed in this story, yet Alicia learns to 'read' the very different design culture which she finds in France, and to benefit from it.

During the same decade, numerous commercial and editorial texts in the magazines reinforced Canada's active role in the garment industry. The clothing sections in some issues of *Chatelaine* were titled 'Canadian Fashions,' while a June 1932 advertisement for the magazine's mail-order pattern service read 'Paris inspires the mode ... Canada makes the pattern' (Chatelaine Pattern).[10] By buying these patterns from a Canadian firm, and using them for home dressmaking, the magazine's readers were themselves participating in their nation's creative and industrial development. This advert, like many others, reveals that Canada's effort was principally focused on the manufacturing or dressmaking side of the process, rather than the design side. Nevertheless, as early as 1930, hints that Canadian taste and Canadian products might begin to influence the international fashion trade, were already legible in the pages of the magazines. An advert published in the April 1930 issue of *Chatelaine* read: 'The latest thoughts of Paris. Expressed in fabrics by Canadian Celanese Ltd. Fabrics so beautiful, so aware, so arresting that even Paris is thrilled and inspired' (Canadian Celanese). This does seem a rather extravagant claim, but it models a two-way influence which the magazines were just beginning to celebrate. The word 'aware' invests the Canadian fabrics with a kind of intelligence—the 'ideas' may come from Paris, but they encounter an alert response on the other side of the Atlantic.

The Canadian magazines place a particularly strong emphasis on the need to be selective, not only to avoid eccentricity but also to adapt Paris and New York fashions so that they suit both the Canadian environment and the person who will wear them. An article on wartime fashion in *Chatelaine* for April 1940 recommended 'canteen-shaped bags with red lining,' but added: 'A smart French woman was seen in the Ritz the other day with a black bag on which was inscribed, "It must stop once and for all." But we probably won't go that far in Canada' ('The Three Ages' 10). The value of simplicity is reiterated, and the style ideal disseminated through these middlebrow periodicals is a notably muted, balanced one. This was compatible with what were seen as mainstream Canadian values, as is evident in the *Globe & Mail*'s report on the Association of Canadian Couturiers' 1957 show, which commented on 'that touch of restrained individuality which is distinctly Canadian' (Dickason). Whilst occasional fashion reports presented the more wildly imaginative Paris designs, many more concentrated on those which exhibited a restrained elegance.

Canadian fashion sense, in general, was evoked more in terms of a set of distinctive choices amongst available options, than as an original style in itself. In March 1932, *Chatelaine* ran an article by Gwenyth Barrington entitled 'Is the Canadian woman better dressed than her American sister?' Barrington rather

---

[10] *The Chatelaine* initially offered the *Vogue* pattern service, but launched its own in January 1930.

indignantly outlines the process by which particularly popular Paris models are copied by US manufacturers:

> These 'runners' or 'flivvers,' so called by the sorority of better shops, have reproduced themselves so widely that a select house would not touch anything resembling their original lines with a ten-foot pole, and yet the style idea will be repeated everywhere until it is as epidemic as checker cabs. (8)

The vocabulary of contamination appears quite often in anti-American discourse in these magazines. In later decades, a couture design that was knocked off in the mass market, became known not as a 'flivver' but a 'Ford' (Palmer, *Couture* 44), a term which reinforces the disparaging association of American clothes with cheap mass production. Barrington's article argues that the Canadian woman, in contrast to the American, possesses 'the gift of wearing clothes which depend for their appeal on some ineffable quality of individuality which defies the quick turn-over of mass production' (8), and that she is prepared to spend a long time searching for the exact item she wants, adding every detail to her outfit 'with the sure, clear touch of the artist' (8). The piece strongly resists the stereotypical image of Canadians as rural, traditional, even naïve, substituting an urbane, modern ideal of Canadian femininity:

> Canadian women have learned to look beyond the mere statement of a fashion style—and to analyze its possibilities for personal adjustments. Perhaps it is the sheer geographic necessity of blending American chic with English practicality which has produced this success, which, mingling with unconfessed worldly wisdom, has led them past the easy allure of 'flivver' dressing, to the very sound conclusion that, as there is only one of each of them, it is the subtlest sophistication to capitalize on the fact. (8)

In Canada, the legacies of colonialism, and the twentieth-century experience of neo-colonialism, inflected fashion 'borrowing' with politicised meanings. Barrington strategically evokes the notion of Canada as a middle space, able to combine the best of American and European cultures and to adapt foreign ideas, styles, and approaches to a local environment.

The coming of war had a major impact on patterns of international trade and exchange in the garment industry. In the early part of the war, Canadian magazines—in a gesture of solidarity—celebrated French fashions more enthusiastically than ever: 'so long as the French couturier sets the fashions, women's clothes will echo the heartaches and triumphs of France,' wrote Lotta Dempsey in *Chatelaine* in February 1940, adding: 'Our shoes become sensible ... don't France's smartest women wear low heels for new hard-working days?' (9) But a few months later, Paris, now under German occupation, was largely cut off from the North American fashion world,[11] and by October 1940, Kay Murphy was claiming in *Chatelaine* that 'the French influence in Canada should contribute much towards carrying on the tradition of French couture in the Western Hemisphere' (26). A rapprochement between English and French Canada through the medium of couture was not the only potential benefit of the European conflict. As Alexandra Palmer points out, the war 'gave impetus to local designers [...] working in good, high-end ready-to-wear' in the US and also in Canada (*Couture* 19). An article in *Chatelaine* claimed that 'the Dominion was going to stop following Paris and New York slavishly, and formulate some of her own ideas for clothes' (Damon), while J. Herbert Hodgins wrote in *Mayfair*'s 'The Cosmopolite' for January 1940 that Florida was expecting a 'bumper season' for tourism, adding: 'As the Rivieras will not be actively concerned with resort styles, as in peacetimes, we can expect an interesting tendency toward developing our own styles this side of the Atlantic' (4).

At a distance from the theatres of war, Canadian magazines could continue to showcase holiday resort clothes, even though the location of the resorts had changed. But the extent of such apparently frivolous coverage was gradually reduced as the conflict proceeded, and both the English- and French-language magazines began to foreground the connection between fashion and politics. In February 1941, the 19-year-old Huguette Oligny, future actress and daughter of Odette Oligny, contributed a fashion report to *La Revue Moderne* in which she recommended simple, elegant black dresses for a wartime spring:

> Voyez-vous, il y a une raison à cette simplicité des modèles du printemps 1941. Les circonstances ne se prêtent pas à une élégance faite de tout petits raffinements, qui sont charmants, certes, mais dont l'entretien est toujours difficile. Il vaut mieux, en ce moment, être simple, c'est-à-dire chic, car les véritables élégantes ne s'y trompent pas. (19)

---

[11] Sixty of the couture houses continued to operate in Paris, in spite of a Nazi attempt to move the industry to Berlin or Vienna (Caton 250), and during the first year of the war, Canadian magazines could still report on Paris fashions. In January 1940, *La Revue Populaire* published an article titled 'Paris reste la capitale de la mode,' but in March, the magazine's first ever 'La mode de New York' spread appeared, and soon afterwards, the Paris reports disappeared for the remainder of the war.

Since elaborate fashions are 'difficult' to wear and maintain, a simple style, Oligny suggests, is more appropriate for a period when women have more important things on their minds. Simpler dresses allowed for economies in fabric, and were faster to make: 'Too many workmen have been called to service to allow for hours of fussing over a single tuck or gusset,' as Lotta Dempsey put it in *Chatelaine* (9). Department store fashion shows were largely suspended from 1941 to 1945, and Dempsey describes 'the mass movement of Canadian women back to the sewing machine and the knitting needles' (9). In August 1944, *La Revue Populaire* ran a similar piece on the importance of maintaining dressmaking skills.

Immediately the war was over, however, journalists resumed their attention to foreign fashions, and to shopping. The travel necessitated by the conflict was turned into an opportunity to scoop fashion stories on the spot. In its April 1945 issue, *Mayfair* claimed to have provided 'the first authentic description of the Paris Spring Collections, the first to indicate the trend of Paris fashions since the Liberation'; the report was sent by its war correspondent, via bomber mail (Thompson 27). Yet, though coverage of the Paris openings was restored, the magazines did not lose interest in the New York and Montreal fashion news that had sustained them during the war. Indeed, the Paris designers themselves were paying attention to North American trends. Raymonde St-Georges wrote in *La Revue Moderne* in January 1950: 'Et si nous nous tournons encore vers Paris pour y chercher des idées fraîches et originales, Paris jette de plus en plus un regard vers l'Amérique pour découvrir ce qui nous plait et ce que nous aimons à porter' (St-Georges). In the 1940s and 1950s, buyers and retailers in Canada and the US continued to expand their influence on both sides of the Atlantic, and European couturiers became increasingly reliant on the North American market.

In July 1946, *La Revue Populaire* published a fascinating picture spread showing New York and Paris fashion designs on facing pages (see Figure 21). The two descriptive texts are worth quoting in full as they reveal so much about Canadian perceptions of the clothing industries in the two countries, and about the magazine's strategies for cultural alignment with France:

> Nette, soignée, élégante à toute heure, telle est la New-Yorkaise, femme d'affaires qui circule sur Fifth Avenue, sur Park Avenue aussi bien que sur Broadway. Le vêtement sport sied à ravir à sa silhouette élancée et gracieuse, et s'adapte à sa vie active. La robe américaine est simple et du genre fourreau, excentrique et théâtrale quelquefois, mais avant tout pratique. Ingénieux, ses couturiers transforment une petite robe de rue en robe bain de soleil; avec un ruban de brocard, des perles ou de

brillants accessoires, ils en font une robe habillée que l'ouvrière, aussi bien que la femme du monde, peut se procurer. Malheureusement, les créations américaines, taillées rapidement et en grande quantité, ne durent que l'espace d'une saison. La New-Yorkaise est toujours à la recherche d'un arrangement nouveau, d'une décoration différente, d'une fantaisie originale qui mettront en valeur son charme. ('À New-York' 10)

Depuis des siècles, Paris est considéré comme le centre de la haute couture. Ce qui fascine dans la mode parisienne, c'est cette ligne du couturier-créateur, c'est un drapé savant qui épouse la taille, c'est un mouvement qui donne une allure royale, c'est la grâce d'une épaule arrondie, c'est un décolleté coquet et indiscret; c'est le charme séduisant du couturier-décorateur qui joue avec les couleurs; c'est l'ingéniosité du sculpteur qui drape et fait jaillir de ses doigts la coiffure idéale; ce sont les doigts patients et habiles des midinettes qui travaillent amoureusement à la réalisation de ces rêves tant caressés. (11)

The divergence between New York and Paris designs and modes of production emerges not only through the content of the two texts, but also through the contrasting prose styles. The practicality, activity, and professional efficiency of the New Yorker are presented in a series of short, concrete statements, while the languorous elegance of the Parisienne is evoked through a single, slow-moving sentence, which piles up clauses as if to emphasise the tendency towards excess in the Frenchwoman's allurements. The account of American modishness contains plenty of specific detail, while the description of Paris haute couture remains deliberately vague, implying that its fascination cannot quite be captured in words. One effect of this is to present French chic as more enduring and less tied to a specific moment in time, in contrast to the quick-changing 'looks' seen on the New York street. This difference is explicitly connected to the American mass production of cheap clothes, as opposed to the handcrafting of individual garments at the French couture houses. The reference to the dress which both the society woman and the factory worker in the US could wear suggests anxiety about the way that these universalised fashions might erase social differences. The eroticisation of the labour of French seamstresses ('midinettes') is slightly disturbing, but the emphasis on their loving labours is consonant with the French-Canadian support for the Parisian industry following the war.[12]

---

[12] In Anglophone Canada, and in the US, attitudes were ambivalent. As Palmer explains: 'After the liberation, news that the haute-couture industry had not only continued during the war but that designs had been lavish, along with rumours of

While *La Revue Populaire* clearly privileges French over American fashion in this piece, it also acknowledges the attractions of New York style. Texts and illustrations alike imply that the two different approaches to dressing might allow Canadian women to try out different models of femininity. Most of the women in the five photographs showing New York outfits are looking either outwards towards the viewer, or downwards at their own bodies. On the opposite page, there is just one photograph, showing a Frenchwoman in a rural setting, together with two hand-drawn illustrations in a soft romantic idiom. All three women are gazing off into the distance, their eyes closed or shaded, and the contrast with the direct, challenging gaze of the New York girls is striking.

During the decade following the war, fashion coverage in *La Revue Populaire* oscillated between Paris and New York,[13] but from the mid-1950s the magazine, along with the other mainstream titles, began to take notice of Canadian designers. In November 1955, the first of several fashion reports titled 'La mode de Paris, New-York et Montréal' appeared (10), while the August 1956 issue contained a piece entitled 'La mode canadienne existe' (15). By April 1958, *La Revue Populaire* was asking on its cover: 'La mode printemps-été: quoi de neuf à Montréal, Paris, New-York, Hollywood?' This issue contains a series of articles beginning with Odette Oligny's account of the new collections from the best Montreal designers. On the following pages, Lucette Beauchemin reports on New York Fashion Week, Jacqueline Conrad on the Paris openings, and Louise Gilbert-Sauvage on Hollywood fashion innovations, which were just beginning to attract widespread interest. Amusingly, Oligny starts with an account of the popularity of the 'robe-sac,' a loose straight short shift dress, and Beauchemin places this item as the first of her four headlines, while Conrad begins: 'La robe-sac a fait son temps et nous ne verrons plus cette ligne inesthétique' (Conrad, 'A Paris'). This tends to reinforce the conventional model of North American fashion following leads from Paris, and therefore always slightly behindhand. Yet, the prioritisation of Oligny's contribution, and the placing of Montreal first in the list of cities on the cover, reveals a growing tendency to celebrate Canadian design.

This was partly a result of the establishment of the Association for Canadian Couturiers in 1954. Its inaugural show was presented in Canadian cities and in

---

collaboration with the Germans, caused shockwaves in the international fashion world. Canadians had supported the French by food rationing and restrictions on clothing and textiles, only to discover that the luxury and opulence of haute couture had continued' (*Couture* 19).

[13] See for instance coverage of designs from the New York Dress Institute in August 1949, September 1950, and September 1951.

New York; the second show, in 1955, travelled from Montreal to Milan, Paris, and Brussels. In July 1955, the *Canadian Home Journal* published photographs of the clothes which had been exhibited in Europe, and the fashion editor wrote:

> Look long at the stunning fashions on these pages. Would you be happy to wear them? Would you know at a glance where they were made—or by whom? [...] Yet because of an adolescent quality of Canadian thinking that tends to believe other nations create things better than we, there are women who would pass up such fashions if they knew they were Canadian designs, and choose the costume with the New York, London, or Paris label. (Thornton, 'At last' 14)

Palmer comments on this piece: 'The article admonished Canadian women who did not support Canadian design. However, the magazine ran the feature only after the couturiers had been shown in New York and Europe, which showed that the editors were as culpable as their readers' ('Association' 95). She explains that the primary aim of the European shows was not so much to open up foreign markets for Canadian fashion and textiles, but to generate prestige for the industry at home (94). In the magazines' fashion coverage from this era, cultural nationalist discourses are legible in at least three ways: first, in the direct advocacy of Canadian goods, seen in Thornton's commentary; second, in the effort to differentiate Canadian style from American, French, and British trends; and third, in the persistent association of Canadian fashion with mobility and modernity.

Eccentricity, difficulty, expertise

The relationship between fashion and the modern began to be theorised in the later nineteenth century, and is an important focus of current research in both modernist studies and the history of dress. Ilya Parkins and Elizabeth Sheehan offer a lucid summary in the introduction to their collection *Cultures of Femininity in Modern Fashion* (2011): 'fashion is intertwined with many of the changes that have come to define modernity—from the rise of mass production and consumption to the proliferation of popular media and visual culture' (3). In critical accounts published from the later nineteenth century onwards, fashion has been theorised as 'exemplary of the modern' (Parkins and Sheehan 3), partly because of its emphasis on change and on the self in process, and partly because of its foregrounding of tensions between individualism and conformity, and between nostalgia and the desire for the new.[14]

These tensions and emphases are clearly legible in editorial and advertising content in mainstream Canadian magazines. A 1928 'Shops of Mayfair in Hamilton' page includes an advertorial text entitled 'Are you hard to please?':

> So are most well dressed women. They refuse to accept some smattering designer's idea of chic. With them the bizarre, the ridiculous is taboo. They know good style at a glance. They will not be hoodwinked into choosing some freakish frock or extreme hat. They demand sophisticated chic ... styles of the moment ... correct to the last thread. They demand even more ... individuality. They insist on being smart, yet different. In other words, they are out for the exclusive and they are willing to pay for it. These are the women to whom Mayfair shops cater. If you are hard to please, you will be more than pleased at the Mayfair shops. ('Shops of Mayfair in Hamilton')

This dynamic between difference and conformity, creativity and correctness is frequently evident in texts such as this. The notion of 'good style' is presented in this paragraph as something consensual, recognisable, yet achievable only by an elite who possess both taste and money. The word 'correct' partially aligns fashion with etiquette, an arcane yet largely arbitrary system which functions to exclude those without the proper training and credentials.[15] This is balanced against an emphasis on individuality—a move typical of fashion writing in many contexts, and one which attempts to conceal a 'contradiction between the values of etiquette and those of fashion' (Gill 44). In *Eccentricity and the Cultural Imagination in Nineteenth-Century Paris* (2009), Miranda

---

[14] Among the canonical accounts are Baudelaire's 'The Painter of Modern Life' (1863); Sombart's *Economy and Fashion* (1902); Simmel's essays, particularly 'The Philosophy of Fashion' (1905); the sections on fashion in Benjamin's *The Arcades Project*, originally written in the 1920s and 1930s; and, more recently, Bourdieu's chapter 'La Haute Couture et la Haute Culture' in his *Questions de Sociologie* (1980), together with Wilson's *Adorned in Dreams: Fashion and Modernity* (1985).

[15] Quentin Bell, in *On Human Finery* (1947), finds a more explicitly moral resonance in this term: 'It is difficult in praising clothes not to use adjectives such as "right," "good," "correct," "unacceptable" or "faultless," which belong properly to the discussion of conduct, while in discussing moral shortcomings we tend very naturally to fall into the language of dress and speak of a person's behaviour as being shabby, shoddy, threadbare, down at heel, botched or slipshod' (14).

Gill provides a prehistory for our analysis of responses to twentieth-century Parisian fashions. She explains: 'Etiquette represented tradition and stability, necessitating the effacement of the self in the interests of social cohesion. Fashion, in contrast, represented the cult of novelty' (44). Gill points out that the semantic associations of eccentricity include creativity as well as pathology, and that therefore, in the context of nineteenth-century France: 'The violation of collective norms could result in either ostracism or praise, depending on whether it was interpreted as an embarrassing social lapse or the self-conscious inauguration of a new style' (43–44). In a twentieth-century context, nothing so severe as 'ostracism' was likely to result from fashion excesses, yet the passage from 'Shops of Mayfair in Hamilton' does use the words 'taboo' and 'freakish.' And the most extreme Paris trends are explicitly rejected in all the magazines. A 1922 'Modes de Paris' report in *La Revue Moderne* deplored the excesses of some recently abandoned trends: 'On a renoncé presque définitivement aux essais de ballonnement, d'élargissement que l'on tente sans succès à chaque changement de saison, modes adoptées seulement des femmes qui se font une loi d'accepter, les yeux fermés, tout ce qui paraît de nouveau, tout ce qui revêt un cachet d'excentricité absurde' (Micheline). Traces remain of the pathological associations that, as Gill points out, attached to 'eccentricity' in the nineteenth century,[16] and this is perhaps why the Canadian fashion writers insisted so strongly on the difference between distinctive and eccentric style.

Yet the fashion system operates by normalising deviance. As Georg Simmel observes: 'Every growth of a fashion drives it to its doom, because it cancels out its distinctiveness' (192). Simmel was one of the theorists who influenced Pierre Bourdieu's powerful theories of class, taste, and cultural production. Bourdieu's now familiar argument is that the aspirational dimension of middlebrow culture—the desire to be distinguished—results in a constant pursuit of new qualities and new things which your competitors have not yet acquired (*Distinction* 251–52). It makes sense to connect early twentieth-century fashion writing with the middlebrow because of the shared emphasis on activity, attentiveness, learning, and self-fashioning. The magazines insisted that achieving distinction without slipping into the bizarre required both effort and intelligence. This, of course, was a strategy for selling more copies by persuading readers that they needed expert guidance, not only from journalists but also from advertisers. Indeed, the copywriters' style, especially in the interwar years, was closely related to that of the fashion correspondents. In

---

[16] See her discussion of fairground freaks and their influence on journalism and visual culture (27; 132–41).

March 1930, *Chatelaine* ran an advertisement for Canadian Celanese which read:

> When you were thinking of Hallowe'en and St. Andrew's Ball, our stylists were studying the signs of the fashion trend for Spring. Cables from the Paris ateliers, indicating the mode made ready for 'The Season' on the sunny Riviera ... Advice from Celanese House, Hanover Square, recording the style decisions of the smart English woman en route for the early Southern spring ... Rapid notes, from our New York stylists, of the Palm Beach mode, forewarning of Fashion's choice for the coming season ...

This copy has overtones of a weather report, suggesting that the company's stylists are uniquely equipped to read the signs and portents relating to new styles. But it also constructs fashion as a 'study,' requiring specialist 'advice' and 'notes.' Thrift might also be an element—for instance, a colourful Canadian Celanese advertisement in *La Revue Moderne* for March 1931 offered 'Tissus riches et luxueux, d'apparence beaucoup plus coûteuse que le prix que vous payez.' The magazines present fashionability as something requiring constant application and vigilance, as well as careful budgeting and strategic expenditure.

The idea of fashion as a serious and sometimes challenging subject is continually reiterated, even though there was a spectrum of tones, from *Mayfair*'s celebration of the pleasure and spectacle of fashion, to the women's magazines' rather stolidly practical information on the required alterations to hemlines for each season. Imported French styles, in particular, seemed to require interpretation for a Canadian audience. The headline of a fashion page in the March 1931 *Chatelaine*—'Translating the Paris Mode in Patterns of Canadian Make'—is indicative. In this respect, the women's magazines inherited a function which had previously been fulfilled mainly by the daily press.[17] Barbara Freeman says of the women's page columnists in 1890s Toronto:

> women of all classes looked to them for sophisticated guidance and leadership on the variety of styles and choices they could wear. [...] Their role was to translate for their readers, sometimes literally, the finer points of high style, making it accessible, affordable, and locally available. In one of her columns, for example, Faith [Fenton of the

---

[17] There were also, of course, earlier magazines in Canada which covered fashion. For example, the Toronto *Anglo-American* (1852–55), included the oddly named 'Mrs Grundy's Gathering' fashion column.

Toronto Empire] explained a number of fashion terms, most of them French, for the benefit of her less worldly readers, who were no doubt grateful to learn that a 'filet' was not fish or steak, but a waistcoat or vest, and that 'suivez-moi' was not an enticing invitation but the falling ends of ribbons. (301)

The notion of foreign fashions as 'difficult' from the point of view of an ordinary Canadian woman persisted in later decades. Mary Wyndham wrote in the June 1928 *Chatelaine*:

In truth never were the fashions so full of pitfalls for the unwary as now. It is decidedly more difficult to be well-dressed this season than it was last, for instance. I do not mean just *suitably* dressed, but dressed suitably and in the movement. Almost anyone could be smart when frocks were simple, unadorned tubes. [...] With all this new drapery and 'drippery' and so many unsuccessful essays to change the silhouette signed and sent out by the Great Ones, it is the easiest matter in the world to go wrong; I mean for those who follow the fashions like sheep. The woman with a feeling for clothes always knows how to adopt the styles which suit her. (32)

This letter flatters the reader, encouraging her to believe that she is among the few with a real 'feeling for clothes,' but at the same time implying that nearly all women require advice on fashion. 'Colors present many pitfalls even to the sophisticated,' noted Mary McNulty Fix in *Chatelaine* in 1933 (34).

In general terms, the middlebrow magazines which are the focus of this study sold themselves on the basis of the expert knowledge of their contributors in areas such as dress, interiors, health and beauty, cookery, domestic economy, reading, and shopping. They increasingly organised their contents into departments, just as large shops had begun to do: indeed, the rise of the department store coincided with the golden age of the mass-market magazine in Britain and America. Aynsley and Forde point to the shared etymology of magazine and the French 'magasin,' noting that both were sites of consumption 'dependent on accumulation, diversity and distraction' (Introduction 2).[18] In the field of periodical publishing, the move from the miscellaneous accumulation of curious or eye-catching items to issues organised into specialised departments anticipated a broader shift, in the field of periodical publishing, from the generalist to the special-interest magazine. There was also a clear parallel with

---

[18] See also Belisle on Canadian department stores.

the rise of book clubs, evening classes, and other self-improvement activities. Just as the guidance of expert literary critics was welcomed by book club members trying to select from amongst the mass of available reading material,[19] so the guidance of experts in dress was welcomed by women consumers faced with an increasingly wide array of ready-made clothes, fabrics, styles, and 'looks' to choose from.

As well as revealing the participation of fashion and fashion journalism in upwardly mobile middlebrow culture, discourses of expertise and difficulty also suggest a certain convergence between fashion and modernism. In *Modernism, Mass Culture, and Professionalism* (1993), Thomas Strychacz discusses the resemblances between modernists and professionals in terms of a shared attempt to demarcate a space apart from the mass market, while Lois Cucullu in *Expert Modernists, Matricide and Modern Culture* (2004) argues that 'literary modernism's extraordinary designs on redefining the modern imaginary and reshaping quotidian experience may be better understood situated within the broader movement of expert culture' (7). Literary modernism, she suggests, obeyed a similar logic to that of the various scientific and professional 'disciplines' which were formalising themselves during the same period, in order to consolidate the value of their areas of knowledge and the status of their practitioners as specialists. The convergence of fashion and modernism happened not only on the terrain of expert culture, but also on the physical sites of Paris and New York, centres of both international fashion and international modernism, as well as on the pages of magazines. Although haute couture was the form of high culture which most appealed to these magazines, modern art also received attention, particularly from the Francophone magazines. As Saint-Jacques and Robert note in their account of responses to modernism in Quebec's print culture: 'c'est surtout avec Jean Chauvin à *La Revue Populaire* et Henri Girard à *La Revue Moderne*, à partir de 1926 et de 1928, qu'un discours ouvert à l'art moderne et aux courants internationaux émerge' (61). But whilst couture and modernist visual or stage art could be mutually nourishing, it was also true that fashion, with its developing language of specialisation and its aspiration to the status of art, was a threat to modernism. Arguably, it is precisely because fashion was so intimately connected with middlebrow practices of imitation and commodification that an association with fashion could be perceived as trivialising the serious aims of modernist art.[20]

---

[19] For the pioneering studies of this phenomenon, see Radway; Rubin.

[20] This spills over into present-day academic discourse. Wilson engages with debates about the intellectual value of studying fashion (see especially the introduction and third chapter).

Leonard Diepeveen's *The Difficulties of Modernism* (2003) is illuminating here. The book offers an account of the debates which played out in the early to mid-twentieth century between those who felt excluded by difficult art and those who attempted to justify difficulty as a necessary condition of artistic innovation. Diepeveen's focus is on difficulty as an experience, 'a recurring *relationship* that came into being between modernist works and their audiences' (xi). In the chapter 'Difficulty as Fashion' he argues:

> Defenders of modern difficulty quickly distinguished difficult modernism from the newness of fashion and its accompanying insincerity. [...] But modernism's apologists, in response, did not hold on to newness as a virtue in and of itself. First, they distanced themselves from romantic valuations of newness, which conceptualized it as personal originality and uniqueness. They recalibrated it by exploring whether this difficult newness was something more than fashion or even original self-expression, whether it had a direction that could give it value or even make it *necessary*. Modern newness, then, was not so much about personal originality as it was about aesthetic *development*; modernism was difficult because difficulty often accompanied important *developments* in art. (114)

Evidently, modernism's 'apologists' sought to invest modernist art with a purposeful forward momentum which would separate it from the cyclical movements of fashion. This separation might appear rather difficult to sustain, since both modernism and fashion seek the new and distinctive whilst continually returning to the past for inspiration: 'Emprunté au passé pour embellir le présent,' as a headline on a page of dress patterns in *La Revue Moderne* put it in December 1931 ('Emprunté'). But while the recursive movements of fashion are openly acknowledged, the modernists' extensive borrowings from past styles and referencing of ancient sources are partially concealed by the dominant narrative of modernism as a break with the past and a response to a chaotic twentieth-century world.

Novelty, originality, modernity

The fashion columns analysed above undoubtedly, in Diepeveen's terms, celebrate 'newness as a virtue in and of itself.' Such appropriations of the new into commercial discourse arguably tended to devalue newness in the eyes of late modernist artists and writers, but this is rather beyond the scope of the present discussion.[21] It is important, though, to explore the particular shapes which the idea of 'the new' took on in the Canadian magazines. *Chatelaine*'s Paris letters provide rich material. In the magazine's early years, the dispatches were sent by sea and appeared several months after they were written—in the October 1929 number, Einna's letter is dated '*ce mois d'août*,' and begins: 'I am almost neglecting you, as I have missed three mails already, and this letter should be bobbing on the high seas en route for Canada' (11). This strikingly emphasises the slow travel of news across the Atlantic, a delay which gives the new fashions increased allure for the Canadian market. The whirl of life in Paris is starkly contrasted with the supposedly marginalised, half-forgotten world of Canada: In the letter published in August 1929, Einna rather smugly emphasises her own privileged position as a Paris resident:

> I am perhaps giving you very advanced information here, because the hat I have just described will not actually be on the market until the first bright snappy days of autumn appear, although we in Paris will be able to buy them long ere then. […] I have told you of some of the bewitching new things I have seen here in suits, hats, scarves, bags. Now let us consider the new fabric weaves in wools. They are ravishing! […] they exploit a subtle combination of color and verve to achieve new delights. (21)

The insistent repetition of 'new' (and related words such as 'advanced') is typical of *Chatelaine*'s fashion reports. The piece also mentions travel five times; for example, Einna notes: 'This is an outfit that one could wear at practically any time when *en voyage, en voiture ou chez soi*' (21). The insertion of French phrases presents the columnist as cosmopolitan, whilst also flattering the reader through the assumption that she will understand.

Newness did not mean simply being up to date; it was also constructed in terms of 'personal originality and uniqueness' (as Diepeveen puts it). This could be invested in the designer, the dressmaker, or the wearer. Eustella Burke brings together all three in her account of the creative process in *Chatelaine*'s January 1931 Paris letter. She begins: 'The Paris collections always give me little thrills of pleasure. Not because the models are so startling … there are always a few

---

[21] As Hindrichs argues: 'The "new" that underwrote high modernism had become by the thirties and forties impossible or repugnant (co-opted by late capitalist discourse or complicit with the destructive forces of imperialism).' She adds: 'the same perceived threat—the obsolescence of an authentic newness and their own belatedness—informs the poetics of these younger generation late modernists' (850).

highly dramatic ones in every collection ... rather it is because the majority are very simple' (4). (Again, that preference for the plainer, more wearable designs rather than the outré ones.) The letter continues:

> I see a frock so lovely that it takes the breath away. The next reaction is, 'How very simple, but whoever would have thought of using the materials and colors just that way?' Undoubtedly, no one but a French dressmaker.
> Recognizing them as the most skilful designers and cutters in the world, yet it is originality that particularly distinguishes their models, originality that uses and combines materials and colors fearlessly, and trims and finishes them with the same courage and good taste.
> As collection after collection of the mid-season openings passed by, I was convinced that the Canadian woman who has mastered scissors and sewing machine, and who keeps an eye on Paris, has everything at her fingertips that is necessary to be smart. (4)

Although Burke describes models by Lanvin, Patou, Vionnet, and Worth, most of her space is given over to a practical account of the materials and techniques required to make versions of these dresses. The strapline to the piece is: 'Making Original Frocks From Paris Inspirations—[...] *The Chatelaine*'s special correspondent abroad gives some valuable suggestions for interpreting the mid-winter mode' (5). This piece shows up the tension between originality and imitation in the practice of home dressmaking. Patterns encourage a woman to be creative, making her own clothes and adapting them to her figure and style. At the same time, they appeal to the desire to own a replica of a model presented on a faraway catwalk. Burke gives instructions for women to follow, yet her words 'original' and 'interpreting' construct an implied reader who is not simply following fashions but actively engaging with them. This, in fact, becomes an aspect of the narrative of effortful self-improvement which the magazines continually reiterated. In addition to projecting personal identity through imaginative adaptation of adapting Paris styles, Burke's reader is invited to collaborate in the production of national identity. She is encouraged to take inspiration from the famed creativity of the French, for which haute couture often functioned as a sign in nationalist discourse. As fashion scholar Kate Best points out, the interwar years were dominated by a 'paradigm of Couture as High Art and more importantly, French High Culture.'

Best argues, further, that: 'This cultural model was produced through textual and iconographic links with surrealism, as well as the emergence of fashion photography and the illustrations of those such as Erté as an art form.'

Her reference to links between fashion and surrealism directs us to the designer Elsa Schiaparelli, a figure who apparently fascinated the North American fashion world. In the Canadian magazines, she was presented as an exemplar of originality, or, in more conservative accounts, of perversity. Schiaparelli began her famous collaborations with surrealist artists in the later part of the 1930s,[22] but even before this she was being presented as a modernist and an artist herself. In 1932, Janet Flanner, Paris correspondent for *The New Yorker*, remarked that 'a frock from Schiaparelli ranks like a modern canvas in boudoirs determined to be "à la page"' (20). Moving repeatedly between France and America, the Italian-born Schiaparelli had become an icon of transatlantic exchange and cosmopolitan style. The Canadian magazines exhibited her designs right from the early stages of her career, commented extensively on her Paris openings, and profiled the designer herself.[23] In these accounts, Canadian responses to modernism, and to modern aesthetics, seemed to crystallise.

Mary Wyndham, in the 'Paris Letter' for *Chatelaine* in February 1934, reveals a certain cautiousness about avant-garde design:

> Schiaparelli's spring silhouette is quite different from that of everybody else. First, she's put all her shoulders back again into boxes. [...] The Schiaparelli waistline is almost 'wasp' in circumference. Her reason for "boxing" shoulders is to balance the width of her flared hemlines, in case anyone reproaches her on the subject. All the same, Schiaparelli or no Schiaparelli, I wouldn't go in for squared shoulder effects on my new spring coat or tailleur. (33)

It was rare for any of the Canadian magazines to reject an entire season's offerings by any of the leading Paris couturiers. It is interesting that it is this

---

[22] Her collaborative work was undertaken primarily between 1936 and 1939. Schiaparelli's work is now more likely than that of most other designers to be considered as art, and included in exhibitions and museum collections which are not focused on fashion. For example, her shoe hat, her 'Tear' and 'Skeleton' dresses, and the 'bird cage' from her Paris salon, were included in the 2007 'Surreal Things' exhibition at the V&A, London (see Wood). For studies of Schiaparelli, fashion and art, see Evans; Parkins.

[23] Schiaparelli presented her first collection in her apartment in 1927; *The Chatelaine* included photographs of her models in some of its earliest Paris letters, such as Wyndham's 'Paris Patter' in February 1929. Among the examples of written accounts are *La Revue Populaire*'s report on her 1940 lecture tour ('Madame') and its profile of her in 1955 (Rochère). *La Revue Moderne* cited her as an authority on health and elegance in 1934 ('Plaisir').

FASHIONS

particular designer, among the most adventurous of the period and the one who became most closely associated with modernism in the visual arts, who is singled out in this way. Intriguingly, Kay Murphy's 'Fashion Shorts,' which appears just underneath the 'Paris Letter' in this issue, offers a totally different perspective on the same designer:

> Then there's the Storm Blown Silhouette—Schiaparelli's newest contribution to this year of grace. I slipped on one of her coats, and did I feel like a leaf in the wind! Very soignée, and makes you think of Diana out with her hounds. This silhouette is front-blown for daytime, and back-blown for evening: and, of course, always streamline in effect. (Kathleen Murphy 35)

It is perhaps to be expected that Murphy, the magazine's recently appointed New York fashion reporter, would be an admirer of Schiaparelli while Wyndham, the seasoned Paris correspondent, would not. Schiaparelli was associated with 'the Young School in Paris dressmaking' (Flanner 19), and was perceived to combine Old World and New World influences. She had spent time in the US during the war (and had extended her lecture tour to include Montreal), and her aesthetic had been influenced by this experience: as Flanner comments in her profile of the designer: 'one of the explanations of her phenomenal success here was the un-European modernity of her silhouettes, and their special applicability to a background of square-shouldered skyscrapers' (20).

The juxtaposition of Wyndham's report with Murphy's exemplifies one of the ways in which *Chatelaine* exhibits the fundamental ambivalence of middlebrow culture. If the magazine is taken as a whole—that is, a collaborative text with multiple authors—it demonstrates an easy familiarity with the modern and the radical (here, in the form of Schiaparelli) and reports on it in detail. Broken down into its individual articles, *Chatelaine* offers a range of perspectives: Wyndham's distrust of extravagantly experimental fashions corresponds to the middlebrow attachment to tradition and suspicion of modernist posturing, while Murphy's admiration for the new streamlined silhouette exhibits a fascination with modern innovation which is equally characteristic of the middlebrow. In general terms, magazines with middlebrow affiliations may be productively analysed in terms of this balancing between aspiration to the modern and retreat from it.[24]

Mayfair, socially conservative in its reinscription of the rituals of a privileged

---

[24] Here, we build on earlier definitions offered in Hammill, *Women, Celebrity* 9–13 and *Sophistication* 113–29.

elite, was nevertheless, in design terms, by far the most modern of the six magazines, and it was the most receptive to Schiaparelli, reporting with unqualified enthusiasm on her designs of the mid-1930s. One unsigned caption in the April 1935 issue read:

> Spectacular and sensational is Schiaparelli's Celestial silhouette, with its Hindu swathing moulding the figure in soft spiral folds, narrow below the knees, but revealing the full curve of hips and bust, with an Ihram's scarf draped over head and shoulders. [...] Despite the prevalence of gores and pleats elsewhere, by day Schiaparelli unconventionally adheres to her straight, pencil-slim skirts of normal length. [...] There is a [...] glazed floral chintz called Garden of Eden—a dizzy kaleidoscope of the earth's flora. Fabrics are characteristic of Schiaparelli—Dervish tulles, stiffened and printed with bold patterns; Ramadan satins, heavy and double-faced; Ballila hemps from Italy. ('Schiaparelli')

This passage, like Wyndham's account, emphasises Schiaparelli's difference, but frames it as creative originality rather than bizarre aberration. The spectacular quality of the designs moves them towards the status of art works, and the new silhouette is described in terms suggesting a statue. The other keynote of this passage is the exotic—her foreign fabrics, lavish natural imagery, and bold patterns align her with the primitivism of some modernist visual artists. The strongly Orientalist idiom of Schiaparelli's designs may be connected to broader tendencies in modernist cultural production: as Steven Yao notes, modernism 'both in part arose from and developed some of its most distinctive features specifically through a sustained, if decidedly uneven, engagement with the Asian "Orient"' (3). For Schiaparelli, there was also a personal dimension: she acknowledged a lifelong fascination with 'eastern things,' deriving from the work of her father, Celestino Schiaparelli, a specialist in Arabic and Islamic literature (see Tredway 90).

The following month, *Mayfair* reported on Schiaparelli's London opening:

> Wax flowers are a delightful caprice of Schiaparelli who bunches white jasmin boldly forward on a black tulle bonnet with a wisp of veil whiffing off the back. [...] The Hindu drapery of her evening saris is apparent in Schiaparelli's afternoon frock of carbon blue woollen. Draped spirally, it is shorter in front, with a sweeping cape extending over the shoulders in an unbroken harmony of line. The hat in dark blue straw marches briskly forward with the side looped up by a cord. At right: Schiaparelli's

amusing bell-hop jacket in beige woollen is whipped on over a blouse in beige and burgundy. ('Schiaparelli' May 1935)

This time, the designer's modernity is captured through a discourse of mobility and progress. There are a lot of present participles, and suggestions of rapid motion—'whiffing,' 'whipped,' and 'marching briskly forward.' Again, a vocabulary of art criticism is evoked in the reference to harmony of line. The term 'amusing,' as Christopher Reed explains in his article on British *Vogue* in the 1920s, derives from a ubiquitous contemporary usage: 'Like *fashion* or *youth*—two closely related terms in *Vogue*'s lexicon—the criterion of amusement privileged an attitude of transient delight over claims to timeless or essential verities' (383). Reed elaborates on his notion of the 'amusing style' in his book *Bloomsbury Rooms* (2004), relating it to the interior décor and fashion choices of the Bloomsbury group, the Sitwells and their associates. Thus we see *Mayfair*'s own aspirations to both modernity and cultural prestige, and the way that it appropriates modern art into the arena of the fashionable. Indeed, many illustrations in this magazine reveal the way that fashion laid claim to the modern, even to modernism. The May 1928 issue, for instance, featured a page entitled 'Modernistic notes of chic,' showing drawings of scent bottles, scarves, and handbags with abstract designs, sunbursts, and streamlined shapes. This is quite an early use of the word 'modernistic'—the first citation in the Oxford English Dictionary dates from 1927. It is especially interesting to see the word appearing so early in a non-modernist venue, and being applied to the more saleable type of modern design, art deco.[25]

Mayfair aligns itself with the middlebrow by joining haute couture to high culture, presenting fashion itself as art by commenting on it alongside other art forms. This approach constructs fashionability as an imperative to 'keep up,' not merely with the trends in dress but with cultural developments in a broad sense. *Mayfair*'s Soiffield was amongst those who included direct references to modernist art and performance in his fashion columns:

To start with, I saw Anton Dolin and Nemchinova at the new and truly gorgeous Salle Pleyel. I was there the night before as well, to hear 'Le

---

[25] In later decades, the influence of modernist art on fashion illustration became more marked as the visual repertoire of modernism became part of the resources available to commercial artists. Bosnitch, in her account of the new style of fashion illustration developed in the 1950s by three artists working for Eaton's of Montreal, notes that they 'borrowed techniques from the Impressionists (pointillism), the Symbolists (mosaics and ornamental pattern), and the Cubists (collage)' (348).

> Prince Igor' given by the Russian Opera Society. Truly, I have never seen such gorgeously gowned women anywhere outside a dress show. The foyer during the entr'acte was a-glitter with diamonds (some real; others artificial, but 'chic' all the same because *c'est la mode*) ... Nemchinova was, as usual, too delightful. One so often wonders why she severed connection with the great Daghlieff ... ('In Paris' 19)

In Soiffield's writing, fashion is not a practical preoccupation of middle-class women, but a site of fantasy. In his dizzying movements from Russian ballet and opera to jewellery and furs, we can also see the influence of Kate Best's 'paradigm of Couture as High Art.' Reiterating the link between high culture and haute couture, the magic names of the top Paris designers functioned in the same way as the 'imprimatur' of modernist authorship, which is defined by Aaron Jaffe as the 'sense [...] that the modernist literary object bears the stylistic stamp of its producer prominently' (20). The relevance of this to haute couture becomes clear in his comment: 'Imprimaturs sanction elite, high cultural consumption in times when economies of mass cultural value predominate' (20). The institutions of modernism invest the modernist artwork with a value which increases with its rarity and which depends on a rarefied appeal to a select audience. Similarly, the Paris couture system locates individual designers on a scale of value which is inversely proportional to the availability and public visibility of their products. Soiffield enthused in *Mayfair* in 1928:

> I ran in and looked at Caroline Reboux's exclusive collection of hats the other afternoon. I say *exclusive* because anything coming from Reboux on the rue de la Paix is stamped with that distinction. But their exclusiveness goes even further, as Madame Reboux will have neither photographs nor sketches of her models. However, I shall endeavor to give you a pen picture, because as I have said they are exclusive and really worth talking about. ('Paris Swathed' 22)

This brings questions of authorship and originality clearly into focus: the value of the designer's 'signature' is upheld through Soiffield's strategy of trading on the value of his own signature, and this in turn derives from his privileged access to the 'exclusive' spaces of Paris, and his ability to replace the prohibited illustration with a skilful 'pen picture.' The importance of fashion *writing* is therefore endorsed. Soiffield's address to his Canadian readers draws them partially into the charmed circle, whilst reminding them—by their inability to see the hats for themselves—that they are dependent on him for access to the most valuable knowledge.

Elizabeth Outka, in her study of the marketing of authenticity in the early twentieth century, argues that:

> what I term the 'originary authentic,' equated authenticity with the original or the one-of-a-kind, something that was not a copy and was not derived from previous traditions. The mystique of the originary object had long been felt, but the turn of the century saw its rapid emergence as a powerful advertising strategy. [...] The originary authentic was in part defined by and valued for its alleged separation from the mass market, and it was likewise aggressively marketed in what are now familiar strategies: appeals to the coterie, to high fashion, to the limited edition. Part of the originary's allure was its evocation of the prototype [...] the authenticity that was evoked was one of novelty, of being the first, the cutting edge, the new. [...] The power of selling the originary authentic lay in its paradoxical promise: middle-class consumers might (allegedly) have both the genuine article and something that they could easily purchase, both the exclusive and the accessible, the original and the perfect reproduction. (9–10)

Whilst Outka is not talking about magazines, her account seems to describe exactly what is happening in the passage just quoted from *Mayfair*, and more broadly in the fashion articles in these aspirational Canadian magazines in the interwar years. The coterie appeal of Madame Reboux's hats derives from their 'originary' status: that is, their unavailability for purchase, or even viewing, by mass audiences. The implication of such marketing strategies is that originality will somehow be transferred from the designer of the clothes or hats to the woman who has the imagination and the means to buy and wear them. In many of the fashion features analysed in this chapter, the resistance to mass production, which is of course a hallmark of modernist rhetoric, is directly echoed. Yet the magazines insist that the woman who wants an individual, non-reproducible 'signature' on her look will achieve this not by eschewing the marketplace but by operating cannily within it: that is, by shopping intelligently and thinking analytically about clothes, and by keeping ahead of mass fashion trends. In disseminating news of the Paris fashions to a wide, middle-class Canadian audience, the magazines participate in the kind of imposture Outka describes: upholding the mystique of Paris style by suggesting that it is unobtainable, yet covertly offering it for sale via couture copies, dress patterns, and local shops in Kingston or Hamilton.

Conclusion

In her influential *Adorned in Dreams: Fashion and Modernity*, originally published in 1985, Elizabeth Wilson writes:

> In the twentieth century fashion, without losing its obsession with the new and different, with change and exclusivity, has been mass-produced. The mass production of fashionable styles—itself highly contradictory—links the politics of fashion to fashion as art. It is connected both to the evolution of styles that circulate in 'high' and avant-garde art; and to popular culture and taste. (8)

The territory where high and popular culture meet, and where art encounters consumerism, is the middlebrow. The magazines explored in this book encompass a broad cross-section of cultural and commercial production. They publish, sell, or comment on products from opera to romance fiction, haute couture originals to department store bargains. Since the shift to mass production which Wilson describes took place over the period covered by our study, it is not surprising that the Canadian magazines present a range of responses to the changing fashion industry, and exhibit a clear preoccupation with questions of individuality and imitation, correctness and creativity. Their extensive offerings of dress patterns co-exist with an increasing attention to shopping, and since mass-produced clothes were becoming widely available, home dressmaking was reconfigured as a mode of creativity as opposed to a necessary chore, and also—during wartime especially—as a thrifty, patriotic practice. But whether mass-produced or intended for home production, the clothes illustrated in these magazines are almost invariably based on Paris or New York models. While the shopping and dressmaking guides exhibit a resolutely practical attitude, disseminating the knowledge and skills necessary for the middle-class woman, the fashion reports from foreign cities appeal to readers' fantasies and aspirations, associating the latest outfits with modernity, newness, distinction, and cosmopolitanism.

One of the ways in which the magazines constructed travel as something to aspire to was through the glamorous figures of their fashion correspondents, who addressed stay-at-home readers from a point of view of superior knowledge and experience: '*Mes Chères Chatelaines!*,' writes Einna in a January 1930 dispatch, 'After much travel I am at home again.' (12). For Einna, 'home' is now Paris, the city to which she returns, after visiting several other European destinations, in order to 'write back' to her former home, Canada, about developments at the centre of the fashion world. The couture trade was an international industry, and the study of Canadian fashion reporting reveals a great deal about cultural exchange across the Atlantic and across the 49th parallel. The discourse of fashion became entwined with the discourse of Canadian nationhood through the magazines' fascination with foreign styles, their complex negotiations of shifting relationships with French, British, and American culture, and their ambivalent responses to the incipient Canadian couture industry. Many of the fashion features are interesting in themselves, as pieces of original writing and artwork, and, indeed, the relatively high status of the staff fashion reporters and editors attests to the serious attention given to this subject in the Canadian periodical press. Dress, in Canadian periodicals, was not only a mode of middle-class self-fashioning; it could also be a form of gossip, an outlet for creativity, a nationalist practice, and an exotic tour.

Chapter Four

CONSUMERS

> *Starve to death on our wedding trip. Not another cent in the world ... after all these years of saving ... thirty years and all our talk ... boasting ... And now the first boat back ... and maybe have to wire the bank and everybody know ... and Ma president of the Literary. [sic] Elected over Mrs Chet just because of Europe—They've never forgiven us ... and Chet working beside me in the bank all the rest of my life, with his mean face in mine. And his wife's talk ... They'd laugh us out of town ... and where then? We're getting old ... no one in Shooter must ever know. It would kill us both.*
> —George Pearson, 'Jack-Pots,' *Maclean's* 1925

SUCH are the thoughts of Ed Roman, an elderly bank clerk from Shooter, Saskatchewan, as he wanders the deck of a cruise ship bound for Europe. He has just lost the money that he and his wife, referred to only as 'Ma,' have been saving to pay for a 'wedding trip' that, as Roman nears retirement, the couple can finally afford. Roman's shame over ruining the trip, combined with his fear of the gossip at home that his folly will provoke, have him contemplating suicide—an action that, the narrator bleakly informs us, he 'lack[s] the courage' to take (70). The Romans—their long years of scrimping and saving, their fantasies of how the trip would be, and the ease with which disaster overtakes them—raise questions about the significance of a journey abroad. The short story appeared in the 15 June 1925 issue of *Maclean's*, and its latter pages were positioned within the Travel Section, so that it was framed by advertisements for cruises and hotels that romanticised travel as a 'pilgrimage' (White Star Line), a chance to 'cool off' (Canadian Pacific), or 'trade dull routine […] for zestful enjoyment' (Canadian National). The story thus reveals many cracks in the fantasy of fulfilment that travel companies were keen to generate, offering us a means of exploring the key questions of this chapter: what kinds of consumption, both material and cultural, were fundamental to travel, and what were the perceived benefits of spending money on such things? How did the experience of travel correlate (or not) with the desires inculcated in lavish advertisements published by companies such as Canadian Pacific? How were magazine readers encouraged to imagine themselves into the role of the traveller-consumer, and what made this imagined role so appealing?

The figure of the traveller-consumer

It is striking just how much of the discussion surrounding the figure of the traveller intersects with discussions of shopping. But perhaps this should not surprise us, since travel can be reduced to a series of expenditures: a cruise, railway journey, or road trip; accommodation; dining and drinks; sightseeing and tours; souvenirs and photographs—all have a price tag attached. Moreover, the editorial attention to linking advertisements with non-advertising content generated an apparently natural connection between a variety of activities, travel included, and an overarching consumer ethos. In mainstream Canadian magazines, travel is treated primarily as an opportunity for consumption, and readers were invited to seek pleasure in consumption itself—in learning about different possibilities, and then choosing amongst them—in addition to anticipating what travel offered in terms of potential edification and symbolic capital.

To those readers who lacked the means to travel, magazines offered a vicarious experience of it and, in the process, educated readers about desirable, fashionable locations in which to imagine themselves. The periodicals operated through a logic of exclusion: the reader may not have been entitled to a given experience, such as a trip to Paris, but he or she was able to gaze on it from a distance, and hear rumours of its pleasures, by buying the magazine. The notion of travel was romanticised and simplified in both the advertisements and the editorial material. Clear blue skies over the Louvre, well-dressed passengers on the deck of a cruise ship, delectable menus, and nights at the opera emphasised the highlights of a possible trip, and left out such realities as rain, sea-sickness, or the difficulties of communicating in a foreign language. There are exceptions to this rule, including the story 'Jack-Pots,' but they only throw into relief the overarching representation of travel as glamorous, exciting, and, ultimately, 'a sound investment,' to use the words of *Maclean's* editor H. Napier Moore ('Holiday Dividends'). As far as the magazines were concerned, travel as a form of consumption served one main purpose: self-improvement, whether in the form of socio-economic self-advancement, cultural engagement, or insight into oneself. Madge Macbeth's series on European travel illustrates these themes.

Macbeth, a successful author and well-connected Ottawa socialite, was singled out in early issues of *Mayfair* as an exemplary traveller. She wrote 14 travel features for the periodical. They appeared between 1927 and 1929, and took the reader with her through France, Italy, and Spain. She was not a typical Canadian; rather, she was a typical *Mayfair* figure: she belonged to the literary, political, and economic elite of Canada, and her travel writing reflected her elite associations. To readers less privileged, Macbeth's work is highly suggestive of the relationship between magazines and the middlebrow culture of aspiration: she provided a combination of entertainment and information, and she was engaged with questions of material and cultural consumption throughout the series. To the upwardly mobile reader, she offered a vicarious experience of the best European restaurants, couturiers, and historic sights.

Peggy Kelly discusses Macbeth's engagement with the social elite, noting that she counted 'the wives of two Governors-General (Lady Bessborough and Lady Tweedsmuir)' as her friends (50). Indeed, Macbeth knew the internal politics of Ottawa well enough to satirise them in her 1924 book *The Land of Afternoon*, to be a dinner guest of Prime Minister MacKenzie King when he hosted a papal delegation in 1939, and to be selected to interview diplomats and European aristocrats for *Mayfair* throughout the 1930s. Macbeth's association with *Mayfair* was not, however, derived solely from her social and political connections. By 1927, she was a successful novelist and author, and while she was born into money, most of it had been lost through a series of bad investments by the time she was an adult. Widowed early in her marriage, she supported herself and her two sons entirely through her writing. She published several novels and produced plays for stage and radio, and helped to found the Canadian Authors Association in 1921, becoming its first female president 18 years later. The CAA, however, had by then become associated with a pejorative notion of the middlebrow as antimodernist and sentimental, principally through the contempt expressed by F. R. Scott in his 1927 poem 'The Canadian Authors Meet' (see Irvine, 'Introduction' 1–2). In 1936, Macbeth was photographed by Yousuf Karsh, who would go on to photograph an impressive set of political leaders, celebrities, and artists ranging from Winston Churchill to Audrey Hepburn and Ernest Hemingway. According to a 2006 newspaper article reporting on a new edition of Macbeth's 1926 novel *Shackles*, when the author died at age 86 in 1965, 'she left $800,000, none of it inherited, all of it earned. She also left a house in Sandy Hill, a large Victorian home that had become a social magnet. [...] Macbeth entertained everybody who was anybody' (Kennedy). Despite her status and connections, Macbeth has all but vanished from Canadian literary history because of the ways in which she positioned herself within Canada's literary field while she was alive (Kelly 29–31; Mason

109) and the ways in which the Canadian canon was constructed in the years following her death (Gerson).

The tone of her *Mayfair* features is frothy and ebullient, tailored to fit the new magazine. The fact that Macbeth was featured in the inaugural issue, and published ten pieces—eight on travel and one each on food and fashion—in the magazine's first year suggests that she was instrumental in striking the right tone for the Maclean Publishing Company's latest endeavour. The travel pieces were autobiographical, and she modelled, for readers, ways of understanding the consumer and cultural nuances of modern living—and using them to one's advantage. Macbeth was 48 at the time, but no mention is made of her widowhood and long career: indeed, the pieces have a decidedly youthful air to them. She plays up her femininity, commenting on the flirtatious nature of European men and cheerfully acquiescing in having her bags carried for her. Yet, she was a woman travelling alone, a bold move for this period. She writes fluently about her mobility in the public medium of print, and her professional capabilities as an author are foregrounded, as are her command of several languages, and her grasp of tasteful cultural and material consumption.

Macbeth's first *Mayfair* article on Paris was published in May 1927 and titled the 'The Only Paris' (see Figure 24). She writes:

> In Paris adventure is unavoidable even to the unadventurous. New … or atrophied … emotions are stimulated. Smiling becomes a habit; laughter, spontaneous. Politeness is national and leisure inescapable in a land where the busy business man takes two hours for his lunch! One can scarcely imagine a Frenchman complaining that he hadn't time to eat. A thousand thunders no! He makes the time, meticulously chooses his food and enjoys it. He has little dyspepsia, rare misanthropia, and practically no ennui. This is the life! (14)

In a Parisian setting, Macbeth suggests, civility and good manners do not conflict with the pursuit of individual gratification, but are compatible with it. Her vision of the elegant leisure of a Paris life is then related back to the fine art of consumption. Macbeth takes the reader into various spaces devoted to shopping, naming some of the city's well-known locations—rue de Rivoli, Place Vendôme, rue de la Paix, and l'Opéra—and commenting: 'Behind an exquisitely wrought-iron [sic] grille, on the far side of a spotless courtyard, a famous costumer's name steals out; or a furrier's, or an art dealer's. There is no gaudy display. That would be second class and vulgar. Indeed, one has to penetrate, to explore' (15). According to Stephen Scobie, literary texts set in Paris often insistently repeat the names of particular streets and districts, because:

even for those who have never been there, there must be a cloud of cultural resonance gathered around certain names—Champs-Elysées, the Seine, the Eiffel Tower—while other, lesser-known names evoke magic simply by their specificity, by the allure of the unknown, their ambivalent appeal to an expertise that the reader may or may not share. (61–62)

Macbeth's feature exhibits this tension between specificity and the allure of the unknown, as she lists famous place names even while insisting that an authentic knowledge of Paris requires more than merely standing on a well-known street and glimpsing things through grilles or across courtyards. Relying on advertisements or openly displayed goods is explicitly categorised as a second-class approach to shopping. The intelligence and initiative required to gain access to hidden realms identifies her style of shopping as upper crust.

Indeed, an introduction was necessary to enter the kind of salon Macbeth describes. As Alexandra Palmer explains, 'a woman who wanted to buy directly at an *haute couture* salon could not just walk in. The social contacts required and the etiquette code surrounding the couture system were steeped in traditions resembling gaining membership to an elite club' (*Couture* 42). The aspiration to belong to this elite, and to gain the specialised understanding that enables tasteful consumption, underwrites Macbeth's travel pieces. In 'Printemps à la Paris,' she describes visiting a couture salon, explaining that it is the custom for the *vendeuses* employed there to model the clothing for shoppers, who then ask for the outfits they prefer—only to be told that this or that one-of-a-kind creation has already been sold. Eventually, a handful of items that are actually for sale will be modelled, at which point, according to Macbeth, 'the scramble is frantic.' She herself manages to 'triumph over a lady with flashing dark eyes and bear off a creation of sea-foam tissue' (19). To shop successfully in Paris, it seems, is not only a semi-occult activity, but also an aggressively competitive one. It is, moreover, an experience in exclusivity, both in the sense that one needs to be accepted into the salons, and in the sense that what one purchases there is unique. Macbeth, then, displays her insider's knowledge of Paris, without imparting it in any useful detail to *Mayfair*'s readers. Rather, she gives an impression of her experience, but keeps her specialised knowledge to herself.

Macbeth goes on to note the Parisian disdain for mass-produced clothing: 'it seems that Parisians are not educated (or is it barbarized?) to the extent of buying from cases or racks that contain a wide choice of garments. They still regard with contempt the ready-made' ('Printemps' 18). Individual tailoring is preferred, and Macbeth's word 'barbarized' shows that she endorses this preference. Her criticism of modern mass production is not presented in leftist terms (what is fair to the worker), but rather in snobbish ones (what is beneficial to the consumer). Mass production undermines individuality, resulting in an unstylishness that mars self-presentation. Erin Smith, in her work on the working-class readers of pulp magazines, describes such concerns with clothing and self-presentation as 'impression management' (64), and notes that it was a preoccupation that ranged across the social spectrum during the interwar period. Anxiety over appearance is grounded in the culture of aspiration, and while advertisers have always exploited this, they did so with increasing intensity during the period following the First World War. Roland Marchand, in his study of American advertising in the 1920s and 1930s, names advertisers' play on impression management 'The Parable of the First Impression.' As he argues, advertisers were 'capitalizing on an increasing public uncertainty that true ability and character would always win out in the scramble for success. [...] Far from deploring the apparent trend toward judging people on superficial externals, advertising tableaux often suggested that external appearance was the best index of underlying character' (210). Social status was indexed to clothing, and Macbeth's articles remind us that Paris had long occupied the highest rank in the hierarchy of fashion. To be able to shop in Paris was a sign of one's privileged position; to shop wisely and well, Macbeth suggests, was a finely honed skill that set one apart.

Macbeth expresses ambivalence towards high culture and, especially, the representations of Paris in works by her contemporaries. Her trip to Paris in 1927 situates her writing within the emerging discussion of 'brows' that began around that point. She was in the city at a time now closely identified with the development of international modernism, when writers and publishers such as Hemingway, Fitzgerald, Stein, Pound, and Sylvia Beach were based there. Yet, her acknowledgement of these associations is absent or oblique. Citing, for instance, the expertise of Michael Arlen and Ernest Hemingway on club and café culture, respectively, she notes that Arlen's portrayal of night clubs 'will give you a fair estimate of the clubs (which are the same in any city)' and that

> a glance at Mr. Hemingway's productions will furnish an erroneously picturesque idea of the cafés ... principally the Rotonde and the Dome which lie *en face* in the *Boulevard Montparnasse*. I state, without fear of contradiction, that the average transient would be bored beyond telling in either of these places. ('Various Cities' 17)

By grouping together Hemingway, a writer strongly linked to the modernist movement, and Arlen, who achieved fame with his melodramatic and hugely popular novel *The Green Hat* (1925), Macbeth momentarily enacts a middlebrow 'vantage point from which high culture, popular culture, and middlebrow culture could be critically observed' (Hammill, *Women* 12). While 'middlebrow' is not a term she uses outright, 'highbrowism' is, and Macbeth reveals an awareness of the 'the battle of the brows' which was gaining intensity in this period.[1] In a discussion of how to spend an evening in Paris, Macbeth remarks that the 'average transient' will naturally wish to attend the opera 'which is produced in one of the most ornately beautiful buildings on the continent' ('Various Cities' 17). After acknowledging the aesthetic appeal of the opera house, however, she wryly comments that 'when the sacrifice to highbrowism has been made, then the average transient fetches a relieved sigh, and says "Now for a bit of life." Then she—"she" meaning equally often "he"—looks up the night clubs and an occasional café' (17). Here, Macbeth playfully articulates the sentiments expressed in one of the earliest uses, in 1925, of the term middlebrow, to describe 'people who are hoping that some day they will get used to the stuff they ought to like' ('Charivaria').

Macbeth modulates between an emphasis on individuality (personal experiences, unique purchases) and an awareness of the superficiality of the tourist experience. At several points, she acknowledges that her travels glance across the surface of the city—she does not work there, nor does she have friends or family there. She is not a part of the community in any long-term way; rather, she is an outside observer who, as far as the actual inhabitants of Paris are concerned, serves primarily as a source of income. As she puts it, in Paris, 'the foreigner is courteously, but nonetheless efficiently, separated from his dollars' ('Various Cities' 17). She comments also on the way that Parisian society consciously exploits tourists through manipulating its own image:

> I asked a newspaper man why I saw so few wounded men in Paris. He answered me something after this fashion: 'Paris is the show-window of France. Only the best and most attractive exhibits are displayed. To continue to attract the tourist, unpleasant sights must never be shown, so the wounded were sent to the provinces where they work, if possible, on farms. ('Where in—Paris' 15)

---

[1] This phrase is used in the title of Erica Brown and Mary Grover's collection of essays that attends to the contestation of literary taste and cultural hierarchy. As Brown and Grover point out in their introduction, 'the term "middlebrow" itself, first used in the 1920s, is the product of powerful anxieties about cultural authority and processes of transmission. It is a nexus for prejudice towards the lower middle classes, the feminine, and the domestic, and towards narrative modes regarded as outdated' (1).

Her articles suggest that what is on offer in Paris is not so much authenticity as style. Her first piece, 'The Only Paris,' suggests that this is what tourists are really seeking: 'long accustomed to the presence of strangers, the Parisian is skilful in catering to their wants, in making them comfortable. No food can equal theirs. No serving of it is more artistic and pleasing. Graciousness of manners puts Anglo-Saxons to shame.' She concludes: 'It is an axiom that Frenchmen know how to live—knowledge well worth traveling mountainous seas to acquire' (48). While the tourist is given the chance to have his or her desires gratified for the duration of the trip, she or he is also expected to return home with a worldly knowledge of luxurious hotels, fine food, gracious manners: in short, *l'art de vivre*. This knowledge will set the returning traveller apart from her friends back home.

The desire for individual distinction, and the power of travel to confer it, is a theme that runs through 'Miss Abigail Duloge ... Traveller,' published in the *Canadian Home Journal* in May 1933. It was the fifth in a series on 'modern women' contributed by 'Lady Willison' (Marjory MacMurchy), and though fictional, the narrative evokes the genre of the celebrity portrait. It relates how Miss Duloge is invited to give a lecture on her extensive travels at a distinguished tea. Willison indicates that her protagonist is independently wealthy, and that her journeys are one of the chief features of her privileged life, thus forging a strong link between travel and upward mobility. Miss Duloge believes that it is her desire to travel, rather than her unlimited freedom to do so, that makes her unique—until she gives her talk in Toronto. There, she discovers that 'every single or married woman with whom she speaks has dreamed of travel; and is convinced that she only, in her own mind and heart, has been born more exceptionally a traveller than anyone else' (Willison).

The discovery throws her elitist worldview into turmoil: 'Had she studied, travelled, trained her mind in aesthetics all these years to find herself now one of a mob? Was there nothing exclusive, transcendental, esoteric, left in the world? Had everyone visited the Pyramids, ridden on camels, brought home a tiny bottle of sand from the Red Sea?' This article acknowledges the tension between the longing for individual prestige and the collective nature of the tourist experience. As Dean MacCannell explains: 'In the establishment of modern society, the individual act of sightseeing is probably less important than the ceremonial ratification of authentic attractions as objects of ultimate value, a ratification at once caused by, and resulting in, the gathering of tourists around an attraction' (14). In the wake of the archaeological discoveries in Egypt in the early decades of the twentieth century, the Pyramids rapidly became 'authentic attractions' in this way. By 1933, when Willison's piece was published, Egypt was already being included on cruise itineraries and advertised as an increasingly popular tourist destination. 'It occurred to me,' says Miss Duloge, 'that I had been thinking of myself as an exception all my life. But [...] we all want to see the Pyramids.' Miss Duloge's mode of travel is luxurious and expensive; she has her own car and a chauffeur. But two examples of travellers who are not wealthy convince her that there are alternative ways of moving about in the world, and also that the motivation to do so is universal. One example consists of two friends, a nurse and a cook, who travel together and stop to work when their funds run low. The other is Miss Duloge's music teacher, who plays his violin on street corners to finance his travels. Her conclusion is: 'I mean to change my will. Not a home for pets. A fund to send people abroad. In memory of dear Father and dear Mother.' This short but important piece emphasises travel as both a mode of escape from ordinary life *and* as a beneficial, educational experience for ordinary people, for which it is worthwhile to work hard and save up.

In June 1950, a *Chatelaine* feature by Mildred Spicer described a journey to Italy taken by a young opera singer, Mary Morrison of Winnipeg. A figure inherently connected to high culture, Morrison was chosen from the Opera School of the Royal Conservatory of Music to be 'the model for *Chatelaine*'s travel story' (5). Morrison is young, with a career before her that promises independence and geographic mobility. She is accompanied by *Chatelaine*'s fashion editor and a photographer who documents the trip, showcasing Morrison's 'nylon travel trousseau,' the BOAC 'Stratocruiser' that flies them all to Rome via London, and the destinations that Morrison visits. The highlights include the Foro Romano in Rome, the Villa d'Este at Lake Como, and La Scala in Milan. Because she is modelling fashions for *Chatelaine*, the trip itself is construed as productive labour with a nationalist angle: Spicer notes that 'we had photographed a Canadian wardrobe against an Italian background' (9). At the same time, Morrison is experiencing culture as a part of her education, and this will presumably further her career. In addition to being presented as cultured and career-oriented, Morrison is positioned as a consumer. The inexplicit aspects of consumption include, of course, her air and car travel, her stays at hotels, and the food she eats. More explicitly, Morrison is shown in a full-skirted chiffon dress and large hat as she 'ponders over a day's shopping' whilst drinking coffee in her hotel. The caption notes:

> Rome, like all other interesting tourist cities, has its unique shops. For women they're a shopper's paradise. Italian silk in lingerie and blouses ... tiny leather jewel boxes ... unusual mosaic jewelry and dainty cameos. Each shop specializes in one type of merchandise. There are no department stores as we know them. (7)

Though over 20 years have elapsed, the passage resonates with Macbeth's 1927 features, since small individual shops and unique items of merchandise are presented as a counterpoint to the growth of mass production. The goods that Morrison apparently ponders are all luxury items, though they are not constructed in terms of excess but in terms of delicate, discriminating, 'dainty' femininity. Cultural consumption is no less important, as Morrison takes in stunning views and glimpses of history in the form of ruins and gardens. The trip culminates with an opera performance at La Scala where, according to Spicer's caption, 'the photographer caught us dazed and enchanted by the beauty, reluctant to admit that it was all over' (9). Two kinds of beauty are presented in this article: the modern allure of Mary Morrison in her 'palest blue nylon marquisette' (9) and the historically resonant beauty of the Renaissance palaces, terraced gardens, and grand opera house. Beauty and history here exist to be consumed by the tourist, yet Italy is constructed as somewhat decadent, in contrast to Canadian modernity. The travellers admire the Italian people for 'their pride of Italy's past glories' rather than for their contemporary lifestyle: 'Their slow, easy-going ways are sometimes annoying to the bustling North American' (9).

'Sur Les Canaux de Grande-Bretagne,' a 1955 piece by Madeleine Vaillancourt for *La Revue Moderne*, revels in the joys of slow, easy-going journeys. The fifties was the decade in which travel articles and advertising became key content in *La Revue Moderne*. Vaillancourt's piece draws our attention to the ways in which magazines situated the tourist within the broader economy. Yet it resists a straightforward linkage between travel and consumption and suggests, instead, that the traveller is free to create an individual experience that defies the speed, sights, and shopping increasingly associated with modern mass tourism.

Rather than presenting an autobiographical account of her own trip, Vaillancourt encourages readers to imagine themselves as travellers going along Britain's canals. She advocates adopting a slow pace and avoiding urban centres, in order to get to know the country intimately: 'les canaux se faufilent à travers prés et bois jusqu'à de vieux villages oubliés; ils longent parfois des châteaux historiques, des abbayes ou tout simplement les paysages de carte postale, ravissants et pittoresques de la campagne anglaise' (6). This statement is accompanied by a photograph of two women and a man taking tea aboard a barge—they are comfortable and undoubtedly civil, yet independent, even Bohemian, in their chosen mode of adventure. That said, the trip is necessarily discussed as a commodity available for purchase, with Vaillancourt explaining that renting a barge costs $30 per week and reminding us that the barge is essentially a floating house with all necessary amenities, making the price reasonable (7). She goes on to suggest that the barge traveller, in his or her role as consumer, becomes an essential figure in maintaining local economies and generating a connection between modernity and tradition:

> Le nombre des bateliers a aussi beaucoup diminué. Mais ils constituent toujours une petite société très spéciale, très unie qui maintient vivantes les traditions anciennes de la vie errante. Plusieurs petites villes situées trop loin des grandes routes ou des voies principales des chemins de fer n'ont encore que les canaux pour assurer l'expédition de leur marchandise, et partant leur prospérité. (7)

As a reward for making this contribution to communities that might otherwise be eroded, the traveller attains 'une expérience profonde et enrichissante qui n'est possible qu'en Europe. Les durs portages, la solitude extrême, la sauvagerie de nos nappes d'eau et de nos forêts n'existent pas ici' (46). The canal trip is thus a happy medium—it offers an escape from the pressures associated with modernity but avoids arduous immersion in the wilderness. In this way, Vaillancourt's traveller-consumer becomes a genteel patron, one who will appreciate the peace and tranquillity that travelling the canals bestows, in which 'tout n'est que réflexion, rêverie, poésie, un réel paradis' (46).

Canada's mainstream magazines consistently connected women travellers, in particular, to consumption. Women were much more likely than men to be featured in photo spreads, interviews, and fictional portraits which situated them as shoppers, wherever they went in the world. This fits with the broader construction of women as the primary consumers in Western societies, dissipating any unease resulting from women's new agency as independent travellers by recuperating their experiences into the productive, even edifying, 'work' of shopping. Travel abroad is characterised as educational and rewarding, not least because of one's power as a consumer to select experiences and items for purchase. Travel, however, was not always as idyllic as the pieces we have discussed so far made it out to be and, as we explore next, social and financial crises arise when travellers fail to be savvy consumers.

The fantasy of travel and its flaws

Travel advertisements, in the decades covered by this study, effectively map the relationship between middlebrow aspiration and travel. The advertisements for Canadian Pacific's shipping line offer an ideal way of grasping the travel fantasies that were most often promoted to Canadians in the interwar years. The cruise liner's very structure reflects the era's social stratification, in which the wealthy were literally stacked on top of the workspaces (kitchens, boiler rooms) and living quarters of those who laboured to provide them with their elegant journey. Servants, boiler men, and cooks are all rendered unobtrusive, and their labour is never acknowledged in ads. It is telling that an advert in the April 1931 *Mayfair* for CP's new luxury liner, the *Empress of Britain*, includes an aerial view of the floor plan, showing only the promenades and lounges, rather than a cut-away view of the ship's internal workings (see Figure 23). Luxury is evoked partly through the main image, depicting passengers in elegant evening dress in a club room, and partly through an emphasis on spaciousness. The perspective used for the drawing of the club room makes the ceiling appear extremely high, and the headline for the article reads 'Size ... speed ... plus Space,' with 'Space' printed in a much bigger font (Canadian Pacific). The list of spaces described are specialised according to activity, but all of the activities are organised around socialising—drinking, dining, smoking, playing tennis, dancing. This constant social interaction is, however, mitigated by the significant emphasis on the ship's provision for personal space. The private suites are described as 'smart metropolitan apartments,' a phrase that draws attention to contemporary urbanity as a part of the travel experience.

In the 1950s, advertisements for air travel to Europe replicated some of the characteristics of interwar ocean travel promotions. The September 1954 issue of *La Revue Populaire*, for instance, features Notre-Dame de Paris on its cover, and named Paris 'la plus belle ville du monde' in an advertisement for the French exhibition about to take place in Montreal (Paris-Montréal). Unsurprisingly, this issue also contains several advertisements for air travel, including one for Trans-Canada Air Lines, which was positioned on the page facing the French exhibition advert. The Trans-Canada ad features a large illustration of Mont St Michel, with a stylish young couple standing in the foreground (see Figure 25). The advertising copy notes the 'vignobles de la Bourgogne,' the 'plages de Bretagne et Normandie,' and the 'sites historiques de la vieille Europe' as enticements to travel. It describes the aeroplanes in excitable terms: 'Les énormes et nouveaux SUPER Constellation d'Air Canada vous conduiront en Europe rapidement et en tout confort,' and offered 'le choix entre le luxueux service de première classe ou l'économique et confortable classe "touriste."' The advertisements for both the *Empress of Britain* and Trans-Canada Air Lines suggest that a combination of modern efficiency with old-world culture defined travel's appeal, though CP's additional emphasis on upper-crust elegance was missing from the airline promotion. Both advertisements employ an impressionistic rather than highly detailed style of illustration that generates an idea of a sophisticated lifestyle. The anonymity of the liner passengers encourages readers to picture themselves in their place in the heady surroundings of the Cathay Lounge, while the figures in the

Trans-Canada Airlines advertisement have their backs to us, so that their point of view on the French scene before them is aligned with that of the reader of the magazine.

The text of the advert for the *Empress of Britain* mentions several well-known contemporary artists who contributed to the design of the ship, forging an association with high culture. The lounge itself was designed by the French-born book illustrator Edmund Dulac. Intriguingly, the lounge's decor draws from an idea of the exotic—'Cathay' was a term used for China in some poetic contexts, most famously in Ezra Pound's *Cathay* (1915)[2]—as well as from a tradition of London book publishing, since Dulac illustrated many books for Hodder and Stoughton, including a 1907 edition of *The Arabian Nights*. The lounge of a Canadian cruise ship was thus styled on a mixture of the foreign and the imperial, yet structured on the modern comfort and efficiency that was associated with North American industry. The shipping lines also highlighted the opportunities for upwardly mobile networking whilst travelling. In July 1931, *Mayfair* ran a two-page piece on the *Empress of Britain* that fell between direct advertising and an article. It featured four social spaces in the ship: the Knickerbocker Bar and the card room were designated spaces 'for the naughty nautical landsman', the pool was for 'trans-Atlantic swimmers' to gather in, and the ballroom was meant for 'hours of play' ('For Hours' 21). The implication, always, is that social interaction will be rewarding and easy, whereas in fact it required the specialised skills of gambling, dancing, and smart conversation. Whilst an overseas journey was marketed as a symbol of achievement and success, the tensions surrounding aspiration could easily be exacerbated by the physical, psychological, and social demands of travel.

In George Pearson's 1925 short story 'Jack-Pots,' discussed in the opening to this chapter, the fantasy of travel is exposed as flawed—largely for reasons connected with class and economic status. The story works along three central themes that intersect with other articles and advertisements published in *Maclean's* and in the other magazines in this era. First, the Romans suffer from anxiety over their status and fear that their supposed inferiority will be apparent to others; second, networking, class prejudice, and (mis)reading fellow passengers all come into play within the compressed social space of the cruise ship, demonstrating that travel cannot offer a complete escape from social stratification; and, third, the preoccupation with illness, boredom, and financial difficulties undermines the ideal of travel as an experience in luxury. At the start of the story, we see the influence which fantasies of modern travel hold over

---

[2] For a very good discussion of *Cathay* in relation to modernist Orientalism, see Yao 19–28.

the protagonist, Ed Roman. During his first evening on board, 'a pervading light-heartedness intoxicated him; so many people intent solely on pleasure,' and he 'ardently embraced the freedom of [the ship's] curiously detached relationships, its sinking of pasts, its opening of vistas to parched souls' (21). The way in which Ed and his wife are described alludes to their temporary change in status, as they 'strolled about the deck like victors, as though all they saw belonged to them; the promenading passengers, the hurrying stewards, the bare-footed sailors still struggling with a mountain of baggage over the ship's hold, and the ship itself, stupendous to their eyes' (20). Yet anxiety over status is almost immediately raised as an issue in the story, as Ed remarks to his wife, 'You'll have something to tell the Literary Society about. You mustn't forget your notes for your lectures to them. They won't need to know we started from here instead of New York because it's cheaper' (20). 'Here' is Montreal, indicating that a Canadian port is considered less glamorous than its American counterpart.

Indeed, right from the start, the trip fails to match fantasies about travel, as the narrator points out the 'unbeautiful lines of the freight shed' (20) that is the couple's view as they sit in deckchairs awaiting departure. Their arrival in Europe is equally unimpressive, as the narrator tells us that the couple 'took in the low-lying mud shores of the Mersey, clusters of squat grey buildings, and the rain of Liverpool' (72). Long before they reach Liverpool, however, Mrs Roman is struck down by seasickness. This is not only less than glamorous, but also, when combined with Ed Roman's uncontrollable gambling, hints that there is something pathological lurking beneath the fantasy of escape abroad. The social alienation that the couple experience, and the industrial ugliness of both ports, point in this direction as well. Indeed, even Mrs Roman's recent election as president of her literary society has a tainted quality. We are told that her plans to tour Europe have given her an elevated social status at home, not least by qualifying her to write lectures to present to the society, and that this led to her being favoured over another candidate for president, the wife of Ed Roman's rival at the bank, Chet. This fact rankles with Chet and his wife, who, if Ed Roman's fears are accurate, appear to be waiting for a chance to ruin the Romans through rumour and innuendo.

Ed Roman's plight illustrates the perils of shipboard socialising for someone attempting to appear worldlier than he truly is. His preoccupation with appearances causes him to misread the gambler Starret. Roman identifies him as upper crust, mentally dubbing him 'Stuck-up,' though he is nonetheless 'impressed by Starret's clothes and general air of material well-being and at-homeness in surroundings so confusing to himself' (21). When Starret's fellow poker players worry that Roman might not be sufficiently well off to join their game, Starret reassures them that Roman represents 'the usual type, though, I suppose ... probably rotten with money. Out to do Europe with his wife—Art galleries on the run, and all that sort of thing. We can't hurt him' (70). When Starret realises his mistake, learning that Roman has gambled away his life's savings and will arrive destitute in Europe, he steps in and rescues Roman by persuading him to play another game that, by cheating, he ensures Roman wins. No one can prove that Starret cheated, but the suspicions of the other players lead to his social condemnation on the ship. Roman, unaware of Starret's heroic, if slightly nefarious, protection of him, eventually shuns his saviour: we are told that 'a haggard Starret passed and bowed. Roman, about to acknowledge the salute, was checked by his wife' (72). The gossip about Starret's cheating (but not her husband's involvement) has reached her, and she decries him as 'a bad man' (72). '"That's right," Ed Roman agreed as he too turned from Starret' (72). Roman and Starret both fail to interpret class markers correctly, and Roman is likewise unable to decipher the characters of those around him. The fact that he exits the ship unscathed is the result, literally, of blind luck. The conclusion suggests that the cruise ship is a treacherous place because it disrupts the categories which structure social experience on land, allowing people to masquerade as members of a class to which they do not belong. In this sense, 'Jack-Pots' may be read as a conservative story, one in which people who try to step out of their place in the social hierarchy risk punishment.

The scenario in the story illustrates some of the dangers inherent to social climbing, and in this respect, it resonated with many other pieces in the magazines. For example, the unsigned 1949 *Chatelaine* feature 'My Wife is a Social Climber' revealed the angst of a husband over his wife's determination to move up their small town's social scale. She is preoccupied with keeping up a 'smart' house, inviting the 'right' people to dinner, and having her children associate with the sons and daughters of 'the best people' in town. The husband argues that his wife's

> social ambitions would be okay if they were just byproducts of a normal human desire for us to do better and better so as to have more security, give our children greater advantages, have time and money to travel and things like that. They aren't just byproducts, though. Little by little they're becoming an end in themselves. (27)

He eventually consults a physician, who blames the wife's behaviour on her own feelings of inadequacy, and warns that the strain she is causing to her family may drive her husband to a mental breakdown. Ironically, the wife's efforts reflect not so much a pathological tendency on her part (despite the physician's diagnosis) but the attitudes that magazines exhorted readers to adopt. The article reveals the potentially destructive effects of this pressure, and it also evokes the shame associated with the open pursuit of social success. This shame is evident in the author's choice not to sign the piece.

The more practical challenges presented by travel are examined in a 1929 *Chatelaine* piece titled 'What Do You Know About Travel? Problems of baggage, customs, tipping, and tripping explained' by Archie G. Wynne-Field, and a similar article published two years later in the *Canadian Home Journal*, 'Off to Europe' by Phyllis Isabel Mackay. The aim of both articles was to assuage fears by offering advice, and the advice was tied to purchasing power. Wynne-Field begins by citing 'one very travelled Englishwoman,' who tells him:

> If I had to pack up tonight, I shouldn't worry. For a trip around the world I'd just throw a few things in a bag, have my passport viséd, [sic] buy a few Travellers' Cheques, and sail. I wouldn't even stop to buy clothes. I'd get a hat in London, a suit in Paris, and so on as I required things. (58)

He goes on to discuss the practicalities of obtaining a passport, shipping souvenirs home from Europe, purchasing travel insurance and traveller's cheques, paying for meals and hotel rooms, and tipping taxi drivers, porters, shoe-shiners, and waiters. Mackay echoes his advice on tipping, and reminds the reader of the embarrassment which can result from getting this wrong. For travellers unused to being waited on, the question of how to acknowledge assistance tactfully and tastefully was problematic, serving as a reminder of class divisions. Mackay's emphasis is on comfort, both physical and social. She advises in detail on selecting the right class of ticket:

> There is a difference of around a hundred dollars on the return trip between First, or Cabin Class, and Tourist Third; and about fifty dollars between the latter and the regular Third Class, which is more restricted in every way. Tourist Third Cabin has its own reading and dining rooms, its own deck space. Students, teachers, and educational tours are its usual passengers. (8)

The quality of one's tourist experience depended on getting this selection correct: it required an accurate self-identification of class, and where one belonged. Her advice on clothing further exposes the more trying aspects of travel, as she suggests dark clothes because they disguise dirt better than light ones, and recommends a warm wool coat, as the deck will be cold. A dinner frock, she notes, is only needed if travelling first class, but sensible shoes are essential for any class of traveller: 'The delight of spending one's first day in the Louvre, for instance, can be forgotten in the pain of tired feet in those new, high-heeled slippers. Sight-seeing is one of the most fatiguing pastimes on earth' (8). An illustration shows two weary women in high heels, standing before a wall of paintings. Unsuitable shoes were, literally, an impediment, and could reduce one's mobility, as well as one's intellectual capacity to take things in. The piece, in recommending that tourists pack aspirin, hot-water bottles, and 'a comfortable pair of Oxfords' (8), rather contradicts the glamour that advertisers attributed to travel. Mackay was honest about the things that could go wrong, and both she and Wynne-Field address the anxiety that emerges around a temporary change in location and social position.

In 1946, the European travel experience was taken up in 'Nostalgia,' a *Chatelaine* piece about postwar life in Canada. The article was by Margaret Ecker Francis, who had lived in London with her husband during the war, and it concentrates on the long-term results of spending time abroad. Service personnel, of course, experienced an enforced geographical movement involving many horrors, but the magazines shied away from these, choosing instead to represent the pleasures of time spent off-duty. Canadians who served overseas, Francis claims, developed 'a taste, and often a cultivated one, for a way of life that is not Canada's' (29). She construes her home country as a place of emotional constraint and cultural impoverishment: 'Canadians who inherited an austere, God-fearing land from serious-minded pioneer ancestors found another way of life' overseas (29). Servicemen, she adds, 'tasted a life that was gayer, more amusing than anything they'd known in Canada' (36). Once they returned home, the European culture they had experienced when on leave from duty became a nostalgic fantasy, marked by relaxed social mores and *joie de vivre*. Francis suggests, then, that travel abroad was a disruptive and potentially destructive force, since it provoked unhappiness with one's ordinary lot in life, and could even lead to disloyal feelings towards one's country. At the same time, the article subtly reinforces the more commercial messages of the mainstream magazines. Their travel promotions deliberately encouraged a degree of dissatisfaction in readers, generating a sense that everyday life was lacking in comparison to the fantasy of travel with which they were repeatedly tantalised.

Consumerism: locating the tourist

Kathleen K. Bowker's article 'Walks Abroad About London' ran in the April 1935 *Mayfair* alongside a detailed list of the events marking the Silver Jubilee Year in London. The piece was, in part, a form of veiled advertising, with Bowker recommending certain shops, and the shops themselves taking out advertisements on the surrounding pages. Bowker remarks of Burberry that 'it is fun to sit luxuriously on one of their long, green sofas [...] and to hear them tell you of what they can do for you, personally' (91). The company had a full-page advertisement between the pages of Bowker's text, and it echoed her attention to the pedestrian tour by employing the language of pilgrimage. The copy claimed that Burberry was 'A famous name and a famous house. The Mecca of all those who seek comfort and weather protection' (95). Entwined, the tourist sights (such as Buckingham Palace), the Jubilee events, and the idea of pilgrimage to a celebrated shop endowed the walking tour with grand associations. The tourist here is oriented towards taking in culture and history, but encouraged to seek rest and revitalisation in shops. In her discussion of perfumes, lingerie, gloves, hats, and other small items, Bowker details which shops provide the most personalised attention and offer items of the best quality and craftsmanship. The result was not only the purchase of a unique or stylish item to bring home as a souvenir and status symbol, but also a London tour with a clearly defined purpose: the accumulation of goods.

The magazines related their discussion of travel to the acquisition of knowledge, social connections, and material items. Bowker's piece showcases the ways in which this aspect of the period's middlebrow ethos was invested in the most basic activity of the tourist—walking. Intriguingly, the tourist on a walk resonates with the *flâneur*, a key figure of high modernism who is defined primarily by wandering the city (especially Paris) in an apparently aimless way.[3] The *flâneur* is an observer, and thus an antithesis to the middlebrow consumer who seeks attention from sales staff and, in turn, attentively picks out and purchases goods. *Mayfair*'s suggested walking tour separated its presumed readers from the modernist ethos by insisting on a purpose, an itinerary, a shopping list. Bowker instructs the reader on a method of walking that involves being able to locate oneself not only within London, but within an imaginary map of the high-end consumer world. This positioned the reader within the broader aesthetic and intellectual terrain of the period; she was asked to make choices regarding her status and aspirations, and express them in relation to

---

[3] Much has been written about the *flâneur* in literature: see for instance Benjamin; Higonnet; Parsons; Scobie; Tester.

where she wished to go, whether on a large scale (travel abroad) or small scale (a particular shop). Metaphorically, the accumulation of goods whilst travelling added weight to the consumer, thus grounding him or her physically in the place being toured and suggesting a substantial quality to his or her experiences that the *flâneur* did not possess.

Advertisements for The Dorchester, The May Fair, Queen Anne's Mansions and Hotel, Park Lane Hotel, the Lancaster Gate Hotel, and the Great Western Royal Hotel were integrated into the broken up columns of Bowker's article. Geographically, all the hotels were situated in the more prestigious London neighbourhoods, from St James's Park to Hyde Park. In terms of socioeconomic hierarchies, they were situated in a more middling position. The May Fair Hotel, for instance, offered: 'Modern refinement and service at a moderate price.' By contrast, in a feature on Claridge's, 'Hotel of Kings and Queens', in the November 1952 *Mayfair*, Naomi Bristol describes the hotel as a 'castle-away-from-home' (50). In order to stay at the hotel—a favourite amongst royal visitors to London—it was necessary to be 'either old clients or recommended by an impeccable authority familiar to the management' (52). Unlike the many other hotels advertised in the magazines, Claridge's claimed to turn away most potential guests, and its exclusivity placed it outside the realm of mass consumption. Indeed, Claridge's professed a disdain of advertising, and Bristol notes that the hotel 'employs a public relations officer whose standing orders are to make sure the hotel gets no publicity of any kind' (101). There is a certain irony in this statement, given the placement of this article in a consumer-oriented magazine; this reminds us that while many hotels invited readers to enjoy an elite lifestyle on a temporary basis, mechanisms remained in place to maintain the boundary between those who were truly elite and those who were merely aspirational. Bristol goes on to describe the lengths to which hotel staff would go to cater to their guests, noting that 'when a great personage arrives [...] the manager, who's on friendly terms with most of the world's royalty, rushes to the entrance to welcome him' (98), and that staff 'devoted three days to unpacking the Dutch royal family's china, silver, and linen in preparation for the family's arrival' (98). Hotels like Banff Springs or The May Fair promised comfort, but the promise was made to all readers of the magazines. Readers who could afford to stay in such hotels, or who were encouraged to imagine doing so, were thus addressed as a homogenous consumer clientele. In contrast, Bristol's piece granted readers an opportunity to gaze on a world to which it was unlikely they would ever be admitted, reasserting the boundaries that designated the readers of *Mayfair* and similar periodicals as 'middlebrow.'

Food was, of course, another important preoccupation in magazine travel articles, which served to orient readers in relation to possible choices. For armchair travellers, the heady descriptions suggest that culinary delights were key elements of an imagined trip. In the case of *Chatelaine* and the *Journal*, such descriptions also offered a fanciful respite from the everyday demands of home cooking.[4] Indeed, 'The Art of Having Something to Eat' was stressed in a 1929 set of CP advertisements, in which elegantly dressed men and women sat in a train dining car at neat tables complete with centrepieces and white tablecloths. In the ad published in *Mayfair* for August 1929, the copy noted: 'The difference between "dining" and just having something to eat, is artfully revealed in the superb and spacious surroundings of the new Canadian Pacific Dining Cars' (see Figure 26). Customers, the ad promised, would benefit from 'carefully guarded culinary secret[s]' as well as 'the traditional excellence of appointments and service' (Canadian Pacific). The potential of travel to refine one's palate is elaborated in an article called 'We Dine and Wine in London,' from the June 1935 *Journal* (see Figure 27). It was written by Claire Wallace, who would later publish the successful etiquette guide for Canadians, *Mind Your Manners* (1953). She suggests in her 1935 article:

> You get into the habit of good food—if you haven't had it anyway—on the way over. I mean, you don't spend seven days crossing the sea on the Duchess of Bedford, for instance, living on the luscious fare of an ocean liner, without feeling you want to keep it up. After consuming sole with mushroom sauce every day or so, who wants plain bread and butter? So, out you go in search of good food, interestingly served. (23)

Travel here becomes a way of elevating taste, and seeking out excellent food abroad becomes part of the experience of exploring a destination. As in Bowker's article, the middlebrow tourist defines her tastes, and delineates her route, through a series of purchases and sensory experiences.

Wallace's description of London coffee stalls reminds us of the importance of the social aspect of consuming:

> You stop off at one of these funny little caravan-restaurants on your way home from theatre or dance, lean against a wheel and drink a grand

---

[4] Cookery was a major department in both magazines, and provided recipes and seasonal advice on such topics as organising picnics or hosting Christmas dinner. At times, the advice appears overwhelmingly detailed, as with *Chatelaine*'s 'Meals of the Month,' which suggested a full meal plan for each day of the month. Many of the suggestions reinforce the British connection: Scotch eggs, roast beef, and Yorkshire pudding are often recommended.

cup of coffee for a penny. On your right you'll probably have a real down-and-outer, on your left a slick gent who has just stepped out a Rolls-Royce; both are chatty because it is a London night, and London nights are that way. (23)

In this convivial setting, the tourist can witness social hierarchies, as well as interacting with individuals he or she would not encounter at home. Wallace goes on to relate dining to literature, noting that in the Cheshire Cheese pub, diners can sit in the very seats formerly preferred by Samuel Johnson and Charles Dickens, and that it offers an 'important English dish, steak-and-kidney pudding, or the special dish of cheese moistened with beer and melted to a golden lusciousness' (23). Today, she notes, a lucky tourist 'might see G. K. Chesterton at the next table, or other famous folk' (23). She thereby shows readers how the mixture of travel and dining gives an exciting glimpse of celebrity, or an authentic experience of the English past.[5] She proceeds through a list of expensive restaurants, explains which meals at the Savoy one ought to 'dress' for and which are more relaxed, and gives the prices of various dishes, mostly traditional English ones such as saddle of mutton or roast beef. She includes, however, two Italian restaurants, one Chinese, and one Japanese restaurant, suggesting that London offered an experience of cosmopolitanism as well as Englishness.

A September 1954 article in *La Revue Populaire*, 'Cuisine Française,' reviewed three Parisian restaurants: La Tour d'Argent, Le Restaurant Prunier, and Le Café de la Paix (see Figure 28). The piece described the history of each restaurant, the reputation of the head chef, and the clientele likely to dine there. Each review was accompanied by an image of the chef and a photograph or two of his signature dishes, with recipe details. The first review begins:

La Tour d'Argent n'est pas seulement l'un des restaurants les plus luxueux de Paris. Sa renommée a depuis longtemps franchi les frontières et il n'est que de voir parmi la clientèle élégante qui s'y presse chaque jour, la proportion d'étrangers venus de tous les continents pour se convaincre que ce temple gastronomique possède une réputation mondiale.

International prestige is key: this restaurant attracts many foreigners because it

---

[5] As MacCannell notes: 'The rhetoric of tourism is full of manifestations of the importance of the authenticity of the relationship between tourists and what they see: this is a *typical* native house; this is the *very* place the leader fell; this is the *actual* pen used to sign the law' (14).

is one of the famous attractions on the tourist itinerary. The food is consumed along with a 'magnifique panorama sur Notre-Dame et la Seine,' so that the restaurant becomes part of the picturesque experience of Paris. The review of Le Restaurant Prunier focused on tradition, noting that the chef had inherited the restaurant from his father, and that it possessed 'caves personelles' filled with 'vénérables bouteilles des plus grands crus de France.' The discussion of Le Café de la Paix referred to its attraction for celebrity authors of the past, such as Maupassant and Zola, drawing a connection between high art and haute cuisine. The piece concludes: 'L'idéal, en tout cas, serait plutôt qu'elles puissent, un jour, venir visiter la France et déguster sur place toutes ces excellentes choses.'

The piece resonates with *La Revue Moderne*'s May 1955 article 'Restaurants de Paris,' by Yvan Christ. He begins by arguing that: 'La France compte autant de capitales gastronomiques que de grandes villes, mais Paris résume à lui seul cette diversité culinaire provinciale et, tout compte fait, les gourmets les plus subtils s'accordent à proclamer la cuisine parisienne la meilleure de France.' The article aimed to familiarise readers with what they ought to look for in a good restaurant, noting the importance of a *sommelier* and a set daily menu. On this last point, Christ cited the 'prince des gastronomes,' Brillat-Savarin, who remarked that the set menu was 'd'un avantage extrême pour tous.' The piece continued to name-drop as it provided a brief history of the most famous Paris restaurants, including the Grand Véfour, frequented by poets and revolutionaries in the eighteenth and nineteenth centuries; Véryon, used as a setting by Honoré de Balzac; and Flore and the Deux-Magots, favoured by the 'jeunesse intellectuelle cosmopolite.' In a sense, the article was a brief tourist's guide to Paris that drew together historical figures with celebrated dining establishments, and gave street locations for each restaurant. It provides detailed information for the tourist, as well as plentiful romantic associations for the armchair traveller. Throughout this, and the other articles discussed in this section, the reader is reminded that travel to, or knowledge of, Paris brought prestige. That was presented as the defining feature of the city at every level, from the demands of the stomach to the intellectual achievements of its inhabitants.

Claiming ownership of place: souvenirs, photo-narratives, and travelogues

Souvenirs were another facet of consumption that was revealed time and again in travel features. The *Mayfair* article 'Treasures to Take Home' by Edmund Finch, published in January 1955, illustrates the key points that run through these features. It focuses on Britain, identifying the goods traditionally produced in each region, and recommending the best items to purchase. For instance, Finch advocates woollens from Yorkshire, the west of England, and Scotland (especially Harris Tweed) as worthy investments. The article relies on a nostalgic notion of good quality, associating it with traditional, usually handcrafted, production (see Outka 8–9). Finch notes that in Yeovil in Somerset, gloves are produced 'at home in scattered cottages and hamlets around the town' (58); this suggestion of pre-capitalist production connects goods to the private, domestic realm, and hints that the tourist has a duty to support tradition and the local economy. Moreover, the association of objects with an exact location becomes a means of interpreting a place. Scottish leather working, for example, is embedded in the ethos of wilderness, as women, 'working in their homes, take the staghorn and hides from deer killed in the surrounding mountains and make them into bags, purses, belts, sporrans' (58). Scotland here is associated with aristocratic hunting lodges, wild glens, and snowy mountains—and Finch's shopping suggestions reinforce these stereotypes by identifying particular objects as representative. As the many references to home-based labour suggest, mass-produced items are to be avoided; equally, the goods he singles out are luxury items made from costly materials, and are therefore meant to last, and to be displayed as markers of the tourist's engagement with, and even expertise in, their various destinations.

As well as purchasing objects to substantiate memories, readers were encouraged to use photographs and travel journals to make a place 'their own.' Photography and writing, like shopping, invested travel with a clear and productive purpose, assimilating sights and experiences into a coherent story and a store of knowledge. Journals and photographs helped to maintain a set of memories that complemented tangible purchases and enhanced symbolic capital. These documents can become a symbol of achievement, as Mrs Roman's travel notebooks, which are intended to be shared with her literary society, suggest. Photography also offered the tourist a private respite. As Susan Sontag notes, pausing to take a photograph is a moment in which tourists may 'take possession of space in which they are insecure [...] The very activity of taking pictures is soothing, and assuages general feelings of disorientation. Unsure of other responses, they take a picture' (9–10). The attention to taking possession of a space is central to understanding how mainstream magazines conceptualised the goal of travel. Smoothing over any uncertainties that geographical mobility, and its attendant issues of social mobility, stirred in readers, magazines played on the imaginary ownership of a destination as a source of pleasure and security.

'Les jours les plus heureux que nous ayons jamais eus' remarks an advertisement for Kodak Verichrome film in *La Revue Populaire* for August 1935. The accompanying photograph shows two women and a little girl on a beach, and the ad copy advises: 'il faut prendre Aujourd'hui—les instantés que vous voudrez Demain.' Leisure time and holidays were thus capitalised as meaningful time that merited preservation and that ought to be celebrated both in the moment and after it had passed. Indeed, Carole Crawshaw and John Urry point out that photographic technology developed in tandem with the rise of middle-class leisure tourism, which perhaps explains why they are interconnected in ways that we now see as natural (179). Cameras and photographs encouraged the materialisation of a given moment so that it could be re-consumed later. According to a 1955 piece in *La Revue Moderne*, 'N'oubliez pas votre caméra,' 'il est rare que le souvenir garde exactement ce qu'on voulait préserver de l'oubli: tel visage, tel regard aimé, tel moment' (J. L.). Unlike a souvenir, a photograph was a unique object, and a series of photographs that traced the contours of a trip had a creative element, turning the picture-taker into a pictorial author. Photographs, as well as travel journals, highlighted the unique qualities of a given trip, and contributed to the traveller's individual self-fashioning. One of the curious paradoxes, of course, is the tendency of travellers to photograph and write about the same sites, and these are typically the ones most readily recognisable through the repetitive imagery of advertising—the Tower of London, for instance, or the Eiffel Tower.

The published travel memoirs of authors such as Madge Macbeth, Wallace Reyburn, and Mollie McGee were predicated on recording a unique experience. Reyburn, a New Zealand-born author and humourist, served as assistant editor at *Chatelaine* before the war. In 1941, he left Canada for London, telling readers in an article entitled 'A Day in London' that 'out of the mass of newspaper and magazine material I couldn't form a clear conception of just what London is like now. I felt I had to come over and see for myself' (18). He proposes to take the reader on a one-day tour of the damaged city, and his account, written in the style of an ordinary travel piece, substitutes bomb sites for tourist attractions and air raids for theatre visits. He describes how, 'in the City, around St. Paul's, in the East End, you will stand aghast at the sight of whole blocks of buildings razed to the ground' (18), yet he notes with astonishment that 'buildings not totally destroyed are put back into commission in amazingly short order' (18). He admires the resilience and determination of the British people under attack. Normality is not something one can expect to find in wartime London, but Reyburn's discussion of the availability of consumer goods maintains continuity with the pre-war decades and with the consumption-based ethos at *Chatelaine*:

> The confectionery shops have elaborate displays in their windows of what look like boxes of chocolates and chocolate bars. But when you go

in to make a purchase, you'll find they're all dummies. [...] However, the food you eat in London restaurants will be much more varied and plentiful than you expected. (18)

He also discusses cultural consumption, including books ('except for cheap editions there are few new books coming out, and booksellers have perforce to do their best with tattered oldies' [60]), cinema and theatre (both shut down for the duration), night clubs (too expensive for the average person), and radio (the airwaves now dominated by German broadcasting). He notes that Londoners now spend their evenings either dancing in a restaurant, or staying at home. When the sirens sound while he is eating at the house of some friends, Reyburn cannot resist going out into the street to see what an air raid is like. Without a proper helmet to wear, he opts for an 'old-fashioned silver-plated meat cover' (60), introducing levity to a dire situation. Reyburn's travel/war reporting combined his flair for humour, his personal experiences, and an overview of consumer goods shortages. The motivation for the journey, and the article, is to present 'his' London to readers.

This idea of a documenting a travel experience to mark its unique quality had two dimensions: the narrative expressed the individuality of the author, and it marked an unrepeatable experience in the author's life. Mollie McGee, the *Globe and Mail*'s war correspondent in London, occasionally also contributed pieces to *Chatelaine*, and one of these appeared in the November 1944 issue. The title, 'I'll Always Remember My Two Weeks in Paris,' initially suggests a holiday memoir, but the article in fact takes readers on a tour of Paris during the fortnight following the Liberation. The journal-like entries, each one starting with the words 'I'll always remember,' recount experiences such as having lunch with Rosette de Pourtalès, daughter of the author Guy de Pourtalès:

> when we sat around the table of one of the most beautiful flats in Paris and divided a can of sardines, a few fried potatoes from last year's crop, bread and a bit of stale cheese which had been received from Switzerland. (It was strange to watch the progress of the meal reflected in an almost priceless antique mirror hanging on the wall.) (13)

McGee visits the same famous sites as Madge Macbeth—the Champs Elysées, Place de l'Opéra, Place de la Concorde—but her account necessarily incorporates the grim realities of recently occupied Paris: 'I'll always remember those rooms on the top floor of the former Gestapo headquarters in Rue Sausannes. The room with the splotched wallpaper and the four great iron rings sunk in the plaster and connected by greasy reddened streaks where spread-eagled bodies had fought their confinement' (62). Against descriptions such as this, she contrasts the celebratory spirit of the French, and the gratitude they express to Canadians and Americans. A young girl whom she asks for directions 'reached into her shabby handbag and brought out a well-thumbed guidebook to Paris and insisted I take it. "It is so little, Mademoiselle,—so little in exchange for so much!"' (62). The piece provided a rare and immediate first-hand account of Paris immediately after the Allied victory. It was emotive, and rich in details, drawing readers in whilst retaining the spontaneous, fragmented quality of a diary. The wording of the title, 'My Two Weeks in Paris,' reminds us of the question of ownership in travelogues. McGee's experiences, unique because of the timing as well as the itinerary she follows, lead to a travel account in which the city imaginatively 'belongs' to her. No one else can possess it in quite the same way. Moreover, the city will continue to belong to her in memory: it is now a part of her identity, articulated via the travelogue.

McGee's article inverts the 'show-window' quality of Paris that Macbeth comments upon, in which uncomfortable truths and ugly images are hidden away so as not to disturb the tourist's pleasure. McGee takes us into a few of the horrific spaces of the Second World War, and these places are juxtaposed with the conventional sites invoked by interwar travel features. Yet it was not long before the Canadian magazines began, once again, to encourage travel to Paris. This was particularly true of the French-language titles: the co-authors of *Quebec Women: A History* note that between 1946 and 1956, *La Revue Populaire* published 114 articles on Paris (Clio Collective 320). By the 1950s, the city was once again being represented as a site of fantasy and delight. For instance, Jean Le Guével, in his 1956 article for *La Revue Moderne*, observed, 'le ciel semble plus proche et la gaieté plus à l'aise dans ces beaux jardins de Paris où s'ébattent les oiseaux et les enfants sous le regard lointain des statues' (12). Like Yvan Christ's article on Parisian restaurants, Le Guével's piece melded together a summary of the city's squares and gardens with information on the influence that various celebrated figures had had on them; as he put it, 'chacun des grands jardins de Paris a son histoire, son charme propre, ses habitudes' (12). He explains the role of Marie de Medici in designing the Jardin du Luxembourg and that of Richelieu in constructing the Jardin du Palais-Royal. The recent events of the Second World War are ignored in favour of presenting a distant, romanticised past.

'A Holiday in Europe,' which appeared in the October 1949 *Mayfair*, centres on the journey of two Canadian couples, the Burtons and the Finlaysons. They are friends, but after arriving together in Britain, they travel separately. The Finlaysons proceed from London to Paris, then on to Switzerland and northern Italy (Milan, Venice, Florence). Meanwhile, the Burtons see more of southern

England before travelling through Brussels to Paris and following much the same itinerary as their friends. The couples meet up in Genoa before returning home. The purportedly separate trips of the Burtons and the Finlaysons demonstrate that the tourist route is an essentially repetitive structure. Travel, according to the magazines, was an event; yet, the well-trodden tourist track correlates with the repetitive nature of periodicals, which reported on nearly identical journeys from season to season, year after year. Certain destinations, activities, and points of interest are endowed with special meaning and mystique that the magazines promised to impart to readers. The author of 'A Holiday in Europe,' Frances Paul, was the travel editor of *Mayfair* at the time. Her description of the couples' activities is illustrated with photographs which they took during the trip. Both couples visit sites associated with high culture and the upper classes, including the playing fields at Eton, the Longchamps racetrack, the Uffizi Gallery, and Buckingham Palace. The Finlaysons stay in a former Doge's palace on the Grand Canal in Venice, suggesting they adopt temporary travelling identities that give them the freedom to live out fantasies of privilege and prestige. The venues which the travellers prioritise are associated with a specific set of values: beauty and history are mentioned in connection with each place. Canadians abroad could thus improve themselves through immersion in the varieties of artistic and natural splendour that Europe offered, simultaneously developing their understanding not only of historical events but also of the canons of taste.

Travelling within Canada

Canadian Pacific advertisements presented Canada as a pristine space in which the natural beauty of the wilderness blended together seamlessly with modern, even glamorous, elements of conspicuous consumption and contemporary living. Canadian Pacific Railways is, of course, famous for building a trans-Canada railway line, thus, as they liked to remind Canadians, making a united coast-to-coast Canada possible. With the rail line in place, the company sought ways to make money from their investment, and one of the most profitable ventures was the creation of luxury hotels placed at attractive locations along the route. The first was the Banff Springs, built between 1886 and 1888 and situated in the Rocky Mountains of Alberta; the second was the Chateau Frontenac, built between 1892 and 1893 and set in the oldest quarter of Quebec City, with a view of the Gulf of St Lawrence. Even though CP's hotels division would build several other hotels, these two remained their flagship resorts, and in the 1920s through to the 1950s an ad for at least one of them appeared in many issues of the six magazines. The architecture of CP's hotels unabashedly borrows from European models. The Banff Springs, for instance, was intended to be in the style of a Scottish castle, while the Frontenac was meant to be reminiscent of a French chateau.

Canadian Pacific Hotels' promotional campaigns presented Canadians to themselves as a class of people with a certain degree of refinement to which the resorts could cater for an affordable price. As one ad in *Chatelaine* for June 1932 argued, readers could have '6 Glorious Days in the Canadian Rockies, All Expenses, $60.' The advertisement was accompanied by photographs of the 'incomparable Lake Louise,' as well as Emerald Lake and Takkakaw Falls, and it quoted 'Edward Whymper, the famous Alpinist, who called the Rockies "fifty Switzerlands in one."' Similarly, a June 1938 issue of the *Journal* ran an ad with pictures of people swimming, hiking, golfing, horseback riding, dining, and dancing at CP's Banff Springs Hotel and the Chateau Lake Louise. The copy described 'snow-capped peaks towering into the blue—jade green rivers—vast unspoiled forests—tangy mountain air to set you up ... Banff Springs Hotel, like a Scottish Baronial Castle—gracious—replete with all the niceties of modern living, is Canada's mountain summer capital.' As with some of the fashion features discussed in Chapter Three, the hotel companies looked to Europe for their definition of elegance and taste, and then created a Canadian equivalent. There was even a suggestion that the Canadian versions outdid their European models—as in the comment about 'fifty Switzerlands in one.'

Canadian Pacific tapped into a tourist market that wanted a vicarious experience of Europe—its music, its sports, its cuisine—without the trouble of an overseas journey, and the advertisements play to a nostalgia for the so-called old world. Stripping out the realities of European history, the CP campaigns offered, in their place, a dream of fairy-tale castles and sumptuous dining halls with grand views from the floor-to-ceiling windows. As a 1930 advertisement for the Banff Springs Hotel in the July 1930 issue of *La Revue Populaire* stressed, 'Les gens qui savent vraiment jouir des plus belles choses de la vie, viennent ici durant la belle saison, pour se reposer, oublier les soucis de l'existence et admirer les plus grandioses panoramas d'une région merveilleusement pittoresque' (see Figure 29). The experience of the grandeur of nature was presented as quite compatible with the pleasures of civilisation and luxury. A 1925 issue of *La Revue Moderne* included an article by Charles Heidsieck, whose very name connoted luxury consumption, describing a rail trip from Montreal to Vancouver. (CP offered free trips to journalists and to artists, and this no doubt explains why so many magazine articles described cross-continental rail journeys and illustrated the scenery that could be viewed along the way). Arriving in the Rockies, Heidsieck writes:

> Ces montagnes énormes ont des arrêtes tourmentées, sombres et terribles. [...] Cet un spectacle désordonné mais magnifique. Le tout est grand et immense et l'homme se sent petit et étouffe sous cette atmosphère écrasante.
>
> L'arrivée à Banff, la fameuse station d'été créé par le 'Canadian Pacific' vous tire de votre muette admiration. La vie semble reprendre tout à coup et c'est un village coquet et élégant qui vous accueille. [...] Dès l'arrivée à l'hôtel, le touriste bien impressionné est saisi par l'atmosphère de luxe qui y règne et c'est l'existence des palaces qui vous attend. Les relations mondaines se nouent vite et bientôt ce ne sont plus que parties joyeuses. (18)

The discourse of the Romantic picturesque here modulates abruptly into that of contemporary worldliness. The promotion of Canada to Canadians by means of a European writer, who refers to the Rockies as 'cette Suisse merveilleuse' (18), reinforces the notion that domestic travel could offer a simulated experience of Europe. In essence, the advertisers sought to extract and commodify appealing features of European culture for a home market; for those unable to pay for train fare and hotel rooms, the magazines—consumer products in themselves—offered the images for consumption.

During the war, this kind of consumption became even more escapist: it drew power from looking away from the conflict and conjuring up ease and security, not to mention pleasure and self-indulgence. It is true that CP and its cruise ships, including the *Empress of Britain*, were part of the industry that supported the war effort, and consumer support of the company could therefore be presented as a patriotic investment. Yet, the advertising campaigns continued to capitalise on a fantasy of travel which had been dominant across the early to mid-twentieth century, generating continuity in the ways in which middlebrow magazines appealed to readers over these decades. Returning, for instance, to the 1930s advertisements for the *Empress of Britain*, we can see that the appeal of the images and text used during the war years is not significantly different. The focus, as a 1940 advertisement in *Mayfair* for the Banff Springs suggests, is on the desire to be among 'those who make the news,' to be cultured and surrounded by beauty, to be free of the demands of labour and able to meet the expense with ease. The advertisement offered the reassurance that some things, like resort hotels, were unshaken by the war; moreover, it maintained the aspirations of the Canadian populace, and ensured that consumer desire for conspicuous leisure did not wane in an era when many consumer advertisements were drawing from war images and rhetoric to align their products with patriotic effort, austerity, and thrift.[6]

The promotion of domestic travel resonated with the magazines' nationalist priorities. Their attention to informing readers about current events, and presenting histories of different regions, dovetailed with discussions of travelling within Canada. An article in the July 1930 issue of the *Journal*, by former editor Jean Graham, urged readers to 'See Canada First!' and argued that 'we cannot imagine any country more liberally endowed with lakes, hills, and streams, where we may fish and ramble to our heart's delight, and build up a store of health that may last for many months' (10). She went on to enumerate Canada's attractions from Prince Edward Island, 'with its roses and its salt air,' to 'picturesque Quebec, with the lordliest river in the world giving its freshness for a thousand miles' to 'Banff the Beautiful, mak[ing] Alberta glorious, and Jasper Park having every attraction that nature can bestow' (10). She concluded:

> there is no land on earth that can give us fairer views or happier days. North, south, east, and west, the prospect is the same, with the bluest of lakes, the brightest of streams, and mountains that kiss the clouds. We certainly do not need to cross our own boundaries, in order to find all that human nature demands. (11)

A more masculine, rugged vision of Canadian wilderness circulated through *Maclean's* in articles such as Edward E. Bishop's 'Mountain Road,' published in the 15 July 1938 issue. He describes a journey on foot along the route of the uncompleted Jasper–Banff highway, which at this point had a 35-mile gap in the middle. To reach the mid-point of the highway's route, at Graveyard, took Bishop and his companions 'almost three days of steady hiking, on top of an eighty-mile automobile drive from the town of Banff.' Their heavy rucksacks, and the necessity of wading across deep rivers, added to the challenge, but they were rewarded by scenes of startling beauty: 'This, we considered, was nature at its best, and constituted perfection to us in spite of the weariness induced by the many miles of trail behind us' (17). The emphasis here is on effort rather than ease, but the celebration of Canada and its unspoilt wilderness is consistent with other articles and advertisements.

A month later, *Maclean's* published a feature on youth hostelling by James Harman. This piece, too, showed a new kind of travel infrastructure in the

---

[6] This emphasis continued after the war, even when austerity was no longer so necessary. Korinek reflects on the way that *Chatelaine*'s attention to thrift in the 1950s and 1960s was attributed, by readers, to its Canadian values (193).

process of construction: the Canadian Youth Hostel Association (which used the acronym C. Y. H., rather than C. Y. H. A.) had been in existence only five years, and had so far established just four hostel trails. It was, on the one hand, a nostalgic or antimodern movement, seeking to discover the untouched natural world of pre-contact North America, and to escape the effects of modern urbanisation and industrialisation.[7] The article evokes 'the romance of travelling inexpensively, the thrill of undergoing a Spartan routine, of physical hardship or at least the absence of luxury, the lure of movement, contact with new scenes' and so on (16). At the same time, and paradoxically, the promise of the C. Y. H. was associated with youth and national progress: 'Youth hosteling,' writes Harman, 'bids fair to give young Canadians an opportunity to know Canada as they have never known it before' (16). This undertaking is given a more explicitly political edge by one of the founders of the C. Y. H., who tells Harman: 'There is in Canada a certain amount of unhealthy provincialism, which must be broken down. We believe that the better understanding of each other's problems, and the exchange of ideas which inevitably comes with travel, will do much to consolidate the national and political life of the Dominion' (35).

It was not until the 1950s that articles on camping, and other budget holiday options, became more prominent in the women's magazines. Irene Pump's 1958 *Chatelaine* piece 'We Camped Our Way Through Europe,' for example, was prefaced by a blurb that asked: 'Why don't you do as this young couple did—take a lighthearted and unusual grand tour—for ten dollars a day (for two)?' Pump explained that 'for two glorious months in the spring of 1957, my husband and I traveled by car through six European countries, enjoyed comfort, privacy, and freedom, cut tips to a bare minimum, and returned triumphantly to Canada with a surplus of money.' While they had initially projected a trip centred on 'hotels, restaurants, and conventional sight-seeing,' they abandoned their plans in favour of 'living under the olive trees with a panoramic view of Florence' and 'sharing a bottle of Medoc with your next-door neighbors under the stars of a French sky.' *Chatelaine*'s 1950s travel pieces reflect a youthful verve, one that marks a turning point in how travel is related to middlebrow aspirations—the need to budget was no longer a source of shame (rather, money

---

[7] Jessup defines antimodernism in terms of 'the pervasive sense of loss that often coexisted in the decades around the turn of the century along with an enthusiasm for modernization and material progress.' She adds that it 'was in effect a critique of the modern, a perceived lack in the present manifesting itself not only in a sense of alienation, but also in a longing for the types of physical or spiritual experience embodied in Utopian futures and imagined pasts' (4). On Canadian antimodernism, see Hammill, 'Wilderness'; Rifkind. See also Renato on imperialist nostalgia.

was saved with pride); flexibility and individuality mattered more than visiting prescribed locations; the goal was to enjoy oneself, and return with a set of unique memories. In a July 1959 editorial on the best way to make the most of holiday time, Doris Anderson expressed a fantasy which contrasted markedly with the ideals embodied by Hilda Pain's chatelaine of 1928:

> Resolve to sleep in if you can, or make onion sandwiches at midnight, if it pleases you. Bury your girdle in the bottom drawer, or buy a lipstick brush and while away an hour trying it out. Read poetry in solitude or fill the house with people. Walk barefoot in the sand or take the children to the park. See only the people you like most, and would enjoy even if the house is a mess and you have left off your lipstick.
>
> Time enough, come September, to be stern about your obligations in life. It's summer now. It's holiday time. Resolve to let the part of you that often gets lost in the squeeze of household demands luxuriate in a little self-indulgence. Resolve to take the best (however brief) vacation you possibly can—from your dutiful, workaday self.

The emphasis on the productive use of leisure time which had dominated the women's magazines in the earlier decades of the twentieth century had given way, by this time, to an emphasis on relaxation and self-discovery.

In *Maclean's* during this period, an increasing number of features on remote destinations appeared, and these were strongly associated with antimodernism, and with what we would now call environmentalism. The desire to keep the wild areas of Canada free from the incursions of 'civilisation' presents an interesting inversion of the colonial project of importing civilisation to the wilderness. Fred Bodsworth, in his piece 'The Fight to Keep the Wilderness Wild,' for the 15 May 1951 number of *Maclean's*, wrote about Quetico in north-western Ontario, which had been established as a provincial park in 1913. In the early 1950s, road access to the wilderness park was being planned, and this provides the occasion for the piece, which begins: 'In Quetico Park a canoeist can sometimes slap a moose on the rump with his paddle. And deep in the lake-and-forest fastness he can forget the civilized world and its worries.' The area is now the focus of campaigning: 'Trying to keep this piece of nature in the raw, an ardent band of wilderness lovers are fighting off the speedboats, dance halls and hamburger stands' (12). Bodsworth goes on to reflect on his own trips there:

> I have experienced the restful soul-cleansing sense of escape that only the wilderness traveler can know. I love Quetico—the raw and rough Quetico that far-sighted authorities have so far seen fit to preserve. I

hope my grandchildren, and their grandchildren, will be able to know and love the wild untracked Quetico which I can know today. We owe them at least one unspoiled fragment of the primitive mid-continental America that is now all but gone. (13)

The article insists on the distinction between wilderness *travel* and commercial *tourism*, and it also speaks to the contradictory mandate of the national and provincial park authorities in Canada. The process of establishing official, protected wilderness areas had begun towards the end of the nineteenth century, but it was only in the later twentieth century that ecological imperatives took over from recreational ones. As Claire Campbell writes: 'By the middle of the twentieth century, the National Parks Branch held a stated commitment to environmental protection but typically was preoccupied with managing parks for tourism and recreation,' which led to a contradiction, as suburban populations made increasing demands on park space (7). Intervening in this debate, articles such as Bodsworth's get caught up in the contradictions which Campbell mentions. The piece extols the beauties of Quetico at length, yet simultaneously laments the fact that increasing numbers of people wish to visit it. In publicising the attractions of park areas, the magazines inevitably contributed to pressures for development, even when their contributors argued against it. Indeed, the magazines' construction of the wilderness in antimodern terms only throws into relief the tourism industry's increasing commodification of wild spaces.

Conclusion

The presentation of the Canadian wilderness as a place of escape and respite from modern, commercialised culture is in tension with the consumer-oriented types of travel writing and advertising discussed throughout this chapter. Travel was presented predominantly as an opportunity for both luxury consumption and the consolidation of social and cultural capital. These practices were bound up with the idea of the magazine itself as a site of both entertainment and improvement. For some readers, a journey abroad, or across Canada, was actually possible, enabling them to adopt a temporary 'travelling self,' free to live out certain aspirations outside the realm of the everyday. For a much larger category of readers, such travel was not affordable, and it became a fantasy bolstered by the magazines' ability to offer proxy access to a world of prestige and vicarious consumption.

Travel and consumption were presented as twin pleasures by Canada's mainstream magazines. In their pages, both activities offered escapist fantasies that counterpoised the more mundane aspects of everyday life. Yet both activities were also constructed as part of the programme of continual self-improvement which magazines proposed for their readers. Many travel features struck a note of dissatisfaction about everyday life, and this fed the desire to have and to do more upon which consumer culture depended. Readers were encouraged to see their lives, and their journeys, in terms of their ongoing accumulation of knowledge, status, and material goods, but the effort to attain these things was fraught with the risk of failure. Magazines therefore offered advice in tandem with the fantasies they prompted, presenting themselves as experienced guides in the areas of good taste, worldly knowledge, networking, and wise expenditure. This attention to balance is central to the middlebrow ethos generated by the periodicals: a trip abroad might offer unwonted opportunities for self-indulgence, but was likely to require careful saving in advance; and while leisure activities abroad need not be avant-garde, they ought to contribute to self-education, with the proof of one's learning articulated through the purchase of a souvenir or through documenting the trip.

Certain destinations, activities, and points of interest were championed. Discussions of domestic travel celebrated the Canadian nation, with both natural beauty and modern modes of transport presented as a potential source of pride for citizens. The capital cities of Europe, by contrast, were constructed as exotic, cosmopolitan spaces, yet simultaneously as sites of access to old-world history and culture. This culture was presented to readers as being, in some measure, their inheritance as citizens of a country largely settled by immigrants from Europe. Luxury was emphasised in both foreign and domestic travel promotions. A visit to Rome or Paris, or indeed to Lake Louise, promised both mental elevation and sensual pleasure, both betterment and delight.

CONCLUSION

It is the time of year when one has to decide what to do with the summer. It is the time of year when, in the more beautifully printed magazines, the advertisements of the steamship companies in one section and the seedsmen and garden supplies companies in another tear one's heart in two with absolutely incompatible allurements. [...] The man who puts things into the ground in April and May and June is practically rooting himself to the ground until September and October. The mystery of the Orient, the glamour of the Southern Seas, can mean little or nothing to him until the snow has descended upon the last of his tall stalks of half-budded Brussels sprouts and the frost has nipped off the heads of his final show of asters and chrysanthemums.
—B. K. Sandwell, 'Garden while you gad,' *Mayfair* March 1928

B. K. Sandwell's fanciful solution to this problem is that the shipping lines and seed companies should join forces, promoting a new kind of transportable garden. If it is replenished with plants from the different countries visited, it will become, he says, an ideal souvenir of the trip. Sandwell suggests various possible slogans for this new composite advertising, such as 'Garden while you gad,' 'Cultivate your mind and your garden,' 'Culture and horticulture,' and 'Take your garden round the world' (17). But he ends his piece on a more serious note of patriotism: 'Feverishly as I yearn to visit Seringapatam, when I am reading Mr Cook's descriptions of its beauties, I know in my sober moments that there is no place like Hamilton, Ontario, or Three Rivers, Quebec' (58). A dynamic between home and mobility animates Sandwell's article and, likewise, the magazine it appeared in. Indeed, all the magazines explored in this book succeed, as Sandwell does, in balancing fantasies of exotic travel with a strong commitment to domestic life and national community. And they all thrived on the middlebrow culture of progress, self-cultivation, and the accumulation of material goods which Sandwell light-heartedly evokes.

CONCLUSION

The editors of *Mayfair* present the magazine as the purveyor of a Canadian dream. Their vocabulary of aspiration and distinction belongs to the discourse of the middlebrow, and is intertwined with nationalist sentiment in a way which was entirely characteristic of Canada's mainstream magazines. A celebratory editorial looking back on the first year of *Mayfair*'s run asked:

> what true Canadian has not dreamed of seeing his country recognised ... taking its place in the world of arts, of letters ... establishing its individuality ... individual literature ... individual books ... *magazines?* Who has not yearned to see virile young Canada expressing itself ... to see sophisticated, cultured, yea, even distinguished Canada depicted to the life ... charmingly, interestingly, even amusingly! (Editorial, March 1928)

Individuality, or having something unique to say, goes hand in hand with establishing a place on the world stage. The editorial proposes that, in order to gain distinction within a global culture of arts, letters, and fashion, Canada needs a leadership group who will set trends and represent the country abroad. *Mayfair*'s readers were encouraged to see themselves as this group and the magazine as their ally: 'And you ... the fashionable elect of our country [...]. You saw the possibilities, the marvelous scope for a magazine which could do just this.' *Mayfair* set itself the dual task of, firstly, reporting on the lives of Canada's elite, and, secondly, bringing them cultural and style news from abroad. Its role is therefore constructed in terms of perpetual motion: 'Just as *Mayfair* was gasping for breath from the dissipations of the holiday season,' the editorial continues, 'behold the Drawing Room presentations at Ottawa dawn upon the horizon. We packed our little week-end bag ... *and so ... to Ottawa.*' Even the magazine's fashion reporting is presented as a type of expedition: '*Mayfair* has been on a voyage of discovery ... tossing about on the Fashion seas. And for excitement, thrills, adventure, it surpasses any ocean voyage.' *Mayfair* was a magazine with a particular focus on travel. Yet the more domestically oriented periodicals, such as the *Canadian Home Journal* or *La Revue Populaire*, likewise drew extensively on discourses of movement, discovery, and the exotic. Indeed, all the magazines included in this study recast geographical mobility as upward mobility by circulating images of travel in both literary and commercial contexts. They promoted actual journeys, through editorial features and advertising, but they also provided a vicarious experience of the foreign, offering readers the enabling fantasy of the 'travelling self,' free from the restrictions and duties of everyday life.

The presentation of travel was heavily inflected by the nationalist agendas which shaped all six magazines. Foreign travel features often focused on destinations which could enhance many white Canadians' sense of connection with their ancestry (holidays in France, England, and Scotland) or with the 'British world' (for instance, articles on Jamaica and Bermuda). Notions of cosmopolitan sophistication enabled magazines to accommodate nostalgia for the 'Old World' alongside the apparently contrary construction of Canadian identity in terms of modernity. Domestic travel was also extensively promoted, not only as a way for Canadians to get to know their own country, but also as a form of consumer-based nationalism, since some of the largest and most influential Canadian companies were railway and shipping operators. The notion of travel as investment was particularly prominent in the business-oriented *Maclean's*, but was also subtly present in the other magazines. It was an idea which connected nationalist commitment with a more individualist discourse of self-improvement, since buying shares in Canadian National railways, or taking a train to the Rockies for a holiday, would profit both country and individual.

The middlebrow ideal of self-improvement was dominant across the decades covered by our study, though during the later 1950s, it began to give way to an emphasis on self-discovery and individualised travel. Instead of prescribed itineraries and standardised cultural knowledge, the magazines started to recommend unusual or remote destinations, flexible trip planning, and low-budget options. The shift was especially noticeable in the two magazines which would survive into the very different commercial climate of the later twentieth century. As the travel industry fragmented into niche markets, so periodical publishing began to prioritise special interest rather than general titles. The two magazines which successfully navigated this change were *Maclean's*, which ran numerous features on camping and wilderness tourism during the fifties, and *Chatelaine*, with its focus on affordable holidays for families.

Mayfair, by contrast, had retained an atmosphere of luxury and exclusivity, though it seemed to be shading into decadence. In December 1959, *Mayfair* printed a travel piece on Nassau in the Bahamas. It is presented as a fragmented list of sights, smells, and tastes: 'Stepped out of the TCA plane into hot, humid perfumed pink paradise ... Nassau. Fort Montagu Beach Hotel ... hotel's traditional drink ... Hibiscus ... flower placed in drink. Swimming at 3 a.m. in hotel pool' (30). The author, Barbara Lawrey, finds many pleasures in the resort, and does a great deal of shopping—'Monday went to Mademoiselle Shop and Amanda Furs shop to view fashion clothes ... possessed with desire to own all of them' (30). She ends her travelogue: 'returned in special TCA flight ... same stewardess ... seemed like having home with us already ... arrived in Toronto ... bleak and cloudy' (32). *Mayfair*'s style had not changed much since 1928. The travel writing still emphasises indulgent consumption, and the texts are still filled with ellipses, generating an impressionistic feel and a quality of fantasy. The ellipses imply an assumption that the magazine's readers will easily be able to fill in the gaps, since they share a body of tacit knowledge. Yet there is a languidness to this piece: the collective energy of *Mayfair*'s 1920s editorials is missing, and individual gratification is all that is aimed at. Canada seems to be a place to escape from rather than to celebrate. Indeed, this issue of *Mayfair* also contained a portentous article, 'The Last Christmas of the Fifties,' which laments that 'the sun has set even on Britain's dominions; we *are* fat and complacent' (14). Written by the *Globe and Mail*'s Washington correspondent, Philip Deane, the piece articulates the threats of disruptive industrial action, 'spendthrift' western economies, and the growth of communist power, describing these as 'the despoilers tunneling under our lavish castle' while 'the prosperous citizenry of these Atlantic Nations searches only for ever more luxurious gadgets to buy as Christmas gifts' (14). Consumerism had become an end in itself, rather than a means to national advancement. And *Mayfair*, itself always lavish and always full of promotions for luxurious gifts, was now on the point of collapse. It had become a much less substantial publication, in several senses, than it had been at first, and had abandoned its early ambitions on behalf of Canadian arts and letters. The December 1959 number would be its last.

In *La Revue Moderne*'s final issue, in June 1960, a notice to subscribers about the impending merger with *Chatelaine* described the important cultural influence of the two titles, in Francophone and Anglophone Canada respectively, concluding: 'Il est donc évident que la fusion de La Revue Moderne et Chatelaine est une initiative capitale. On espère favoriser ainsi le développement de la littérature, des arts et de la culture au Canada.' As well as articulating this admirable aim, the notice explained the practical reasons for the merger: 'Il est de plus en plus difficile à une publication française du Québec, limitée par ses ressources locales, d'offrir au Canada français le genre de magazine que son développement moderne exige.' One of the greatest challenges cited was foreign competition, and the merger was intended to make the magazine more commercially viable: 'Cette fusion permettra de présenter un périodique plus rentable, mieux illustré et beaucoup plus varié' (Cadieux). There was, of course, a conflict between cultural aspirations and commercial imperatives; the latter won out, and the newly named *Châtelaine* achieved success at the cost of becoming much more similar to its American and English-Canadian rivals. Indeed, there was little room for diversity in what remained of the general interest magazine marketplace in 1960s Canada. The broad tendency in print media was towards specialisation, with editors and advertisers targeting much more narrowly defined audiences. In a country with a relatively small population, only very well capitalised, or generously subsidised, publications could maintain a national scope. By 1963, all three of the surviving titles were owned by the same company. *La Revue Populaire* folded in that year, and the *Canadian Home Journal* had been sold five years previously to Maclean Publishing, which shut it down and used its subscription list to increase sales of *Chatelaine*. A twenty-first-century issue of *Maclean's*, *Chatelaine*, or *Châtelaine* looks very different from an issue published during the interwar or postwar years, and yet there are certain continuities. A consumer-based ethos still predominates. The women's magazines define the primary areas of feminine interest using categories which were established a century ago: fashion, the home, cookery, and so on. In *Maclean's* especially, an emphasis on the distinctiveness of Canadian culture persists. These magazines have been, and remain, extremely influential, and the cultural work they perform includes mediating ideas of nationhood in relation to gender and class, and constructing Canada's relationship to foreign cultures. Their origins and histories deserve to be much better known.

BIBLIOGRAPHY

'À New-York ... À Paris ...' *La Revue Populaire* July 1946: 10–11. Print.

Aliman, Laura. 'Cottage Crafts.' *Canadian Home Journal* June 1951: 4. Print.

'Among Those Present.' *Canadian Home Journal* June 1951: 2. Print.

Anderson, Doris. Editorial. *Chatelaine* July 1959: 14. Print.

Ardis, Ann. 'Making Middlebrow Culture, Making Middlebrow Literary Texts Matter: The Crisis, Easter 1912.' *Modernist Cultures* 6.1 (2011): 18–40. Print.

Ardis, Ann and Patrick Collier. Introduction. *Transatlantic Print Culture, 1880–1940: Emerging Media, Emerging Modernisms*. Ed. Ardis and Collier. Basingstoke: Palgrave, 2008. 1–12. Print.

Aston, Suzy and Sue Ferguson. '*Maclean's*: The First 100 Years.' 2005. www.macleans.ca. Web.

Aubry, Luc. 'Quels sont d'après vous les qualités et les défauts de la jeune fille moderne?' *La Revue Moderne* June 1925: 11–12. Print.

Aynsley, Jeremy. 'Fashioning graphics in the 1920s: Typefaces, magazines and fashion.' *Design and the Modern Magazine*. Ed. Aynsley and Forde. Manchester: Manchester UP, 2007. 37–55. Print.

Aynsley, Jeremy and Kate Forde, eds. *Design and the Modern Magazine*. Manchester: Manchester UP, 2007. Print.

—. 'Introduction.' *Design and the Modern Magazine*. Ed. Aynsley and Forde. Manchester: Manchester UP, 2007. 1–16. Print.

Azoulay, Dan. *Hearts and Minds: Canadian Romance at the Dawn of the Modern Era, 1900–1930*. Calgary: U of Calgary P, 2011. Web.

Baillargeon, Denyse. *Brève histoire des femmes au Québec*. Montreal: Éditions du Boréal, 2012. Print.

Barbour, Noel. *Those Amazing People! The Story of the Canadian Magazine Industry*. Toronto: Crucible P, 1982. Print.

Barnard, Leslie Gordon. 'Successor to Laura.' *Canadian Home Journal* June 1951: 16+. Print.

Barrington, Gwenyth. 'Is the Canadian woman better dressed than her American sister?' *Chatelaine* Mar. 1932: 7–8. Print.

Baudelaire, Charles. 'Le Peintre de la vie moderne.' 1863. Rpt in *Œuvres Complètes de Charles Baudelaire*. Vol. 3. Paris: Michel Lévy Frères, 1868. 51–114. Print.

Beaulieu, André and Jean Hamelin. *La presse québécoise des origines à nos jours.* Vol. 4. Québec: PUL, 1982. Print.

—. *La presse québécoise des origines à nos jours.* Vol. 5. Québec: PUL, 1984. Print.

Beetham, Margaret. *A Magazine of Her Own? Domesticity and Desire in the Woman's Magazine, 1800–1914.* London: Routledge, 1996. Print.

Béland, Emmanuel. 'Catalogues and Consumer Loyalty.' *Before E-Commerce: A History of Canadian Mail-order Catalogues.* Canadian Museum of History, 2004. Web.

Belisle, Donica. *Retail Nation: Department Stores and the Making of Modern Canada.* Vancouver: U of British Columbia P, 2011. Print.

Bell, Quentin. *On Human Finery.* London: The Hogarth Press, 1947. Print.

Benjamin, Walter, *The Arcades Project.* Trans. Howard Eiland and Kevin McLaughlin. Cambridge: Harvard UP, 2002. Print.

'Les Bermudes.' *La Revue Moderne* Sept. 1928: 11. Print.

Bertin, Leonard. 'Are We Winning the War Against Cancer in Women?' Oct. 1958: 28+. Print.

Berton, Pierre. 'Irwin, William Arthur.' *The Canadian Encyclopedia.* Toronto: Historica Foundation, 2007. Web.

Best, Kate Nelson. 'Fashioning the Figure of French Creativity: A Historical Perspective on the Political Function of French Fashion Discourse.' *Web Journal of Media French Studies* 7 (2008). Web.

Bishop, Edward E. 'Mountain Road.' *Maclean's* 15 July 1938: 17+. Print.

Bishop, Edward L. 'Re:Covering Modernism: Format and Function in the Little Magazines.' *Modernist Writers and the Marketplace.* Ed. Ian Willison, Warwick Gould, and Warren Cherniak. Basingstoke: Macmillan, 1996. 287–319. Print.

Blair, Amy L. *Reading Up: Middle-Class Readers and the Culture of Success in the Early Twentieth-Century United States.* Philadelphia: Temple UP, 2011. Print.

Bobb, Yvonne, as told to Jeannine Locke. 'Are Canadians Really Tolerant?' *Chatelaine* Sept. 1959: 27. Print.

Bodsworth, Fred. 'The Fight to Keep the Wilderness Wild.' *Maclean's* 15 May 1951: 12+. Print.

Bornstein, George. *Material Modernism: The Politics of the Page.* Cambridge: Cambridge UP, 2001. Print.

Bosnitch, Katherine. 'A Little on the Wild Side: Eaton's Prestige Fashion Advertising Published in the *Montreal Gazette*, 1952–1972.' *Fashion: A Canadian Perspective.* Ed. Alexandra Palmer. Toronto: U of Toronto P, 2004. 339–63. Print.

Botshon, Lisa and Meredith Goldsmith, eds. *Middlebrow Moderns: Popular American Women Writers of the 1920s.* Boston: Northeastern UP, 2003. Print.

Bourdieu, Pierre. *Distinction: A Social Critique of the Judgement of Taste.* Trans. Richard Nice. Cambridge: Harvard UP, 1984. Print.

—. *The Field of Cultural Production: Essays on Art and Literature.* Ed. Randal Johnson. Cambridge: Polity, 1993. Print.

—. *Questions de Sociologie.* Paris: Minuit, 1980. Print.

BIBLIOGRAPHY

Bowallius, Marie-Louise. 'Advertising and the use of colour in *Women's Home Companion*, 1923–33.' *Design and the Modern Magazine*. Ed. Jeremy Aynsley and Kate Forde. Manchester: Manchester UP, 2007. 18–36. Print.

Bowen, Elizabeth. 'Dress.' Review of *English Women's Clothing in the Nineteenth Century* by C. Willett Cunnington. *The New Statesman and Nation*. 1937. Rpt in *Collected Impressions*. Elizabeth Bowen. London: Longmans, Green, 1950. 111–15. Print.

Bowker, Kathleen K. 'Walks Abroad About London.' *Mayfair* Apr. 1935: 91+. Print.

—. 'London Luminous.' *Mayfair* July 1935: 24+. Print.

—. 'Who Said Safari?' *Mayfair* Oct. 1935: 80. Print.

Boxer, Rosemary. 'Fashions with an Oriental Flair.' *Canadian Home Journal* Mar. 1958: 17–25. Print.

—. 'Spring fashions … in new power colours.' *Canadian Home Journal* Feb. 1958: 16–19. Print.

Boyd, John. 'The Secret of National Unity.' *La Revue Moderne* 15 Dec. 1919: 15–16. Print.

Bristol, Naomi. 'Hotel of Kings and Queens.' *Mayfair* Nov. 1952: 50+. Print.

Brooker, Peter and Andrew Thacker. 'General Introduction.' *The Oxford Critical and Cultural History of Modernist Magazines. Vol. 1: Britain and Ireland 1880–1955*. Ed. Brooker and Thacker. Oxford: Oxford UP, 2009. 1–26. Print.

Brown, Erica. *Comedy and the Feminine Middlebrow Novel: Elizabeth von Arnim and Elizabeth Taylor*. London: Pickering and Chatto, 2013. Print.

Brown, Erica and Mary Grover. Introduction. *Middlebrow Literary Cultures: The Battle of the Brows, 1920–1960*. Ed. Brown and Grover. Basingstoke: Palgrave, 2012. 1–24. Print.

—, eds. *Middlebrow Literary Cultures: The Battle of the Brows, 1920–1960*. Basingstoke: Palgrave, 2012. Print.

Bruchési, Jean. 'Les onze ans de *La Revue Moderne*.' *La Revue Moderne* Nov. 1930: 5. Print.

Bryan, Eva Ruberta. 'Bermuda's Lure for Canadians.' *Mayfair* Jan. 1935: 24+. Print.

Burke, Eustella. 'The Letter from Paris.' *Chatelaine* Oct. 1930: 12+. Print.

—. 'The Paris Letter.' *Chatelaine* Jan. 1931: 4+. Print.

Cadieux, Léo. 'Fusion, dès septembre prochain, de Chatelaine et La Revue Moderne. Message aux abonnés.' *La Revue Moderne* June 1960: 15. Print.

Campbell, Claire Elizabeth. 'Governing a Kingdom: Parks Canada, 1911–2011.' *A Century of Parks Canada, 1911–2011*. Ed. Campbell. Calgary: U of Calgary P, 2011. 1–19. Web.

Cameron, Colin. 'Don't be a Babe in the Woods.' *Canadian Home Journal* June 1951: 10+. Print.

Canada Dry. Advertisement. *Chatelaine* June 1934: 33. Print.

Canadian Celanese. Advertisement. *Chatelaine* Mar. 1930: 85. Print.

—. Advertisement. *Chatelaine* Apr. 1930: 72. Print.

—. Advertisement. *La Revue Moderne*. Mar. 1931: 30. Print.

Canadian National. Advertisement. *Maclean's* 15 June 1925: 74. Print.
—. Advertisement. *Canadian Home Journal* June 1951: 85. Print.
Canadian Pacific. Advertisement. *Maclean's* 15 June 1925: 73. Print.
—. Advertisement. *Mayfair* Aug. 1929: 50. Print.
—. Advertisement. *La Revue Populaire* July 1930: 6. Print.
—. Advertisement. *Mayfair* April 1931: 69. Print.
—. Advertisement. *Chatelaine* June 1932: 32. Print.
—. Advertisement. *Mayfair* Aug. 1935: 48. Print.
—. Advertisement. *Chatelaine* May 1938: 52. Print.
—. Advertisement. *Canadian Home Journal* June 1938: 35. Print.
—. Advertisement. *Mayfair* May 1940: inside front cover. Print.
—. Advertisement. *Canadian Home Journal* June 1951: 62. Print.
Carter, David. 'The Mystery of the Missing Middlebrow or The Co(u)rse of Good Taste.' *Imagining Australia: Literature and Culture in the New New World.* Ed. Judith Ryan and Chris Wallace-Crabbe. Cambridge: Harvard University Committee on Australian Studies, 2004. 173–201. Print.
Cassell, Joan. 'For Your Mad Fling in Europe.' Apr. 1959: 38. Print.
Caton, Susan Turnbull. 'Fashion and War in Canada.' *Fashion: A Canadian Perspective.* Ed. Alexandra Palmer. Toronto: U of Toronto P, 2004. 249–69. Print.
'Ce que l'on pense de *La Revue Moderne*.' *La Revue Moderne* Nov. 1935: 5. Print.
Chapman, Rosemary. *Between Languages and Cultures: Colonial and Postcolonial Readings of Gabrielle Roy.* Montreal: McGill-Queens UP, 2009. Print.
'Charivaria.' *Punch* 23 Dec. 1925: 673. Print.
The Chatelaine. Advertisement. *Chatelaine* Sept. 1931: 28. Print.
'The Chatelaine Pattern Service.' *Chatelaine* June 1932: 70. Print.
Chevrolet. Advertisement. *La Revue Moderne* Jan. 1932: inside front cover. Print.
Christ, Yvan. 'Restaurants de Paris.' *La Revue Moderne* May 1955: 10. Print.
'Circulation Now.' Advertisement. *Chatelaine* Jan. 1933: 3. Print.
Clark, H. C. 'London's Mayfair.' *Mayfair* Jan. 1956: 23+. Print.
'Clean, orderly Switzerland.' *Mayfair* May 1950: 57+. Print.
Clio Collective (Micheline Dumont et al.). *Quebec Women: A History.* 1982. Trans. Roger Gannon and Rosalind Gill. Toronto: Women's Press, 1987. Print.
Cole, Catherine C. 'Eaton's Winnipeg and Toronto Catalogues Compared.' *Before E-Commerce: A History of Canadian Mail-order Catalogues.* Toronto: Canadian Museum of History, 2004. Web.
Cole, Celia Caroline. 'Eve Au Miroir: Où allons-nous?' *La Revue Moderne* Jan. 1932: 20. Print.
'Comment se Donner un Manicure à la Maison.' *La Revue Populaire* Jan. 1932: 62. Print.
Conrad, Jacqueline. 'À Paris, la robe-sac a fait son temps.' *La Revue Populaire* Apr. 1958: 10. Print.
—. 'Lettre de Paris.' *La Revue Populaire* Apr. 1947: 7. Print.
Crawshaw, Carole and John Urry. 'Tourism and the Photographic Eye.' *Touring*

Cultures: Transformations of Travel and Theory. Ed. Chris Rojek and John Urry. London: Routledge, 2002. 176–95. Print.

Cucullu, Lois. *Expert Modernists, Matricide and Modern Culture: Woolf, Forster, Joyce.* Basingstoke: Palgrave Macmillan, 2004. Print.

Cuddy-Keane, Melba. *Virginia Woolf, the Intellectual and the Public Sphere.* Cambridge: Cambridge UP, 2003. Print.

'Cuisine Française.' *La Revue Populaire* Sept. 1954: 15. Print.

Dagenais, John. 'Decolonizing the Medieval Page.' *The Future of the Page.* Ed. Peter Stoicheff and Andrew Taylor. Toronto: U of Toronto P, 2004. 37–70. Print.

Damon, Carolyn. 'How Do We Dress from Here?' *Chatelaine* Feb. 1941: 16. Print.

Damon-Moore, Helen. *Magazine for the Millions: Gender and Commerce in* The Ladies' Home Journal *and* The Saturday Evening Post, *1880–1910.* Albany: New York UP, 1994. Print.

'Dans le Monde de l'automobile.' *La Revue Populaire* Jan. 1932: 62. Print.

Dare, Eleanor. 'I'd Like To Know.' *Canadian Home Journal* Apr. 1945: 30. Print.

—. 'Smiling Through.' *Canadian Home Journal* Jan. 1941: 46–47. Print.

Deane, Philip. 'The Last Christmas of the Fifties.' *Mayfair* Dec. 1959: 12–14. Print.

Dempsey, Lotta. 'Will war affect our fashions?' *Chatelaine* Feb. 1940: 8+. Print.

Des Rivières, Marie-José. *Châtelaine et la littérature, 1960–75.* Montréal: L'Hexagone, 1992. Print.

Des Rivières, Marie-José, Carole Gerson, and Denis Saint-Jacques. 'Women's Magazines.' *History of the Book in Canada. Vol. 3: 1918–1980.* Ed. Carole Gerson and Jacques Michon. Toronto: U of Toronto P, 2007. 248–53. Print.

Dickason, Olive. 'Couturier Show Mixed in Merit.' *Globe & Mail* 6 Feb. 1957: 11. Print.

Diepeveen, Leonard. *The Difficulties of Modernism.* New York: Routledge, 2003. Print.

Distad, Merrill. 'Newspapers and Magazines.' *History of the Book in Canada. Vol. 2: 1840–1918.* Ed. Yvan Lamonde, Patricia Lockhart Fleming, and Fiona Black. Toronto: U of Toronto P, 2005. 293–303. Print.

Djwa, Sandra. *Journey with No Maps: A Life of P. K. Page.* Montreal: McGill-Queens UP, 2012. Print.

Dobbs, Kildare, comp. *Away from Home: Canadian Writers in Exotic Places.* Toronto: Deneau, 1985. Print.

Doig, Ryan Mitchell. 'Protecting Canadian Culture: The Case of Split-Run Periodicals.' MA thesis. U of Calgary, 2001. Web.

Dornan, Christopher. 'Printed Matter: Canadian Newspapers.' *How Canadians Communicate.* Ed. David Taras, Frits Pannekoek, and Maria Bakardjieva. Calgary: U of Calgary P, 2003. 97–120. Print.

Douglas, George H. *The Smart Magazines: 50 Years of Literary Revelry and High Jinks at Vanity Fair, The New Yorker, Life, Esquire, and The Smart Set.* Hamden: Archon Books, 1991. Print.

Dubinsky, Karen. 'Everybody Likes Canadians: Canadians, Americans, and the

Post-World War II Travel Boom.' *Being Elsewhere: Tourism, Consumer Culture, and Identity in Modern Europe and North America*. Ed. Shelley Baranowski and Ellen Furlough. U of Michigan P, 2001. 320–44. Print.

—. *The Second Greatest Disappointment: Honeymooning and Tourism in Niagara Falls*. Toronto: Between the Lines, 1999. Print.

Dumont, Micheline and Louise Toupin, ed. *La pensée féministe au Québec*. Montréal: Éditions du remue-ménage, 2003. Print.

Dupuis, Katie. 'The Way We Were.' *Chatelaine* May 2008: 321–52. Print.

Editorial. *Mayfair* Mar. 1928: 11. Print.

Editorial. *Mayfair* Apr. 1928: 11. Print.

Edmunds, Jean. 'Recession or Boom: How to Live With Either.' *Chatelaine* May 1958: 15+. Print.

Einna. 'A Letter from Paris.' *Chatelaine* Oct. 1929: 11+. Print.

—. 'A Letter from Paris.' *Chatelaine* Jan. 1930: 12–13. Print.

—. 'News from Paris.' *Chatelaine* Aug. 1929: 20–21. Print.

'The Empress of Britain Fashion Story.' *Canadian Home Journal* May 1956: 28–35. Print.

'Emprunté au passé pour embellir le présent.' *La Revue Moderne* Dec. 1931: 31. Print.

'En Route.' *Mayfair* July 1935: 22–23. Print.

Evans, Allen Roy. 'She Hunts Big Cats.' *Canadian Home Journal* May 1949: 98. Print.

Evans, Caroline. 'Masks, Mirrors and Mannequins: Elsa Schiaparelli and the Decentred Subject.' *Fashion Theory* 3.1 (1999): 3–32. Print.

Fiamengo, Janice. *The Woman's Page: Journalism and Rhetoric in Early Canada*. Toronto: U of Toronto P, 2008. Print.

Le Film. Advertisement. *La Revue Populaire* Jan. 1932. 55. Print.

'Financial Queries'. *Maclean's* 15 Jan. 1927: 61–62. Print.

Finch, Edmund. 'Treasures to Take Home.' *Mayfair* Jan. 1955: 36+. Print.

Fisher, Susan. 'Canada and the Great War'. *The Cambridge History of Canadian Literature*. Ed. Coral Ann Howells and Eva-Marie Kröller. Cambridge: Cambridge UP, 2009. 224–43. Print.

Fix, Mary McNulty. 'How to Dress Well.' *Chatelaine* Dec. 1933: 12+. Print.

Flanner, Janet. 'Profiles: Comet.' *The New Yorker* 18 June 1932: 19–23. Print.

Flynn, Eanswythe Rowley. 'They're off to camp.' *Canadian Home Journal* June 1951: 58–62. Print.

'For Hours of Play on the New "Empress."' *Mayfair* July 1931: 20–21. Print.

Ford Cars. Advertisement. *Chatelaine* July 1934: 3. Print.

Francine. 'Voyages.' *La Revue Populaire* May 1937: 80. Print.

Francis, Margaret Ecker. 'Nostalgia.' *Chatelaine* Nov. 1946: 16+. Print.

Freeman, Barbara M. 'Laced In and Let Down: Women's Fashion Features in the Toronto Daily Press, 1890–1900.' *Fashion: A Canadian Perspective*. Ed. Alexandra Palmer. Toronto: U of Toronto P, 2004. 291–314. Print.

Fulton, Gloria. 'Why Aren't There More Canadian Women in Science?' Nov. 1959: 40+. Print.

BIBLIOGRAPHY

Gallichan, Gilles. 'The Newspaper in Quebec: Partisan to Commercial.' *History of the Book in Canada. Vol. 2: 1840–1918.* Ed. Yvan Lamonde, Patricia Lockhart Fleming, and Fiona Black. Toronto: U of Toronto P, 2005. 303–306. Print.

Garvey, Ellen Gruber. *The Adman in the Parlor: Magazines and the Gendering of Consumer Culture, 1880–1910.* New York: Oxford UP, 1996. Print.

Gatenby, Greg, ed. *The Wild is Always There: Canada through the Eyes of Foreign Writers.* Toronto: Knopf, 1995. Print.

Gerson, Carole. 'Middlebrow Modernity and Mid-century Fiction: Fiction by Women, 1920–1950s.' *The Oxford Handbook of Canadian Literature.* Ed. Cynthia Sugars. Toronto: Oxford UP, in press. Print.

Gerson, Carole and Jacques Michon, eds. *History of the Book in Canada. Vol. 3: 1918–1980.* Toronto: U of Toronto P, 2007. Print.

Gianelli, Adele M. 'Olympia, Thermometer of London Fashion.' *Mayfair* Nov. 1927: 7+. Print.

Gill, Miranda. *Eccentricity and the Cultural Imagination in Nineteenth-Century Paris.* Oxford: Oxford UP, 2009. Print.

'Globe-Trotting Canadians.' *Mayfair* Feb. 1928: 88. Print.

Graham, Jean. 'See Canada First!' *Canadian Home Journal* July 1930: 10–11. Print.

Granatstein, J. L. '*Maclean's*.' Revised by Mark Anderako. *The Canadian Encyclopedia.* Historica Dominion Institute, 2012. Web.

Gray, Grattan. 'Banff: A Paradise for Sultans and Stenos.' *Maclean's* 15 June 1951: 16–17. Print.

Green, Anne. 'Paris Opening.' *Canadian Home Journal* Nov. 1938: 13+. Print.

Green, Barbara. 'Complaints of Everyday Life: Periodical Culture and Correspondence Columns in *The Woman Worker*, *Women Folk* and *The Freewoman*.' *Modernism/Modernity* 19.3 (2012): 461–85. Print.

Grover, Mary. *The Ordeal of Warwick Deeping: Middlebrow Authorship and Cultural Embarrassment.* Madison, NJ: Fairleigh Dickinson UP, 2009. Print.

Guillory, John. 'The Ordeal of Middlebrow Culture.' Rev. of *The Western Canon*, by Harold Bloom. *Transition* 67 (1995): 82–92. Print.

'Halcyon Holidays in Muskoka.' *Mayfair* July 1935: 74–75. Print.

Hammill, Faye. 'The Sensations of the 1920s: Martha Ostenso's *Wild Geese* and Mazo de la Roche's *Jalna*.' *Studies in Canadian Literature* 28.2 (2003): 74–97. Print.

—. *Sophistication: A Literary and Cultural History.* Liverpool: Liverpool UP, 2010. Print.

—. 'Wilderness/Sophistication'. Pamphlet. London: British Library, 2012. Web.

—. *Women, Celebrity, and Literary Culture between the Wars.* Austin: U of Texas P, 2007. Print.

Hammill, Faye and Karen Leick. 'Modernism and the Quality Magazines: *Vanity Fair*; *American Mercury*; *New Yorker*; *Esquire*.' *The Oxford Critical and Cultural History of Modernist Magazines. Vol 2: North America, 1880–1960.* Ed. Andrew Thacker and Peter Brooker. Oxford: Oxford UP, 2012. 176–96. Print.

Hammill, Faye and Michelle Smith, eds. *Print culture, mobility, and the middlebrow / Imprimé, mobilité et culture moyenne.* Spec. issue of *International Journal of Canadian Studies / Revue internationale des études canadiennes* 48 (2014). Print.

Hamilton, Evelyn. 'The Invisible Barrier between Men and Women.' *Chatelaine* June 1958: 15+. Print.

Hamilton, Sharon. 'The First *New Yorker? The Smart Set* Magazine, 1900–1924.' *The Serials Librarian* 37.2 (1999): 89–104. Print.

Harker, Jaime. *America the Middlebrow: Women's Novel, Progressivism, and Middlebrow Authorship between the Wars.* Amherst: U of Massachusetts P, 2007. Print.

Harman, James. 'Here Come the Hostelers.' *Maclean's* 15 Aug. 1938: 16+. Print.

Harris, Jane. 'A Fashion Expert Speaks Her Mind: Women Are Cowards about Clothes.' *Maclean's* 1 July 1961: 22–25. Print.

Harrison, Julia, *Being a Tourist*: *Finding Meaning in Pleasure Travel.* Vancouver: U of British Columbia P, 2003. Print.

Hayles, N. Katherine. *My Mother was a Computer: Digital Subjects and Literary Texts.* Chicago: U of Chicago P, 2005. Print.

Heidsieck, Charles. 'De Montréal à Vancouver.' *La Revue Moderne* Aug. 1925: 17–19. Print.

'High Hat and Low Brow.' *Canadian Home Journal* Sept. 1936: 71. Print.

Higonnet, Patrice. *Paris: Capital of the World.* Trans. Arthur Goldhammer. Cambridge: Harvard UP, 2002. Print.

Hilliard, Christopher. *To Exercise Our Talents: The Democratization of Writing in Britain.* Cambridge: Harvard UP, 2006. Print.

Hindrichs, Cheryl. 'Late Modernism, 1928–1945: Criticism and Theory.' *Literature Compass* 8.11 (2011): 840–55. Web.

Hodgins, J. Herbert. 'The Cosmopolite: A Department for Well-Dressed Men.' *Mayfair* Jan. 1940: 4–7. Print.

—. Editorial. *Mayfair* May 1927: 16. Print.

—. Editorial. *Mayfair* June 1927: 16. Print.

—. Editorial. *Mayfair* Oct. 1927: 9. Print.

—. 'Revenue from Tourist Traffic.' *Maclean's* 15 Jan. 1927: 60–61. Print.

Houston, Susan E. '"A little steam, a little sizzle and a little sleaze": English-language tabloids in the interwar period.' *Papers of the Bibliographical Society of Canada* 40.1 (2002): 37–61. Web.

Humble, Nicola. *The Feminine Middlebrow Novel, 1920s to 1950s: Class, Domesticity, and Bohemianism.* Oxford: Oxford UP, 2001. Print.

—. 'Sitting Forward or Sitting Back: Highbrow v. Middlebrow Reading.' *Modernist Cultures* 6.1 (2011): 41–59. Print.

Hurley, Erin. *National Performance: Representing Quebec from Expo 67 to Céline Dion.* Toronto: U of Toronto P, 2011. Print.

Hutchinson, David. 'Cultural Policy and Cultural Production: *Maclean's* Magazine and Foreign News.' *British Journal of Canadian Studies* 17.1 (2004): 44–60. Print.

L'Illustration. Advertisement. *Mayfair* Jan. 1935: 54. Print.

BIBLIOGRAPHY

'In the Editor's Confidence.' *Maclean's* 15 Dec. 1948: 4. Print.

Irvine, Dean. *Editing Modernity: Women and Little-Magazine Cultures in Canada, 1916–1956.* Toronto: U of Toronto P 2007. Print.

—. Introduction. *The Canadian Modernists Meet.* Ed. Irvine. Ottawa: U of Ottawa P, 2005. 1–13. Print.

Italian State Tourist Office. Advertisement. *Canadian Home Journal* June 1951: 83. Print.

Jaffe, Aaron. *Modernism and the Culture of Celebrity.* Cambridge: Cambridge UP, 2005. Print.

Jaffe, Aaron and Jonathan Goldman. Introduction. *Modernist Star Maps: Celebrity, Modernity, Culture.* Ed. Jaffe and Goldman. Farnham: Ashgate, 2010. 1–16. Print.

Jasper Park Lodge. Advertisement. *Chatelaine* May 1930: 65. Print.

Jean-Baptiste. 'La Vie Canadienne.' *La Revue Moderne* March 1932: 10. Print.

Jessup, Lynda. 'Antimodernism and Artistic Experience: An Introduction.' *Antimodernism and Artistic Experience: Policing the Boundaries of Modernity.* Ed. Jessup. Toronto: U of Toronto P, 2001. 3–10. Print.

J. L. 'N'oubliez pas votre caméra.' *La Revue Moderne* Aug. 1955: 36. Print.

Johnston, Russell. *Selling Themselves: The Emergence of Canadian Advertising.* Toronto: Toronto UP, 2001. Print.

'Joint Submission of *Maclean's* Magazine, *Chatelaine* and *Canadian Homes*: Blair Fraser (editor of *Maclean's*), Doris Anderson (editor of *Chatelaine*) and Mr. Gerry Anglin (editor of *Canadian Home*).' *Report of the Royal Commission on Publications: Hearings.* Vol. 21. Toronto: Angus Stonehouse, 1961. Print.

Jones, John Bush. *All-Out For Victory! Magazine Advertising and the World War II Home Front.* Lebanon: Brandeis UP, 2009. Print.

Jones, Richard. 'French Canadian Nationalism.' *The Canadian Encyclopedia.* Toronto: Historica Canada, 2006. Web.

Jordan, Tessa. '*Branching Out:* Second-Wave Feminist Periodicals and the Archive of Canadian Women's Writing.' *English Studies in Canada* 36.2/3 (2010): 63–90. Print.

Karr, Clarence. *Authors and Audiences: Popular Canadian Fiction in the Early Twentieth Century.* Montreal: McGill-Queens UP, 2000. Print.

Kelly, Peggy. 'A Materialist Feminist Analysis of Dorothy Livesay, Madge Macbeth, and the Canadian Literary Field, 1920–1950.' DPhil diss. U of Alberta, 1999. Print.

Kennedy, Janice. 'The Unshackling of Madge Macbeth.' *Ottawa Citizen* 21 May 2006. Web.

Keshen, Jeffrey A. *Saints, Sinners, and Soldiers: Canada's Second World War.* Vancouver: U of British Columbia P, 2007. Print.

Kinahan, Anne-Marie. '"The colored lady knows better": Marketing the "New Century Washer" in *Canadian Home Journal*, 1910–1912.' *Canadian Journal of Communication* 38.2 (2013): 187–205. Web.

Kodak Verichrome. Advertisement. *La Revue Populaire* Aug. 1935: back cover. Print.

Korinek, Valerie. '"It's a tough time to be in love": The Darker Side of Chatelaine during the Cold War.' *Love, Hate and Fear in Canada's Cold War*. Ed. Richard Cavell. Toronto: U of Toronto P, 2000. 159–82. Print.

—. *Roughing It in the Suburbs: Reading* Chatelaine *Magazine in the Fifties and Sixties*. Toronto: U of Toronto P, 2000. Print.

Kröller, Eva-Marie. *Canadians in Europe 1851–1900*. Vancouver: U of British Columbia P, 1987. Print.

—. 'Exploration and Travel.' *The Cambridge Companion to Canadian Literature*. Ed. Kröller. Cambridge: Cambridge UP, 2004. 70–93. Print.

—. '"*Une terre humaine*": Expo 67, Canadian women, and *Chatelaine/Châtelaine*.' *Expo 67: Not Just a Souvenir*. Ed. Rhona Richman Kenneally and Johanne Sloan. Toronto: U of Toronto P, 2010. 61–80. Print.

—. 'Travellers and Travel Writing.' *Encyclopedia of Literature in Canada*. Ed. W. H. New. Toronto: U of Toronto P, 2003. 1128–34. Print.

Kuffert, L. B. *A Great Duty: Canadian Responses to Modern Life and Mass Culture, 1939–1967*. Montreal: McGill-Queen's UP, 2003. Print.

Kuttainen, Victoria. 'Dear Miss Cowie: The Construction of the Canadian Author 1920s–1930s.' *English Studies in Canada* 39.4 (2014): 145–71. Web.

Lamonde, Yvan, Patricia Lockhart Fleming, and Fiona Black, eds. *History of the Book in Canada. Vol. 2: 1840–1918*. Toronto: U of Toronto P, 2005. Print.

Lang, Marjory. *Women Who Made the News: Female Journalists in Canada, 1880–1945*. Montreal: McGill-Queen's UP, 1999. Print.

Latham, Sean. 'Affordance and Emergence: Magazine as New Media.' Conference paper. 'What is a Journal?' Roundtable. MLA 2013. Web.

Latham, Sean and Robert Scholes. 'The Rise of Periodical Studies.' *PMLA* 121.2 (2006): 517–31. Web.

Lassner, Phyllis. 'Testing the Limits of the Middlebrow: The Holocaust for the Masses.' *Modernist Cultures* 6.1 (2011): 178–95. Print.

Lawrey, Barbara. 'Pink Paradise.' *Mayfair* Dec. 1959: 30–32. Print.

Le Guével, Jean. 'Dans les Jardins de Paris.' *La Revue Moderne* July 1956: 12. Print.

Leavis, Q. D. *Fiction and the Reading Public*. 1932. London: Chatto and Windus, 1968. Print.

Lecker, Robert. *Keepers of the Code: English-Canadian Literary Anthologies and the Representation of Nation*. Toronto: U of Toronto P, 2013. Print.

Lemelin, Roger. 'We're closer than we think.' *Chatelaine* July 1951: 8+. Print.

Lewis, Paula Gilbert. *The Literary Vision of Gabrielle Roy: An Analysis of Her Works*. Birmingham: Summa, 1984. Print.

Liddle, Dallas. *The Dynamics of Genre: Journalism and the Practice of Literature in Mid-Victorian Britain*. Charlottesville: U of Virginia P, 2009. Print.

Lloyd, David. *Battlefield Tourism: Pilgrimage and the Commemoration of the Great War in Britain, Australia and Canada, 1919–1939*. Oxford: Berg, 1998. Print.

Macbeth, Madge. 'Sheep Skin and Homespun.' *Mayfair* June 1935: 35+. Print.

—. 'The Only Paris.' *Mayfair* May 1927: 14+. Print.

—. 'Printemps à La Paris.' *Mayfair* Aug. 1927: 18+. Print.
—. 'The Various Cities Called Paris.' *Mayfair* Dec. 1927: 16+. Print.
—. 'Where in—Paris, shall we go for Tea?' *Mayfair* June 1927: 14+. Print.
MacCannell, Dean, *The Tourist: A New Theory of the Leisure Class*. Berkeley: U of California P, 1999. Print.
Macdonald, Kate, ed. *The Masculine Middlebrow, 1880–1950: What Mr Miniver Read*. Basingstoke: Palgrave, 2011. Print.
Mackay, Phyllis Isabel. 'Off to Europe.' *Canadian Home Journal* June 1931: 8+. Print.
Mackie, Ellen. 'What will the new fashions really mean?' *Chatelaine* Mar. 1930: 19, 37. Print.
Maclean Publishing Company. Advertisement. *Chatelaine* June 1928: 59. Print.
Maclean-Hunter. Advertisement. *Maclean's* 1 Jan. 1948: 44. Print.
MacLean's. Advertisement. *Chatelaine* Mar. 1929: 52. Print.
MacLeod, Kirsten. *American Little Magazines of the 1890s: A Revolution in Print*. Sunderland: Bibelot Press, 2013. 4–17. Print.
'Madame Schiaparelli à Montréal' in *La Revue Populaire* Nov. 1940: 70. Print.
Madeleine [Anne-Marie Huguenin]. 'Chez les Canadiens de France.' *La Revue Moderne* May 1925: 9–11. Print.
—. 'Le Courrier de Madeleine.' *La Revue Moderne* 15 Nov. 1919: 33. Print.
—. 'Je reviens …' *La Revue Moderne* Oct. 1929: 5. Print.
—. 'Plus haut encore! En pleine lumière.' *La Revue Moderne* Jan. 1926: 7. Print.
—. 'S'unir pour grandir.' *La Revue Moderne* 15 Nov. 1919: 8–9. Print.
Magazine Publishers Association of Canada. Advertisement. *Maclean's* 15 Sept. 1932. 4. Print.
—. Advertisement. *Maclean's* 1 Feb. 1933. 3. Print.
—. Advertisement. *Canadian Home Journal* Mar. 1936: 66. Print.
Magazines, Travel and Middlebrow Culture in Canada, 1925–1960. U of Strathclyde. 2011. Web
Mapes, Mrs. J. J. W. Letter to the editor. *Chatelaine* June 1934: 94. Print.
Marchand, Roland. *Advertising the American Dream: Making Way for Modernity*. Berkeley: U of California P, 1985. Print.
Marjolaine [Justa Leclerc]. 'Le Courier du Mois.' *La Revue Moderne* Jan. 1932: 37. Print.
Martin, Carol, ed. *Local Colour: Writers Discovering Canada*. Vancouver: Douglas and McIntyre, 1994. Print.
Martin, Geoff. 'Pierre Berton, Celebrity, and the Economics of Authenticity.' *Canadian Literature* 212 (2012): 50–66. Print.
Mason, Jody. 'Anti-Modernist Paradox in Canada: The Graphic Publishers (1925–32) and the Case of Madge Macbeth.' *Journal of Canadian Studies* 45.2 (2011): 96–122. Web.
Mathieu, Jocelyne. '*Châtelaine* à Expo 67: chronique de la modernité.' *Les cahiers des dix* 63 (2009): 257–78. Web.
May Fair Hotel. Advertisement. *Mayfair* Apr. 1935: 90. Print.

'Mayfair Round-About.' *Mayfair* Sept. 1935: 21. Print.
Mayfair's Paris Representative. Advertisement. *Mayfair* May 1928: 73. Print.
Mayrand, Napoléon. 'Impressions de New-York.' *La Revue Moderne* Oct. 1929: 10. Print.
McBrine Baggage. Advertisement. *Canadian Home Journal* June 1951: 89. Print.
McClung, Nellie. *Nellie McClung, The Complete Autobiography: Clearing in the West and The Stream Runs Fast*. 1935, 1945. Ed. Veronica Strong-Boag and Michelle Lynn Rosa. Peterborough: Broadview, 2003. Print.
McCracken, Ellen. *Decoding Women's Magazines: From* Mademoiselle *to* Ms. Basingstoke: Macmillan, 1993. Print.
McGann, Jerome. *The Textual Condition*. Princeton, NJ: Princeton UP, 1991. Print.
McGee, Mollie. 'I'll Always Remember My Two Weeks in Paris.' *Chatelaine* Nov. 1944: 13+. Print.
McKay, Jenny. *The Magazines Handbook*. 3rd ed. Abingdon: Routledge, 2013. Print.
McLuhan, Marshall. *Counterblast*. 1954. Berkeley: Ginko P, 2011. Print.
Mead, Margaret. 'Do Women Like Other Women?' *Chatelaine* Aug. 1958: 13+. Print.
Mendes, Kaitlynn. 'Reading Chatelaine: Dr. Marion Hilliard and 1950s Women's Health Advice.' *Canadian Journal of Communication* 35.4 (2010): 515–31. Web.
Mesch, Rachel. *Having It All in the Belle Epoque: How French Women's Magazines Invented the Modern Woman*. Stanford: Stanford UP, 2013. Print.
Micheline. 'Les Jolies Modes de Paris.' *La Revue Moderne* 15 Feb. 1922: 59. Print.
Mitchell, Peter, comp. *An Index to MacLean's Magazine, 1914–1937*. Ottawa: Canadian Library Association, 1965. Print.
'La Mode.' *La Revue Populaire* Apr. 1932: 58. Print.
Modernist Journals Project. Brown U and the U of Tulsa. Web.
Modernist Magazines Project. De Montfort U and U of Sussex. 2006–13. Web.
'Modernistic Notes of Chic.' *Mayfair* May 1928: 26. Print.
'Modes Parisiennes.' *La Revue Moderne* Dec. 1934: 31. Print.
Moore, H. Napier. 'Holiday Dividends.' *Chatelaine* July 1934: 2. Print.
—. 'In the Editor's Confidence.' *Maclean's* 15 Jan. 1927: 64. Print.
Morgan, Cecilia. *'A Happy Holiday': English Canadians and Transatlantic Tourism, 1870–1930*. Toronto: U of Toronto P, 2008. Print.
Morphy, K. M. [Kay Murphy]. 'The Cosmopolite.' *Mayfair* July 1934: 84–85. Print.
Morrisson, Mark S. *The Public Face of Modernism: Little Magazines, Audiences and Reception, 1905–1920*. Madison: U of Wisconsin P, 2001. Print.
Mulhallen, Karen, ed. *Views from the North: An Anthology of Travel Writing*. Erin: Descant, 1984. Print.
Murphy, Kathleen [Kay Murphy]. 'Fashions for Autumn.' *Maclean's* 1 Sept. 1936: 10. Print.
—. 'Fashion Shorts.' *Chatelaine* Feb. 1934: 34–35. Print.
Murphy, Kay (*see also* Morphy, K. M.; Murphy, Kathleen). 'Fashion Shorts.' *Chatelaine* Mar. 1934: 40–41. Print.
—. 'Fashion Shorts.' *Chatelaine* July 1934: 16+. Print.

—. 'Fashion Shorts.' *Chatelaine* Oct. 1940: 26–27. Print.
Murphy, Michael. 'One Hundred Per Cent Bohemia: Pop Decadence and the Aestheticization of the Commodity in the Rise of the Slicks.' *Marketing Modernisms: Self-Promotion, Canonization, Rereading*. Ed. Kevin J. H. Dettmar and Steven Watt. Ann Arbor: U of Michigan P, 1996. 61–89. Print.
Murray, Heather. 'The Canadian Readers Meet: The Canadian Literature Club of Toronto, Donald G. French, and the Middlebrow Modernist Reader.' *Papers of the Bibliographical Society of Canada / Cahiers de la Société Bibliographique du Canada*: 46.2 (2008): 149–83. Print.
Murray, Tom. *Rails across Canada: The History of Canadian Pacific and Canadian National Railways*. Minneapolis: Voyageur, 2011. Print.
'Muskoka Interlude.' *Mayfair* June 1935: 23+. Print.
Mussell, James. *The Nineteenth-Century Press in the Digital Age*. Basingstoke: Palgrave, 2012. Print.
'My Wife is a Social Climber.' *Chatelaine* Mar. 1949: 26+. Print.
Napier-Moore, H. 'In the Editor's Confidence.' *Maclean's* 15 June 1930: 84. Print.
Neatby, Nicole. 'Meeting of Minds: North American Travel Writers and Government Tourist Publicity in Quebec, 1920–1955.' *Social History / Histoire Sociale* 36 (2003): 465–95. Web.
The News Scout. 'Advertising Newscast.' *Canadian Home Journal* Apr. 1941: 94. Print.
'Night Life.' *Canadian Home Journal* Jan. 1935: 10. Print.
Novak, Dagmar. *Dubious Glory: The Two World Wars and the Canadian Novel*. New York: Peter Lang, 2000. Print.
'An Odyssey of Summer.' *Mayfair* June 1935: 25, 106. Print.
Ohmann, Richard. *Selling Culture: Magazines, Markets and Class at the Turn of the Century*. London: Verso, 1996. Print.
Oligny, Huguette. 'La Mode.' *La Revue Moderne* Feb. 1941: 19+. Print.
Outka, Elizabeth. *Consuming Tradition: Modernity, Modernism, and the Commodified Authentic*. Oxford: Oxford UP, 2009. Print.
Packard Cars. Advertisement. *Maclean's* Jan. 1930: 65. Print.
Pain, Hilda, Mrs. 'Why I Chose "The Chatelaine."' *Chatelaine* Mar. 1928: 30. Print.
Palmer, Alexandra. 'The Association of Canadian Couturiers.' *Fashion: A Canadian Perspective*. Ed. Alexandra Palmer. Toronto: U of Toronto P, 2004. 90–109. Print.
—. *Couture and Commerce: The Transatlantic Fashion Trade in the 1950s*. Vancouver and Ottawa: U of British Columbia P and the Royal Ontario Museum, 2001. Print.
—, ed. *Fashion: A Canadian Perspective*. Toronto: U of Toronto P, 2004. Print.
Panofsky, Ruth. 'At Odds: Reviewers and Readers of the *Jalna* Novels.' *Studies in Canadian Literature* 25.1 (2000): 57–72. Print.
'Paris-Montréal.' *La Revue Populaire* Sept. 1954: 30. Print.
Parkins, Ilya. *Poiret, Dior and Schiaparelli: Fashion, Femininity and Modernity*. London: Berg, 2012. Print.

Parkins, Ilya and Elizabeth M. Sheehan, eds. *Cultures of Femininity in Modern Fashion*. Durham: U of New Hampshire P, 2011. Print.

—. Introduction. *Cultures of Femininity in Modern Fashion*. Ed. Parkins and Sheehan. Durham: U of New Hampshire P, 2011. 1–15. Print.

Parkinson, Isabelle. 'The modernist periodical through time.' The Everyday and the Event. Modernist Studies Association annual conference. University of Sussex. 29 Aug. 2013. Paper.

Parsons, Deborah. *Streetwalking the Metropolis: Women, the City, and Modernity*. Oxford: Oxford UP, 2000. Print.

Paul, Frances. 'A Holiday in Europe.' *Mayfair* Oct. 1949: 63–65. Print.

Pearce, Douglas. *Tourist Development*. Harlow: Longman, 1981. Print.

Pearson, George. 'Jack-Pots.' *Maclean's* 15 June 1925: 20+. Print.

La Petite Revue. Advertisement. *La Revue Moderne* Jan. 1932: back cover. Print.

Phillips, Susan E. *Transforming Talk: The Problem with Gossip in Late Medieval England*. University Park: Penn State UP, 2007. Print.

Pigott, Peter. *Sailing Seven Seas: A History of the Canadian Pacific Line*. Toronto: Dundurn, 2010. Print.

'Le plaisir de la marche pour la femme.' *La Revue Moderne* May 1934: 18. Print.

Pleau, Jean-Christian. '*La Revue Moderne* et le nationalisme.' *Revue Mens* 6.2 (2006): 205–37. Web.

'Les Plus Belles Ruines du Monde.' *La Revue Populaire* Jan. 1932: 10. Print.

Pollentier, Caroline. 'Configuring Middleness: Bourdieu, *l'Art Moyen* and the Broadbrow.' *Middlebrow Literary Cultures: The Battle of the Brows, 1920–1960*. Ed. Erica Brown and Mary Grover. Basingstoke: Palgrave, 2012. 37–51. Print.

Potvin, John. 'Fashioning Masculinity in *Mayfair* Magazine: The Aesthetics of the Male Body, 1927–1936.' MA thesis. Carleton U, 2000. Web.

Pringle, Gertrude. 'Making a Business of Good Taste.' *Maclean's* 1 Oct. 1926: 71–72. Print.

Pump, Irene. 'We Camped Our Way Through Europe.' *Chatelaine* May 1958: 19. Print.

'Quebec Sous la Neige.' *La Revue Populaire* Jan. 1932: 9. Print.

Quedrue, Commandant Maurice. 'Conversation avec Mme Madeleine Huguenin'. *La Revue Moderne* Dec. 1925: 20–21. Print.

Radway, Janice. *A Feeling for Books: Book-of-the-Month Club, Literary Taste and Middle-Class Desire*. Chapel Hill: U of North Carolina P, 1997. Print.

Reed, Christopher. *Bloomsbury Rooms: Modernism, Subculture, and Domesticity*. New Haven: Yale UP, 2004. Print.

—. 'Design for (Queer) Living: Sexual Identity, Performance and Décor in British *Vogue*, 1922–26.' *GLQ* 12.3 (2006): 377–404. Print.

'Renaissance: Quelques mots au lecteur.' *La Revue Moderne* May 1939: 1. Print.

Renaud, Armand. 'Variations sur les toilettes de Pâques.' *La Revue Moderne* Apr. 1928: 3. Print.

La Revue Moderne. Advertisement. *La Revue Moderne* Apr. 1928: 21. Print.

La Revue Moderne. Advertisement. *La Revue Moderne* Dec. 1936. Inside back cover. Print.
'*La Revue Moderne* a douze ans.' *La Revue Moderne* Nov. 1931: 10. Print.
La Revue Populaire. Advertisement. *La Revue Populaire* Jan. 1932: 66. Print.
Reyburn, Wallace. 'A Day in London.' *Chatelaine* June 1941: 18+. Print.
Ricard, François. '*La Revue moderne*: deux revues en une.' *Littératures* (Montreal) 7 (1991): 76–84. Print.
Rifkind, Candida. *Comrades and Critics: Women, Literature, and the Left in 1930s Canada*. Toronto: U of Toronto P, 2009. Print.
—. 'The Returning Reader: Canadian Serial Fiction and Mazo de la Roche's *Jalna* Novels.' *Middlebrow Literary Cultures: The Battle of the Brows, 1920–1960*. Ed. Erica Brown and Mary Grover. Basingstoke: Palgrave, 2012. 171–86. Print.
—. 'Too Close to Home: Middlebrow Anti-Modernism and the Poetry of Edna Jacques.' *Journal of Canadian Studies* 39.1 (2005). 90–114. Print.
Roberts, Gillian. *Prizing Literature: The Celebration and Circulation of National Culture*. Toronto: U of Toronto P, 2011. Print.
Robinson, Judith. *As We Came By*. Toronto: Dent, 1951. Print.
—. 'You cawn't miss it!' *Canadian Home Journal* June 1951: 20+. Print.
Rochère, Jean. 'Elsa Schiaparelli.' *La Revue Populaire* Aug. 1955: 11. Print.
Rogers, Juliette M. *Career Stories: Belle Epoque Novels of Professional Development*. University Park: Penn State UP, 2007. Print.
Rojek, Chris and John Urry, eds. *Touring Cultures: Transformations of Travel and Theory*. London: Routledge, 1997. Print.
Rooke, Constance, ed. *Writing Away: The PEN Canada Travel Anthology*. Toronto: McClelland and Stewart, 1994. Print.
Rosaldo, Renato. 'Imperialist Nostalgia.' *Representations* 26 (1989): 107–22. Print.
Roy, Gabrielle. 'Dead Leaves.' *Maclean's* June 1947: 20+. Print.
Roy, Wendy. *Maps of Difference: Canada, Women, and Travel*. Montreal: McGill-Queen's UP, 2005. Print.
Rubin, Joan Shelley. *The Making of Middlebrow Culture*. Chapel Hill: U of North Carolina P, 1992. Print.
Saint-Jacques, Denis. 'Popular Magazines in French.' *History of the Book in Canada. Vol. 2: 1840–1918*. Ed. Yvan Lamonde, Patricia Lockhart Fleming, and Fiona Black. Toronto: U of Toronto P, 2005. 317–21. Print.
Saint-Jacques, Denis and Marie-José Des Rivières. 'Le magazine en France, aux États-Unis et au Québec.' *Production(s) du populaire*. Ed. Jacques Migozzi and Philippe Le Guern. Limoges: Presses de l'Université de Limoges, 2005. 29–37. Print.
Saint-Jacques, Denis, Lucie Robert et al. *La Vie Littéraire au Québec. Vol. 6. Le nationaliste, l'individualiste et le marchand, 1919–1933*. Québec: Presses de l'Université Laval, 2010. Print.
Sanders, Byrne Hope. Editorial. *Chatelaine* Sept. 1929: 16. Print.
—. Editorial. *Chatelaine* Dec. 1931: 84. Print.

—. Editorial. *Chatelaine* June 1932: 2. Print.
—. Editorial. *Chatelaine* Sept. 1934: 2. Print.
—. 'This Month with Our Advertisers.' *Chatelaine* Dec. 1931: 84. Print.
Sandwell, B. K. 'Garden While You Gad.' *Mayfair* Mar. 1928: 17+. Print.
Sarfati, Sonya and Sandra Martin. 'Magazines.' *The Canadian Encyclopedia*. Historica Foundation, 2007. Web.
Sartre, Jean-Paul. 'Prose et Langage.' *La Revue Populaire* Mar. 1947: 6+. Print.
Savoie, Chantal. '"Moins de dentelles, plus de psychologie" et une heure á soi: les *Lettres* de Fadette et la chronique féminine au tournant du XXe siècle.' *Tendances actuelles en histoire littéraire canadienne*. Ed. Denis Saint-Jacques. Québec: Éditions Nota Bene, 2003. 183–99. Print.
—. 'Femmes, mondanité et culture dans les années 1940: l'exemple de la chronique « Ce dont on parle » de Lucette Robert dans *La Revue populaire*.' Print culture, mobility, and the middlebrow / Imprimé, mobilité et culture moyenne. Spec. issue of *International Journal of Canadian Studies / Revue internationale des études canadiennes* 48 (2014). Ed. Faye Hammill and Michelle Smith. 105–17. Print.
Scanlon, Jennifer. *Inarticulate Longings:* The Ladies' Home Journal, *Gender, and the Promises of Consumer Culture*. New York: Routledge, 1995. Print.
'Schiaparelli.' *Mayfair* April 1935: 44. Print.
'Schiaparelli.' *Mayfair* May 1935: 58. Print.
Scobie, Stephen. *The Measure of Paris*. Edmonton: U of Alberta P, 2010. Print.
Sharman, Lydia Ferrabee. 'Fashion and Refuge: The Jane Harris Salon, Montreal, 1941–1961.' *Fashion: A Canadian Perspective*. Ed. Alexandra Palmer. Toronto: U of Toronto P, 2004. 270–87. Print.
Shevelow, Kathryn. *Women and Print Culture: The Construction of Femininity in the Early Periodical*. London: Routledge, 1989. Print.
'Shops of Mayfair in Hamilton.' *Mayfair* Apr. 1928: 93. Print.
'Shops of Mayfair in Montreal.' *Mayfair* Apr. 1928: 95, 97. Print.
Simmel, Georg. 'The Philosophy of Fashion'. 1905. Rpt in *Simmel on Culture*. Ed. David Frisby and Mike Featherstone. London: Sage, 1997. 187–206. Print.
'Simples réflexions de saison.' *La Revue Moderne* July 1932: 18. Print.
Smith, A. J. M. 'Wanted—Canadian Criticism.' *Canadian Forum* 8.91 (1928): 600–01. Rpt. in *The Making of Modern Poetry in Canada: Essential Articles on Contemporary Canadian Poetry in English*. Ed. Louis Dudek and Michael Gnarowski. Toronto: Ryerson, 1967. 31–33. Print.
Smith, Erin. *Hard-Boiled: Working-Class Readers and Pulp Magazines*. Philadelphia: Temple UP, 2000. Print.
Smith, Michelle. 'Fiction and the Nation: The Construction of Canadian Identity in *Chatelaine* and *Canadian Home Journal* during the 1930s and 1940s.' *British Journal of Canadian Studies* 27.1 (2014): 37–53. Print.
—. 'From "The Offal of Canada's Magazine Trade" to "Absolutely Priceless": Considering the Canadian Pulp Magazine Collection." *English Studies in Canada* 30.1 (2004): 101–16. Print.

—. 'Guns, Lies, and Ice: The Canadian Pulp Magazine Industry and the Crime Fiction of Raymond Chandler and Niel Perrin.' *Dime Novel Roundup* 74.01 (2005): 1–17. Print.

—. '"Mainstream Magazines, Middlebrow Fiction, and Leslie Gordon Barnard's "The Winter Road."' *Studies in Canadian Literature* (2012): 7–30. Print.

—. 'Soup Cans and Love Slaves: National Politics and Cultural Authority in the Editing and Authorship of Canadian Pulp Magazines.' *Book History* 9 (2006): 261–89. Print.

Smith, Michelle and Hannah McGregor. 'Middlebrow Aspiration in Martha Ostenso's Magazine Fiction.' *Print culture, mobility, and the middlebrow / Imprimé, mobilité et culture moyenne*. Spec. issue of *International Journal of Canadian Studies / Revue internationale des études canadiennes* 48 (2014). Ed. Faye Hammill and Michelle Smith. 67–83. Print.

Soiffield of Paris. 'Bienvenu! *Mayfair*'s Paris Letter.' *Mayfair* Oct. 1927: 19–21. Print.

—. 'In Paris ... all that glitters is not pure gold but at least it's chic ... the evolution of a hat.' *Mayfair* Feb. 1928: 19+. Print.

—. 'Paris Swathed in Black and White ... Walks Abroad in Gun Metal Shoes ... Stockings of Silver Gray.' *Mayfair* Mar. 1928: 22+. Print.

—. 'Paris! ... The Tea Hour at Drecoll's.' *Mayfair* Dec. 1927: 24+. Print.

Sombart, Werner. *Wirtschaft und Mode*. Wiesbaden: J. F. Bergmann, 1902. Print.

Sontag, Susan. *On Photography*. Harmondsworth: Penguin, 1979. Print.

Sotiron, Minko. *From Politics to Profit: The Commercialization of Canadian Daily Newspapers, 1890–1920*. Montreal: McGill-Queens UP, 2005. Print.

Spacks, Patricia Meyer. *Gossip*. New York: Knopf, 1985. Print.

Spicer, Mildred. 'Travel Light as Air.' *Chatelaine* June 1950: 5–9. Print.

Stevenson, Iain. 'Atlantic Iconography.' *Montreal-Glasgow*. Ed. Bill Marshall. Glasgow: University of Glasgow, 2005. 53–65. Print.

Steward, Walter, ed. *Canada's Newspapers: The Inside Story*. Edmonton: Hurtig, 1980. Print.

St-Georges, Raymonde. 'Petits Chapeaux, Gros Bijoux.' *La Revue Moderne* Jan. 1950: 13. Print.

Stoicheff, Peter and Andrew Taylor, eds. *The Future of the Page*. Toronto: U of Toronto P, 2004. Print.

—. Introduction. *The Future of the Page*. Ed. Stoicheff and Taylor. Toronto: U of Toronto P, 2004. 3–25. Print.

Strange, Carolyn and Tina Loo. *True Crime, True North: The Golden Age of Canadian Pulp Magazines*. Vancouver: Raincoast Books, 2004. Print.

Straw, Will. 'Traffic in Scandal: The Case of Broadway Brevities'. *University of Toronto Quarterly* 73.4 (2004): 947–71. Web.

Stewart, Mary Lynn. *Dressing Modern Frenchwomen: Marketing Haute Couture, 1919–1939*. Baltimore: Johns Hopkins UP, 2008. Print.

Strychacz, Thomas. *Modernism, Mass Culture, and Professionalism*. Cambridge: Cambridge UP, 1993. Print.

Sullivan, Melissa and Sophie Blanch, eds. *The Middlebrow – Within or Without Modernism*. Special issue of *Modernist Cultures* 6.1 (2011): 1–200. Print.

Sutherland, Fraser. *The Monthly Epic: A History of Canadian Magazines*. Markham: Fitzhenry and Whiteside, 1988. Print.

Szeman, Imre. 'The Rhetoric of Culture: Some Notes on Magazine, Canadian Culture and Globalization.' *Journal of Canadian Studies* 35.3 (2000): 212–30. Web.

Taylor, Charles. *Radical Tories*. Toronto: Anansi, 1982. Print.

Tector, Amy. 'Healing Landscapes and Evolving Nationalism in Interwar Canadian Middlebrow Fiction of the First World War.' *The Masculine Middlebrow, 1880–1950: What Mr Miniver Read*. Ed. Kate Macdonald. Basingstoke: Palgrave, 2011. 104–18. Print.

Tester, Keith, ed. *The Flâneur*. London: Routledge, 1994. Print.

Thacker, Andrew. 'General Introduction: "Magazines, Magazines, Magazines!"' *The Oxford Critical and Cultural History of Modernist Magazines. Vol 2: North America 1894–1960*. Oxford: Oxford UP, 2012. 1–39. Print.

Thompson, Gwenda. 'Paris Spring Collections.' *Mayfair* Apr. 1945: 27+. Print.

Thornton, Margaret. 'At last: Our own Couture.' *Canadian Home Journal* July 1955: 14+. Print.

—. 'Fashions Right for Flight.' *Canadian Home Journal* June 1951: 12+. Print.

'The Three Ages of Women–and that 1940 Look.' *Chatelaine* Apr. 1940: 10+. Print.

Toussaint, Ismène. 'Monique Bosco.' *The Canadian Encyclopedia*. Toronto: Historica Canada, 2012. Web.

Trans-Canada Airlines. Advertisement. *La Revue Populaire* Sept. 1954: 31. Print.

'Translating the Paris Mode in Patterns of Canadian Make.' *Chatelaine* Mar. 1931: 81. Print.

'Travel Light.' *Chatelaine* June 1941: 39. Print.

Tredway, Tom. 'Inside Out: Elsa Schiaparelli, Interiors and Autobiography.' *Biography, Identity and the Modern Interior*. Ed. Anne Massey and Penny Sparke. Farnham: Ashgate, 2013. 87–102. Print.

Urry, John, *The Tourist Gaze*. Second Edition. London: Sage. 2001. Print.

Vaillancourt, Madeleine. 'Sur Les Canaux de Grande-Bretagne.' *La Revue Moderne* Dec. 1955: 6+. Print.

Vance, Jonathan. *Death So Noble: Memory, Meaning, and the First World War*. Vancouver: U of British Columbia P, 1997. Print.

Vautier, Marie. 'Hemispheric Travel from Europe to *las Américas*: the Imaginary and the Novel in Québec and Canada.' *Print culture, mobility, and the middlebrow / Imprimé, mobilité et culture moyenne*. Spec. issue of *International Journal of Canadian Studies / Revue internationale des études canadiennes* 48 (2014). Ed. Faye Hammill and Michelle Smith. 191–212. Print.

Veblen, Thorstein. *The Theory of the Leisure Class*. 1899. Ed. Martha Banta. Oxford: Oxford UP, 2007. Print.

Vipond, Mary. 'Major Trends in Canada's Print Mass Media.' *History of the Book in*

Canada. Vol. 3: 1918–1980. Ed. Carole Gerson and Jacques Michon. Toronto: U of Toronto P, 2007. 242–47. Print.

—. *The Mass Media in Canada*. Toronto: J. Lorimer 1989. Print.

'Virginia Woolf.' *La Revue Populaire* Oct. 1946: 77. Print.

Vollmer, Margaret, 'A Slow Boat to Fun.' *Canadian Home Journal* June 1951: 82–84. Print.

Wallace, Claire. 'We Dine and Wine in London.' *Canadian Home Journal* June 1935: 23+. Print.

'A Welcome to the Tourist.' *Chatelaine* June 1941: 64. Print.

White Star Line. Advertisement. *Maclean's* 15 June 1925: 72. Print.

'Why You Should Buy Advertised Products.' *Canadian Home Journal* Oct. 1930: 1. Print.

Wilcox, Vivian. 'How to Travel by Train.' Feb. 1959: 84. Print.

Wiley, Elizabeth and Anna Davies. 'Do We Need Midwives in Canada?' *Chatelaine* Apr. 1958: 17+. Print.

Willison, Lady [Marjory MacMurchy]. 'Miss Abigail Duloge … Traveller.' *Canadian Home Journal* May 1933: 18. Print.

Wilson, Elizabeth. *Adorned in Dreams: Fashion and Modernity*. 1985. Second edition. London: I. B. Tauris, 2003. Print.

Wood, Ghislaine, ed. *Surreal Things: Surrealism and Design*. London: V&A Publications, 2007. Print.

Woolf, Virginia. Letter to Clive Bell. 6 Feb. 1930. *A Reflection of the Other Person: The Letters of Virginia Woolf 1929–1931*. Ed. Nigel Nicolson. London: Hogarth P, 1978: 133. Print.

—. 'Middlebrow.' 1942. *Collected Essays*. Woolf. Vol. 2. London: Hogarth P, 1966. 196–203. Print.

Wyndham, Mary. 'The Great Designers Dress the Bride.' *Chatelaine* June 1928: 21+. Print.

—. 'The Paris Letter.' *Chatelaine* Feb. 1934: 33–35. Print.

—. 'Paris Patter.' *Chatelaine* Feb. 1929: 18+. Print.

Wynne-Field, Archie G. 'What Do You Know About Travel?' *Chatelaine* Aug. 1929: 58+. Print.

Yao, Steven. 'A Rim with a View: Orientalism, Geography, and the Historiography of Modernism.' *Pacific Rim Modernisms*. Ed. Mary Ann Gillies, Helen Sword, and Steven Yao. Toronto: U of Toronto P, 2009. 3–33. Print.

York, Lorraine. *Literary Celebrity in Canada*. Toronto: U of Toronto P, 2007. Print.

INDEX

Note: References are to page numbers, except where otherwise specified, (e.g. figure numbers are preceded by the abbreviation *fig*). Page numbers followed by *n* refer to information in the page notes.

Acton, James 44
advertising
    aspirational qualities 32, 34, 36–37, 38, 144, 151, 156, 158, 163–64, 183
    cosmopolitan theme 96, 109
    magazines *fig*3, *fig*13, 14, 20, 24, 29–30, 32–34, 35–40, 66, 71–72, 81–82
Allison, Frank Drummond 92
Anderson, Doris 46, 61–62, 177
André, Madame Claude 105
Anglophone 4–5, 12, 19, 33, 37, 41, 42, 114
    comparisons to Francophone magazines 26–31, 38, 46, 50, 56, 81, 95–96, 102–3, 106–7, 117
    magazines *see Canadian Home Journal; Canadian Homes and gardens; Chatelaine; Maclean's; Mayfair*
antimodernism 86, 176–77n
Ardis, Ann 2, 3, 20–21
Argosy 23
Arlen, Michael 151–52
aspiration, middle-class 1, 2, 5, 9, 15, 21, 33, 43, 54, 64, 81, 86–87, 148, 174, 176–77, 181
Atkins, Patsy 73–74
Atwood, Margaret 8–9, 62–63
Aubry, Luc 101*n*
Aynsley, Jeremy 4, 89–90, 133

Barnard, Leslie Gordon 45, 82, 84–85
Barnard, Margaret E. 80
Barnes, Nancy 80
Barrington, Gwyneth 123–24
Baxter, Beverley 51

Beach, Sylvia 151
Beauchemin, Lucette 128
Beaudry, Roland 105
Beetham, Margaret 88
Bell, Quentin 130*n*
Benjamin, Peggy 113
Benoit, Paule 114
Benson, E. F. 8
Berton, Pierre 50
Best, Kate Nelson 137–38, 142
Bishop, Edward E. 175
Black, Martha Munger 74
Black Mask 23*n*
Blanch, Sophie 13
Bodsworth, Fred 177–78
Bornstein, George 67
Bosco, Monique 27
Bosnitch, Katherine 141*n*
Boucher, Lucienne 114
Bourdieu, Pierre 7, 10, 13, 131
Bowallius, Marie-Louise 77–78
Bowen, Elizabeth 120
Bowker, Kathleen K. 90, 94, 163–64
Boxer, Rosemary 46, 47, 120–21
Boyd, John 28
Bristol, Naomi 164
Brooker, Peter 67
Brown, Erica 152*n*
    Comedy and the Feminine Middlebrow Novel 8
    Middlebrow Literary Cultures 12–13
Bruce, Eva L. 60
Bruchési, Jean 101, 104
Bryan, Eva Ruberta 91–92

205

Burke, Eustella 112*n*, 115, 116, 136–37
The Business Magazine 50
The Busy Man's Magazine 26, 50–51, 73

Callaghan, Morley 50, 62–63
Callwood, June 62–63
Campbell, Claire E. 178
Campbell, Helen G. 80
Canada
   influence of American popular culture 29–30
   sense of national 'fashion style' 123–25
   tourism 17–19
   travel writing 172–78
Canada; *see also* nationalism
Canadian Baker and Confectioner 44–45
Canadian Celanese Ltd. 123, 131–32
Canadian Home Journal 1–2, 3, 4, 20, 26, 35, 44–47, 63, 81–88, 103, 175
   advertisements *fig*22, 32, 36, 81
   circulation 30, 45, 81, 184
   contents page 82–83
   cover design *fig*4, *fig*15
   fashion writing 111, 113, 120–21, 121–22, 129
   pricing 41, 81
   promotion of Canadian writing 45
   readers' letters 39
   travel writing *fig*14, *fig*27, 153–54, 165, 181
Canadian Homes and Gardens 26, 27, 50, 59, 63
   circulation 30–31
Canadian Magazine 26
Canadian Pacific *fig*26, *fig*29, 157, 172–73, 174
Candle, Nancy 83
Carroll, Madeleine 80
Carter, David 7, 8
Cartier, George-Étienne 28
Casson, A. J. 50
Chandler, Raymond 23*n*
Chapman, Rosemary 28
Chatelaine 1–2, 3, 4, 6, 11, 13, 20, 26, 27, 47, 59–63, 66
Châtelaine 4, 6, 13, 50, 56, 63, 102, 114
Chatelaine
   advertisements *fig*1, *fig*3, *fig*13, 32, 35–36, 61

aimed at female readers 30, 44, 46
circulation 30, 184
Châtelaine, circulation 183, 184
Chatelaine
   contents page *fig*12, 78
   cover design *fig*19
   fashion writing 111, 112–13, 119, 123, 132–33, 139
   fiction 60–61
   gossip columns 115–18
   letters page 38, 40, 77
   pages 69–81
   pricing 41, 77
   travel writing 154–55, 160–62, 165, 169–70, 176–77, 182
Chauvin, Jean 49, 134
Choquette, Robert 103–4
Christ, Yvan 167, 171
Clare, John 61
Clark, H. C. 57–58
Clement, Caroline 92–93
Cole, Catherine C. 76
Cole, Celia Caroline *fig*7, 55–56
Collier, Patrick 2, 3, 20–21
Colliers 41
Comstock, Louise M. 80
Connor, Ralph 93
Conrad, Jacqueline 128
Consolidated Press 45
consumerism 2, 21, 24, 31*n*, 32–34
   link with travel 146–56
Cooke, Jack Kent 45, 47
Cosmopolitan 25
cosmopolitanism 2, 14, 52, 57, 58, 86, 89–90, 118, 136, 144, 166, 182
Costain, Thomas B. 26*n*
Crawshaw, Carole 169
Crombie, David B. 57
Crombie Publishing Company 57
Crowell, H. C. 73
Cucullu, Lois 134
Cuddy-Keane, Melba 7
cultural hierarchy 24–25
Cunningham, Louis Arthur 45

Dagenais, John 69
Damon-Moore, Helen 26*n*
Dare, Eleanor 39

INDEX

Davies, Marion 49
de Cère, Lise 106
de la Roche, Mazo 3, 8–9, 45, 92–93
   Jalna 8
Deane, Philip 183
The Delineator 55
Dempsey, Lotta 61, 62, 125, 126
Denison, Flora Macdonald, *Sunset of Bon Echo* 16
Depression period 34, 41, 97, 100
Dickens, Monica 8
Diepeveen, Leonard 135–36
Dinsmore, E. J. 73
Dominion Dental Journal 44–45
Douglas, Gilean 82
du Veuzit, Max 48
Dubinsky, Karen 16, 19, 71*n*
Dulac, Edmund 158
Dupuis, Katie 62

Editions Poetry 8
The Edmonton Journal 43
Einna 116, 136, 144–45
elite culture 14, 24, 57, 91, 95, 122, 130, 142, 148, 150
elitism, perceived elitism of magazine readers 40, 54, 58, 87, 89, 119, 122, 164, 181
Elliot, Minerva 52
Esquire 95
Evans, Allen Roy 46
Everywoman's World 26

fantasy
   created for readers 34–35, 52–53, 58, 80, 103, 118–22, 142, 178, 181
   flaws 156–62
fashions 21, 32–33, 83–84, 109–45, 150–51
   advertising 111
   eccentricity and modernity 129–35
   effect of Second World War 122–28
   forms of coverage 110–18
   French and American fashions 127–28
   links with foreignness and mobility *fig*14, 109–10, 118–22
   relationship with modernity and modernism 129–35, 135–43

   sense of 'Canadian fashion style' 123–25, 128, 144–45
Femina 54
Finch, Edmund 167–68
Fish, Anne Harriet 115
Fix, Mary McNulty 133
Flanner, Janet 138, 139
Fleming, Patricia 2–3
Forde, Kate 4, 133
Fort William Times-Journal 43
Fournier, Jules 49–50
Francine (Surveyer, Thérèse) 49–50, 114
Francis, Margaret Ecker 162
Francophone 4–5, 26–31, 33, 37, 42
   magazines *see La Revue Moderne*; *La Revue Populaire*
Fraser, Blair 11, 50
Freney, Thomas P. 73
Frigon, Roger 105
Frum, Barbara 62–63
Fry, Roger 89

Gagnier, Harold 44–45
Garner, Grace 46
Gianelli, Adele M. 118
Gilbert-Sauvage, Louise 128
Gill, Miranda 130–31
Girard, Henri 105, 134
Globe and Mail 170, 183
Goldman, Jonathan 115
Good Housekeeping 25
Graham, Jean 45–46, 175
Gray, Grattan 53
Green, Anne 122
Green, Barbara 38*n*
Greer, Germaine 62–63
Groulx, Lionel 101
Grover, Mary 152*n*
   Middlebrow Literary Cultures 12–13
Guillory, John 11

Hammett, Dashiell 23*n*
Hammill, Faye 121n, 152
Harman, James 175–76
Harper's Bazaar 25, 115
Harris, Jane 120
Harrison, Julia 16
Hayles, N. Katherine 67

207

Heidsieck, Charles 173–74
Hemingway, Ernest 151–52
Henry, Vera 82
hierarchy
    cultural 24–25
    social 59, 160
highbrow culture 7, 9–10, 152
Hindrichs, Cheryl 136*n*
Hodgins, J. Herbert 56–57, 58, 71, 73, 75, 89, 106, 109, 125
The Home Publishing Company 44
Hubbard, Mina 16
Hucks, M. Frances 80
Huguenin, Anne-Marie *see* Madeleine
Humble, Nicola 9
    The Feminine Middlebrow Novel 8
Hurley, Erin 5, 29
Hutton, Eric 57

interwar period 19, 98, 111, 114, 131–32, 137, 184
    advertising 37–38, 143, 151
    travel 17–18, 156–57, 171
Irvine, Dean 16
Irwin, William Arthur 70*n*

Jaffe, Aaron 115, 142
Jameson, Anna 16
Jaques, Edna 13–14
Jaunière, Claude 48
Jessup, Lynda 176*n*
Johnston, Russell 31, 33*n*, 51
Jones, John Bush 42
Jones, Richard 5

Keaton, Buster 49
Kelly, Peggy 148
Knister, Raymond 3
Korinek, Valerie 50, 61, 62, 175*n*
Kossoff, Paul 73
Kröller, Eva-Marie 18
    Canadians in Europe 1851-1900 15
Kuffert, Len 13, 69
Kuttainen, Victoria 13, 17

La Revue Moderne 1–2, 3*n*, 4, 5–6, 11–12, 26, 28, 53–56, 63, 66, 97–107
    advertising 35, 37–38, 40, 98, 103, 104–7

changes in appearance over time 102–5
circulation 30, 99, 105*n*, 183
cover design *fig*16, *fig*17, *fig*18, 98–99
fashion writing 111, 113, 114, 119, 125–26, 132
influence on liberal thought in Quebec 101–2
pricing 40, 41, 98
readers' letters page 39*n*, 42
travel writing *fig*7, 155–56, 167, 171, 173–74
La Revue Populaire 1–2, 3*n*, 4, 5–6, 12*n*, 26, 47–50, 63, 66
    advertisements *fig*5, *fig*25, *fig*28, *fig*29
    circulation 30–31, 49, 184
    cover design *fig*5
    fashion writing *fig*21, 111, 113–14, 119–20, 126–28
    market position 50, 73
    pricing 41
    travel writing 157, 166–67, 168–69, 173, 181
La Vie Canadienne 103–4
La Vie Heureuse 54
L'Action française 26, 101
L'actualité 63–64
Ladies' Home Journal 25, 41
Lang, Marjory 45–46
Latham, Sean 3–4, 67
Laurence, Margaret 16
Lawrey, Barbara 182
Le Film 49
Le Guével, Jean 171
Le Samedi 26*n*, 47, 49
Le Terroir 26
Leacock, Stephen 50
Leavis, Q. D. 7
Lecker, Robert 14
Leclerc, Justa *see* Marjolaine
Lee, Annabelle 80
Lemaître, Michèle 114
Lemelin, Roger 28–29
Lemire, Maurice 3
    'La Vie littéraire au Québec' 3
Lismer, Arthur 50
little magazines 3, 16, 24–25
Livesay, Dorothy 3, 60
Livesay, Florence Randall 115

INDEX

Lloyd, C. F. 73
Longstaff, Alan 73
lowbrow culture 7, 9–10, 23

Macbeth, Madge *fig*24, 94, 147–53, 155, 169, 170, 171
McCall's Magazine 25
MacCannell, Dean 153, 166*n*
McClung, Nellie 3, 45, 62–63, 115
McClure's 25*n*
MacDonald, J. E. H. 50
Macdonald, Kate, *The Masculine Middlebrow* 12–13
McGann, Jerome 67
McGee, Mollie 46, 90, 169, 170–71
MacKay, Douglas 73
Mackay, Phyllis Isabel 161–62
Mackie, Ellen 112*n*, 113, 115
McKishnie, Archie 73
McKnight, Miller 45
Maclean, James Bayne 50–51
Maclean Publishing 1–2, 27, 31*n*, 45, 56, 59, 89, 184
Maclean-Hunter 27, 30
Maclean's 1–2, 3, 4, 5–6, 11, 12, 19, 20, 26, 27–28, 47, 50–53, 60, 63–64, 66, 182
  advertising *fig*2, 32, 33–34, 35
  circulation 30, 31
  cover design *fig*6
  literary and artistic content 50, 75, 111*n*
  nationalism 43
  pages *fig*11, 68–81
  pricing 40–41
  readers' letters page 38–39, 73
  travel writing *fig*6, 146–47, 175–76
McLuhan, Marshall 65, 108
MacMurchy, Marjory *see* Willison, Lady
Macpherson, Mary-Etta 46, 47, 75–76*n*, 81, 89
Madeleine (Huguenin, Anne-Marie) 28, 39, 53–55, 97, 99–100, 101, 103–4
Magali (Philbert, Jeanne) 48
Magazine Publishers' Association of Canada (MPAC) 31, 41–42, 51
magazines 7
  advertising *fig*3, *fig*13, 14, 20, 24, 29–30, 32–34, 35–40, 66, 71–72, 81–82
  aspirational 12, 14, 25, 131, 143

bibliographic codes 67–68
Canadian *see Canadian Home Journal*; *Chatelaine*; *La Revue Moderne*; *La Revue Populaire*; *Maclean's*; *Mayfair*
categorisation 3–4, 8–10, 11–12, 20, 23–24
circulation 20, 30–31
content themes 20, 45–46
continuities between editorial and commercial items 67, 71–72, 84, 111, 130, 147
contributions by literary authors 3, 8–9, 27–28, 43, 60–61
editorial contributions 36–37, 51, 69–70, 71
Francophone and Anglophone divide 4–5, 26–31, 33, 37, 42
impact of Second World War 42–43, 46–47, 71*n*, 122–28, 171
influence of American popular culture 29–30
influence of fashion 109–10
marketing to female readers 29–30*n*
miscellany format 65–66
pages 68–81, 107–8
position within 'middlebrow culture' 11–12
pricing 20, 70
readers' letters 38–40, 73
readership 11–12, 29–31, 38, 45, 47, 49, 51, 77, 100, 117
society gossip 115–18
structure 20, 107–8, 133
table of contents *fig*11, 66, 69–70, 71
travel writing 146–56, 180–83
magazines; *see also* little magazines; mainstream magazines; pulp magazines
mainstream magazines 23–25*n*
  advertising 31
  aspirational 24
  nationalism and patriotism 43
Manning, Herbert C. 57
Marchand, Roland, *Advertising the American Dream* 34–35, 151
Marjolaine (Leclerc, Justa) 39–40, 104–5
Martel, Yann 13*n*

209

Massey Commission 63
Mathieu, Joyce 13
Mayfair 1, 3*n*, 4, 12, 18, 20, 26, 47, 50, 56–59, 60, 63, 88–97
  advertisements *fig*20, *fig*23, *fig*26, 32–33, 35
  aspirational ethos 57–58, 89, 96, 141
  circulation 30–31*n*
  cover design *fig*8, *fig*9, *fig*10
  emphasis on luxury and exclusivity *fig*23, 111, 182
  fashion writing *fig*8, 111–12, 119, 126, 132, 139–40, 141–42
  pricing 40, 89
  style 58–59, 89–90
  themed issues *fig*9, 90
  travel writing *fig*9, *fig*24, 148, 163–64, 167–68, 171–72, 181, 182–83
Mead, Margaret 62–63
Mencken, H. L. 23*n*
Mesch, Rachel 54
middlebrow culture 1–2, 7–14, 13*n*
  'battle of the brows' 152*n*
  ideal of self-improvement 12–13
  influences of modernism and modernity 140–42
  origins of term 7–8
Mistry, Rohinton 13*n*
Mitchell, W. O. 3, 50
mobility, social and geographical 1–2, 7, 14–20, 21, 33–34, 35, 43, 52–53, 56–58, 68–69, 79, 99, 112, 118–22, 153, 168–69
modernism 14, 21, 110, 134–35, 138–42, 151–52, 163
  cover design 99
  and fashion 129–35
modernism; *see also* antimodernism
Modernist Journals Project (MJP) 8–9
Montgomery, L. M. 3, 45, 60, 62–63, 115
Montpetit, Edouard 49
Morgan, Cecilia 15–16, 17, 18
Morphy, Kay *see* Murphy, Kay
Morrison, Mary 154–55
Morse, Ann 80
Munro, Alice 60
Munsey, Frank 23, 25*n*
Munsey's Magazine 25*n*

Murphy, Kay (Kathleen) 80, 113, 117–18, 125, 139
Murray, Heather 13

Napier-Moore, H. 70*n*, 74–75, 78–80, 147
Nathan, George Jean 23*n*
National Home Monthly 26
nationalism 2, 20, 28–29, 41–44, 69, 89, 123–24, 144–45, 175, 181–82
Neatby, Nicole 16
The New Yorker 138
Newsweek 53
1920s 1, 6, 7, 10, 17–18, 20–21, 32, 40–41, 47, 55, 73, 98, 111–12, 151
1930s 18, 32, 47–48, 55, 98, 111–12, 151
1940s 18–19, 29–30, 49–50, 98, 106, 111, 125, 126
1950s 19, 20–21, 30, 50, 98, 111, 126

Oakley, Virginia 82
Ohmann, Richard 10, 25, 60, 65–66, 76, 79
  refers to 'reading' advertisements 81–82, 95
O'Leary Commission 63
O'Leary, Grattan 63, 73
Oligny, Huguette 125–26
Oligny, Odette 114*n*, 125, 128
Ondaatje, Michael 8–9
Ostenso, Martha 3, 8–9, 45, 50, 60
  Wild Geese 8
Outka, Elizabeth 143

Pain, Hilda 59–60, 177
Palmer, Alexandra 110*n*, 125, 127*n*, 129, 150
Paris, as primary cultural reference 29
Parkins, Ilya 129–30
Paul, Frances 172
Pearson, George 146, 158–60
periodicals *see* magazines
Persephone Books 8
Pettit Hill, Maud 80
Philbert, Jeanne *see* Magali
Pleau, Jean-Christian 28, 53–54, 100, 101–2
Poirier, Bessette Publishers 47, 49
postwar period 46, 58, 88, 112, 114, 162, 184
Pound, Ezra 151, 158
Pringle, Gertrude 52

INDEX

print culture *see* magazines
pulp magazines 23, 24–25, 151
Pump, Irene 176

Quedrue, Maurice 42

Raddall, Thomas 50
Raine, Norman Reilly 73
readership 11–12, 29–31, 38, 45, 47, 49, 51, 77, 100, 117
Reed, Christopher 141
Renaud, Arnaud 119
Reyburn, Wallace 169–70
Rifkind, Candida 13–14
Robert, Lucie 26, 98, 99, 134
Roberts, Charles G. D. 3
Roberts, Gillian 13*n*
Robinson, Judith 83, 86–87
Rogers Media conglomerate 63, 64
Rooke, Bill 44
Rouse, William Merriam 73
Roy, Gabrielle 3, 27–28, 106
Roy, Wendy 16

Saint-Georges, Raymonde 114, 126
Saint-Jacques, Denis 26, 37, 98, 99, 134
Salverson, Laura Goodman 3, 45
Sanders, Byrne Hope 11, 13, 35–36, 40, 46, 47, 60–62, 70*n*, 75*n*
Sandwell, B. K. 180
Sartre, Jean-Paul 12*n*
The Saturday Evening Post 25–26*n*, 41
Saturday Night 26*n*, 44–45
Schiaparelli, Elsa 138–41*n*
Scholes, Robert 3–4, 67
Scobie, Stephen 149–50
Second World War 60–61, 171
 impact on fashions 122–28
 impact on magazines 42–43, 46–47, 58, 71*n*, 122–28, 171
Seton, Edwina 73–74
Shearer, Norma 49
Sheehan, Elizabeth 129–30
Simmel, Georg 118, 131
Smart, Elizabeth 8
Smith, A. J. M. 75
Smith, Erin 151
Smith, Michelle 6*n*, 82

social hierarchy 59, 160
Soiffield (Swaffield, Richard G.) 112, 115–18, 141–42
Sontag, Susan 168
Spacks, Patricia Meyer 116
Spicer, Mildred 154–55
Stead, Robert 3
Stoicheff, Peter 107
Strychacz, Thomas 134
Sullivan, Alan 73
Sullivan, Melissa 13
Surveyer, Thérèse *see* Francine
Swaffield, Richard G. *see* Soiffield
Szeman, Imre 64

Tait, Catherine Wilma 46, 47
taste, cultural discernment 14–16, 19–20, 38, 43, 52, 57, 66, 81, 130–31, 165, 172
Tate, Bertram 57
The Tatler 58
Taylor, Andrew 107
Taylor, Elizabeth 8
Taylor, H. Weston 73
Tector, Amy 13
Thacker, Andrew 10, 25, 67
The Home Journal see Canadian Home Journal
The Smart Set 23*n*, 25*n*
Thompson, Anne 80
Thornton, Margaret *fig*14, 83, 84–85, 113, 129
Time 53
Tit-Bits 66*n*
Town, Harold 86
travel 1–2, 7, 14–20, 35, 52–53
 advertising *fig*3, 156–61
 as a form of self-improvement 65–66, 153, 154, 181, 182
 romanticisation 146–47, 156–61
 souvenirs and photo-narratives 167–72
 tourism 17–18, 52–53, 71
 travel writing *fig*7, 15–17, 146–79, 180–83
travel; *see also* mobility
Tyndall, George H. 70*n*

urban 2, 18, 32, 60, 85, 89, 93–94, 112, 157
Urry, John 17*n*, 169

211

Vaillancourt, Madeleine 155–56
Valentine, A. C. 73
Vanity Fair 95, 115
Vautier, Marie 28
Vipond, Mary 42
Virago Press 8
Vogue 141
Vollmer, Margaret 87–88

Wallace, Claire 165–66
Western Home Monthly 32, 44
Whipple, Dorothy 8
Whiting, Elizabeth 80
Whitton, Norah 80
Williams, Raymond 31

Willison, Lady (MacMurchy, Marjory) 153–54
Wilson, Anne Elizabeth 60, 73, 80, 144
Woman's Home Companion 77–78
Women's Wear 44–45
Woolf, Virginia 7n, 12n, 89
Wyndham, Mary 112n, 115, 116, 117, 119–20, 133, 138–39
Wynne-Field, Archie G. 161–62

Yao, Steven 140
York, Lorraine 8–9
  Literary Celebrity in Canada 8–9
Young, Scott 50